China–U.S. Relations Transformed

"This book tackles a most complex subject, one that is critical to the United States in the 21st Century. The rise of China is fraught with contradictions, from a successful superpower to a huge nation state bogged down by domestic problems. Of particular interest in the book are the views of the Chinese scholars with their unique insights and their cultural predispositions. It is a valuable work and a must read for those who care about the most important bilateral relationship in the world."

James R. Lilley, Former American Ambassador to China and South Korea

China's emergence in the twenty-first century to the status of great power has profoundly transformed its relationship with the U.S.A. and compelled leaders in both countries to redefine their positions towards each other. This book, written by leading scholars and policy analysts from both the U.S.A. and China, explores the transformation and multifaceted nature of U.S.–China relations, including how the political elite in both countries have defined their strategic objectives in response to China's rise and managed their relations accordingly. It provides an up-to-date analysis on the policy adjustments and strategic interactions during the last decade, and covers the most important issue areas, including security, nuclear deterrence, military modernization, energy, trade and economic interaction, and Asia-Pacific power reconfiguration. It does not seek to confirm either an alarmist or optimistic position but presents different perspectives and assessments by foreign policy specialists with the hope that leaders in Washington and Beijing may make positive adjustments in their policies to avoid confrontation and war. It will also be an invaluable resource for students and scholars of U.S. and Chinese politics, international relations and comparative politics.

Suisheng Zhao is Executive Director of the Center for China–U.S. Cooperation and a Professor at the Graduate School of International Studies, University of Denver, U.S.A. A founding editor of the *Journal of Contemporary China*, he is the author and editor of eight books, including *Debating Political Reform in China: Rule of Law versus Democratization* and *A Nation-State by Construction: Dynamics of Modern Chinese Nationalism*.

Routledge contemporary China series

China–U.S. Relations Transformed

Perspectives and strategic interactions

Edited by Suisheng Zhao

Routledge
Taylor & Francis Group

LONDON AND NEW YORK

First published 2008
by Routledge
2 Park Square, Milton Park, Abingdon, Oxon OX14 4RN

Simultaneously published in the U.S.A. and Canada
by Routledge
270 Madison Ave, New York, NY 10016

Routledge is an imprint of the Taylor & Francis Group, an informa business

Transferred to Digital Printing 2009

© 2008 Selection and editorial matter, Suisheng Zhao; individual chapters,
the contributors

Typeset in Times by Wearset Ltd, Boldon, Tyne and Wear

British Library Cataloguing in Publication Data
A catalogue record for this book is available from the British Library

Library of Congress Cataloging in Publication Data
A catalog record for this book has been requested

ISBN10: 0-415-43867-5 (hbk)
ISBN10: 0-415-49580-6 (pbk)
ISBN10: 0-203-93478-4 (ebk)

ISBN13: 978-0-415-43867-4 (hbk)
ISBN13: 978-0-415-49580-6 (pbk)
ISBN13: 978-0-203-93478-4 (ebk)

To William S. Jackson, Jr.

for his support to my efforts of building bridges between the U.S.A. and China

and

to Lillian, Sandra, Justinian, and Yi

for their love that has sustained my search for a better world

Contents

Illustrations

Chart

Tables

About the editor and contributors

The editor

Suisheng Zhao is Professor and Executive Director of the Center for China–U.S. Cooperation at Graduate School of International Studies, University of Denver. He is founder and editor of the *Journal of Contemporary China* and a member of the Board of Governors of the U.S. Committee of the Council for Security Cooperation in the Asia Pacific. A Campbell National Fellow at Hoover Institution of Stanford University, he was Associate Professor of Political Science/International Studies at Washington College in Maryland, Associate Professor of Government/East Asian Politics at Colby College in Maine. His most recent books are *Debating Political Reform in China: Rule of Law versus Democratization* (M. E. Sharpe, 2006), *A Nation-State by Construction: Dynamics of Modern Chinese Nationalism* (Stanford University Press, 2004), and *Chinese Foreign Policy: Pragmatism and Strategic Behavior* (M. E. Sharpe, 2003). His articles have appeared in *Political Science Quarterly, The Wilson Quarterly, Washington Quarterly, International Politik, The China Quarterly, World Affairs, Asian Survey, Asian Affairs, Journal of Democracy, Pacific Affairs, Communism and Post-Communism Studies, Problems of Post-Communism, Issues and Studies*, and elsewhere.

Contributors

Baohui Zhang is an Associate Professor of Politics at Lingnan University, Hong Kong. He received his Ph.D. from the University of Texas at Austin. His research interests include democratization, U.S.–China relations, and political reform in Hong Kong. He has published in journals such as Comparative Political Studies, Democratization, Theory and Society, and Asian Perspective.

Pieter Bottelier is a visiting Associate Professor at the School of Advanced International Studies (SAIS) of Johns Hopkins University. He was an Adjunct Lecturer at Harvard University (KSG) and at Georgetown University. He has authored many articles on China's economy. Bottelier worked for the World Bank as the Senior Advisor to the Vice President for East Asia;

Chief of the World Bank's Resident Mission in Beijing; consecutive director for Latin America and North Africa; Division Chief for Mexico; resident Chief Economist in Jakarta, Indonesia; and had various assignments as desk economist for East and West African countries. He received Drs degree (M.A. equivalent) from the University of Amsterdam and attended M.I.T. Ph.D. program.

Bernard D. Cole is Professor of International History at the National War College in Washington, D.C., where he concentrates on the Chinese military and Asian energy issues. He previously served 30 years as a Surface Warfare Officer in the Navy, all in the Pacific. He commanded USS *Rathburne* (FF 1057) and Destroyer Squadron *35*, served as a Naval Gunfire Liaison Officer with the Third Marine Division in Vietnam, as Plans Officer for Commander-in-Chief Pacific Fleet, and as special assistant to the Chief of Naval Operations for Expeditionary Warfare. He has written numerous articles and four books: *Gunboats and Marines: The U.S. Navy in China; The Great Wall at Sea: China's Navy Enters the 21st Century; Oil for the Lamps of China: Beijing's 21st Century Search for Energy;* and *Taiwan's Security: History and Prospects*, published in January 2006. Dr. Cole earned an A.B. in History from the University of North Carolina, an M.P.A. (National Security Affairs) from the University of Washington, and a Ph.D. in History from Auburn University.

Dongxiao Chen is a Senior Fellow and Director of the Department of American Studies at the Shanghai Institute for International Studies (SIIS). Prior to this position, he was director of Department of International Organizations and International Law, and deputy director of Dept. of American Studies. He specializes in studies on American foreign policy and international collective security regimes.

June Teufel Dreyer is Professor of Political Science at the University of Miami. She received her M.A. and Ph.D. from Harvard University. In addition to energy issues, her research interests include China's ethnic minorities, Sino-Japanese relations, and cross-Strait relations. She is a senior fellow of the Foreign Policy Research Institute. From 2001 through 2005, Dreyer served as commissioner of the congressionally-established U.S.–China Economic and Security Research Commission.

Elizabeth Economy is C.V. Starr Senior Fellow and Director of Asia Studies at the Council on Foreign Relations. She has published extensively on both Chinese domestic and foreign policy, including *The River Runs Black: The Environmental Challenge to China's Future* (Cornell University Press, 2004); articles in foreign policy and scholarly journals such *Foreign Affairs* and *Survival*; and op-eds and book reviews published in *The New York Times, The Washington Post, The International Herald Tribune* and others. She serves on several China-related boards and consults frequently for the U.S. government. Dr. Economy received her Ph.D. at the University of

Michigan, her M.A. at Stanford University and her B.A. at Swarthmore College.

Jean Anne Garrison is Associate Professor of Political Science at the University of Wyoming. She is the author of two books, *Making China Policy: From Nixon to G.W. Bush* (Boulder, CO: Lynne Rienner 2005) and *Games Advisors Play: Foreign Policy in the Nixon and Carter Administrations* (College Station: Texas A&M University Press, 1999), and several book chapters and journal articles (including publications in the *International Studies Review, Political Psychology, Cooperation and Conflict, Asian Affairs, and Asian Perspective*. In 2003, she was the recipient of a Council on Foreign Relations International Affairs Fellowship and several months in 2004 posted with the State Department's Bureau of East Asian Pacific Affairs working on the China desk. She received her Ph.D. and M.A. in political science from the University of South Carolina.

Jian Xu is Vice President of Institute of International Studies in Beijing and a senior research fellow. He received his B.A. and M.A. degrees in history from Peking Normal University and a M.A. degree in law from University of Sussex and a Ph.D. in law from University of Bristol. From 1993 to 1999, Mr. Xu worked in the International Studies Center of the State Council. He joined CIIS in 1999. Before taking the current position, he was Director of Division of International Politics. His research areas cover international politics, Asia-Pacific security and globalization.

Phillip C. Saunders is a Senior Research Professor at the National Defense University's Institute for National Strategic Studies since January 2004. He previously worked at the Monterey Institute of International Studies, where he served as Director of the East Asia Nonproliferation Program at the Center for Nonproliferation Studies and taught courses on Chinese politics, Chinese foreign policy, and East Asian security. Saunders has conducted research and consulted on East Asian security issues for Princeton University, the Council on Foreign Relations, RAND, and the National Committee on U.S.–China Relations. Saunders has published numerous articles on China and Asian security in journals including *International Security, China Quarterly, The China Journal, Survival, Asian Survey, Pacific Review*, and *Orbis*. Saunders attended Harvard College and received his M.P.A. and Ph.D. in International Relations from the Woodrow Wilson School at Princeton University.

Qingguo Jia is Professor and Associate Dean of the School of International Studies of Peking University. He received his Ph.D. from Cornell University in 1988. He was a research fellow at the Brookings Institution between 1985 and 1986. He has taught in University of Vermont, Cornell University, University of California at San Diego, University of Sydney in Australia as well as Peking University. He has published extensively on U.S.–China relations, relations between the Chinese mainland and Taiwan, Chinese foreign policy as well as Chinese politics. He is a member of the editorial board of *Journal of Contemporary China* (U.S.A.), *Political Science* (New Zealand), *International Relations of the Asia-Pacific* (Japan) and *China Review* (Hong Kong). He is also Vice President of the China Association for Asia-Pacific Studies, a board member of the China Association of American Studies, and a board member of the National Taiwan Studies Association.

Wei Li is an Associate Research Fellow and Director of the Department of American and Oceanian Studies at the Chinese Academy of International Trade and Economic Cooperation (CAITEC). Before joining the Department of American and Oceanian Studies, he was Deputy Director of the Academy's Department of Asian and African Studies, and his fields of specialization were East Asian economic cooperation, especially trade and economic cooperation between ASEAN and China. He has served as a member of China–ASEAN Economic Cooperation Expert Group.

Acknowledgments

Most of the chapters in this book are selected from papers presented at two international symposiums on U.S.–China relations that I organized as the executive director of the Center for China–U.S. Cooperation (CCUSC) at the Graduate School of International Studies (GSIS), University of Denver in 2005 and 2006. More than 30 papers were presented and a group of outstanding scholars and government officials engaged in dialogue at these symposiums to explore various aspects of the implications of China's rise for U.S.–China relations. I would like to thank all participants for their contribution to the success of these symposiums. In particular, I would like to thank the contributors to this book for their willingness to make revisions and updates in a timely manner. I would also like to thank Dean Tom Farer at GSIS for the support that I have always been able to count on. My staff at the CCUSC provided the most professional assistance, for which I am extremely grateful. Finally, I would like to thank Bill Jackson for his friendship and his generosity in pledging an endowment to partially fund the CCUSC annual conference and speaker series and also thank Diana Lee for introducing Bill Jackson to me and launching the endowment, which has sustained me in pursuing my dream of building an eminent China Center at the University of Denver.

Part I
Introduction

1 Implications of China's rise for U.S.–China relations

Suisheng Zhao

An ancient empire, China was one of the most powerful nations in the world before the spread of the Industrial Revolution that gave rise to modern European powers, the U.S.A., and Japan. A mid-kingdom, accounting for about one third of the world output as recently as the early nineteenth century, China began a steady decline thereafter as it plunged into war, famine, isolation, and revolution. After about 200 years of struggle for national independence and modernization, China reemerged as a global power in the twenty-first century. If China is able to sustain the momentum of the recent decades, it will ultimately regain the glorious position it enjoyed two centuries ago. The Summer Olympics of 2008 is a symbol of this national resurgence from a dark cocoon of decline and isolation into the light of international recognition.

China's rise certainly poses a serious challenge to public policy-makers everywhere in the world, particularly to policy-makers in the U.S.A., the sole superpower in the post-Cold War world. While some Americans welcome China's rise as creating new opportunities for great power cooperation, others worry about a "China threat" to U.S. security and economic interests as China now demonstrates its rapidly rising power as a counterweight to U.S. influence. Has China's rise led U.S.–China relations toward a vicious conflict for war or toward a convergence of interests for cooperation? Can the two countries manage their rivalry and competition to preserve peace by exploring areas in which China's national interests overlap U.S. interests and where cooperation brings mutual benefits? This book represents a modest effort by leading scholars and policy analysts from the U.S.A. and China to examine the dynamics of transformation and multifaceted nature of U.S.–China relations. Focusing on how the political elite in both countries define their strategic objectives in response to China's rise and manage their relationship accordingly, this book looks at strategic issues facing policy-makers in the U.S.A. and China and explores where this crucially important bilateral relationship is heading.

The transformation of U.S.–China relations

In spite of theoretical equality and anarchy in the modern nation-state system, a hierarchical structure often exists among states, reflecting variations in their relative power status. Hegemonic states command dominant positions over other states, resting on a robust economic base and military capabilities, supplemented and solidified by soft normative power. The hegemonic states have a vested interest in maintaining the established international system because their values and interests are often universalized to the point where they largely conform to the rules, values, and institutions of the system. Rising powers, however, often demand a change in the power hierarchy and become challengers to the established system. Historically, the rise of great powers has always been associated with a transformation in the relationship between the rising powers and their more established counterparts. Sometimes this rise has even produced a restructuring of the hierarchy, i.e. a power transition from dominant states to challengers in the international system.[1] Whether or not a systemic power transition took place, the inevitable power competition often caused disruptive conflicts and even large-scale wars. During the twentieth century, except for the competition between the U.S.A. and the U.K. that resulted in a more or less peaceful power transition from a hegemonic Pax Britannica to a Pax Americana, all other great power competitions were violent and disruptive. For example, the rivalry between Germany and the U.K. was one of the causes leading to World War I; the emergence of Germany and Japan was followed by World War II; and the competition between the Soviet Union and the U.S.A. caused a prolonged Cold War.

Now China is rising and its rising power status is recognized by many Americans. A 2006 survey by the Chicago Council on Global Affairs and the Asia Society shows that "60% of Americans believe that China's economy will grow to be as large as the US economy within two decades or so."[2] Utilizing its rising economic power in foreign affairs, China's diplomatic activism has been increasingly observed well beyond its neighboring Asian countries into Latin America, Africa, the Middle East, and Europe. Although China has not reached the position of parity with American power, its rapid rise has profoundly transformed the Sino-U.S. relationship and made the bilateral relationship increasingly strategic and globally significant. Consequently, a profound debate about the implications of China's rise for U.S.–China relations has taken place among scholars and policy-makers in both the U.S.A. and China.

Liberal optimists believe that globalization has produced growing strategic interdependence among great powers. This strategic interdependence constrains the U.S.A. and China from pursuing zero-sum strategies toward each other. As a result, China's rise has increased the common stakes for these two countries to expand cooperation on almost all important international issues, such as trade and investment, fighting terrorism, the proliferation of weapons of mass destruction, trade liberalization, environmental protection, energy, transnational crime, and pandemic diseases. As an American scholar has argued, globalization is reshaping the international strategic environment, in which the interests of the U.S.A. and China will limit strategic competition and compel closer cooperation in response to shared strategic threats and challenges. Although this high-level common interest does not preclude sharp differences over specific issues, it is likely to create pressure on both countries to cooperate in many areas to defend, maintain, and strengthen the international system and to restrain them from pursuing containment or confrontational strategies.[3] Strategic and economic interdependence thus become positive forces for integrating China into the established international system in which self-interests and growing networks of international involvement will impose their own constraints and help ensure its emergence as a responsible stakeholder in the international system. This view is echoed by another American scholar: "Fortified by both globalization and its economic policies, China has thus become an ardent supporter of the existing international economic order."[4] A Chinese scholar also suggests that although China is not a fully satisfied power in the international system because of its historical grievances against the Western powers and unresolved issues such as Taiwan, China is basically a status quo power, eager to be part of the international community because China has benefited enormously from the international political and economic system since the late 1970s. "China's development is shaped by the international system and, most significantly, as an important participant, China is also helping to shape the changing international system at the beginning of the twenty-first century."[5] China's search for a greater role in world affairs, in this case, will not necessarily threaten U.S. interests in the non-zero-sum game.

Realist alarmists, in contrast, argue that "there will be no win-win situation in conflicts among international political entities accompanying the rise of China" because "the rise of a state's power status indicates an expansion of its political power. This in turn causes the fall of other states' power status and political power."[6] By this logic, China's rise will inevitably alter the international status quo as a rising China will want to define its interests more expansively and seek a greater degree of influence. If successfully fulfilling its expected potential, China will join a select group of modern great powers, including Great Britain in the nineteenth century, Germany and Japan during World War II, and the Soviet Union and the U.S.A. during the Cold War. Each of these rising great powers expanded their influence and pursued some form of hegemony to protect its interests or even launched aggressive warfare against rival states. A rising China is likely to engage in an intense security competition with the U.S.A. to maximize its share of world power. This may consequently upset the balance of power and spark realignments particularly in East Asia as well as the rest of the world because most of China's neighbors and other powers will have to decide whether to join the U.S.A. or China in a new round of power competition. It is not difficult for alarmists to find evidence in an unsatisfied China which suggests that China's rise is being fraught with tensions with the U.S.A. For example, America's accidental bombing of the Chinese Embassy in Belgrade in 1999 and China's capture of an American spy plane in 2001 provoked extreme nationalistic responses from both the Chinese public and government. In response to the U.S. policy toward Taiwan, China has determined to prevent U.S. intervention should China have to use force in its efforts towards unification with Taiwan.[7] In addition, China has forged links with the anti-American government in

Venezuela and conducted business with the Sudan's genocidal government, which the U.S.A. has been trying to isolate. In these cases, China is challenging U.S. interests, raising the specter of great power rivalry.

In addition to theoretical debate, the rise of China has profoundly transformed the strategic thinking of policy-makers in both Washington and Beijing. For about a century before China's recent emergence, the U.S.A. either engaged or confronted China for various purposes, but it always regarded China as secondary in significance – important simply in the context of rivalry with other powers, such as imperial Japan during the Pacific War and with the Soviet Union during the Cold War. China's rise has changed the strategic thinking of China in the U.S.A. from "a weak China" to "a strong China."[8] The U.S.A., for the first time, has to deal with China for its own sake and is anxious to see whether or not the latter will challenge U.S. predominance in world affairs. This change has given rise to a sense of fear among some in the U.S.A. that a rising China could become a post-World War II Soviet Union or a nineteenth-century Germany. The Pentagon's 2001 *Quadrennial Defense Report* (QDR), a geopolitical blueprint issued right after the events of September 11, took a capacity-based approach to define enemies and believed that "[a] military competitor with a formidable resource will emerge in the region" and become the long-term threat to the U.S.A. Although the report did not mention the name of China, everyone recognized who was being identified.[9] The 2006 QDR states explicitly that: "Of the major and emerging powers, China has the greatest potential to compete militarily with the U.S.A. and field disruptive military technologies that could over time offset traditional U.S. military advantages absent U.S. counter strategies."[10]

Consequently, many Americans have begun wondering how China as a great power will use its influence globally and regionally. At the global level, China has gone around the world in search of raw materials and has been trying to lock up energy supplies, including pursuing deals with countries under U.S. sanctions or with U.S. security concerns, such as Venezuela, Sudan, and Iran. This development has caused a suspicion that China is not only challenging the U.S.A.'s historic dominance in many parts of the world but also undermining Western efforts to promote transparency and human rights, damaging U.S. interests and values. This suspicion has been intensified by the lack of transparency in China's rapid military modernization program. China has striven to modernize its military forces but has not made its purposes clear nor indicated how far the military modernization program has gone and will go. The 1996 QDR expressed concern: "secrecy envelops most aspects of Chinese security affairs. The outside world has little knowledge of Chinese motivations and decision-making or of key capabilities supporting its military modernization."[11]

At the regional level, China's resurgence has raised some questions about its aspiration in Asia-Pacific. Will it seek to restore the position of ancient dominance and develop a sphere of influence over its periphery for security if Chinese capacities enable Beijing to pursue a regional dominance? Will China challenge U.S. strategic alliances in East Asia and diminish U.S. strategic presence? For nearly every Asia-Pacific economy in recent years, China has replaced the U.S.A. as the largest foreign-trade partner and has become an increasingly more important source of economic growth. With the emerging Asia-Pacific regional manufacturing system, China has served as the main point of final assembly for parts and components produced throughout the region for export to North America and Europe.[12] In the security arena, China has pursued an active regional diplomacy, reflected in the growing bilateral security ties and an increasing activism in multilateral regional organizations. In contrast, although the U.S.A. has vital interests in Asia-Pacific, it has been preoccupied by the war on terror, particularly the Iraq War in recent years, and its influence has declined in the Asia-Pacific region. The contrast between China's active engagement in the region and the U.S. preoccupation somewhere else makes it easy to conclude that China is beginning to replace the U.S.A. as the region's hegemon. These contentious economic and security issues have made the U.S.–China relations in Asia-Pacific extremely complicated.

In addition, the rise of popular nationalist sentiments and China's reluctance to open domestic political competition to build a liberal democracy has exacerbated the sense of unease among some Americans about an increasingly powerful China. Many have concerns about China's aspirations for great power status drawing upon strong nationalism linked with the victim's conviction of a "century of shame and humiliation" at the hands of imperialist powers. A rising China, driving such nationalist sentiments, would be anything but peaceful; China's international behavior would be irrational and inflexible. The lack of progress toward democracy is another concern: many Americans have worried that if China's authoritarian governmment sustains its rapid economic growth, China will challenge the "Washington consensus" concerning free markets and liberal politics with a "Beijing consensus" promoting authoritarian governments producing rapid economic growth and social stability. In addition, many in the West believe that authoritarian governments are more prone to plunge into wars than democracies.

In the late 1990s, the Clinton administration carried out an engagement policy. Its rationale was that because China's rise was inevitable, the goal of U.S. policy should ensure that China's greater role did not threaten American interests by facilitating and perhaps accelerating the changes that China brings about in its domestic affairs and pursues in its international interests. When the Bush administration took over in the early 2000s, it criticized Clinton's engagement policy and came out in favor of a containment policy that interpreted China's rise as a serious threat to the U.S.A., its friends, and the Western way of life and sought to prevent, or at least delay, China's emergence as a peer competitor. The September 11th terrorist attacks softened Bush's position since he had to work with Beijing to deal with the urgent danger of terrorism. However, the Bush administration has never stopped struggling to define its stance on the critically long-term issue facing the U.S.A.: whether to view China as a strategic threat and plan accordingly, or to see it as a strategic partner and work with it to shape a future international system. This is particularly challenging while the

Bush administration is preoccupied internationally with military engagements in Iraq and Afghanistan and concerns about Iranian and North Korean nuclear developments.

Going through swings, Bush finally came to the realization that the U.S.–China relationship is a complex one with a mix of cooperative and competitive interests. Deputy Secretary of State Robert Zoellick elaborated the complexity of the relationship in a September 2005 speech. On the one hand, he raised the concern about how China will use its power, criticized China's "involvement with troublesome states" and its "mercantilist" attempts to "lock up" energy resources, and urged China to adopt democratic reforms. On the other hand, he disagreed with those who view China solely through "the lens of fear" and encouraged China to become a "responsible stakeholder," working with the U.S.A. to sustain the international system that has enabled its success.[13] The Bush administration has hence settled on a policy of hedging against possible China challenges but cooperating with China on many strategically important issues. This is a two-pronged strategy toward China: "America is heavily engaged with China economically, diplomatically, and culturally, but at the same time is trying to contain its regional and global ambitions."[14]

Similarly, Beijing's position toward Washington has experienced some important changes in recent decades. Before the 1990s, as a relatively weak power unable to seriously compete with the U.S.A., China positioned itself as one of the developing countries in a collective struggle against the superpower hegemony. Although China gained some diplomatic weight in the strategic triangle of Beijing, Moscow and Washington during the 1980s, as the weakest pole among the three, China's main diplomatic thrust was to retain as much strategic leverage as possible in its relationships with the two superpowers. Since the mid-1990s, China's rising power status has given it more leverage in its relationship with the U.S.A., but, as a *Time* magazine article indicates: "The most immediate priority for China's leadership is less how to project itself internationally than how to maintain stability in a society that is going through the sort of social and economic change that, in the past, has led to chaos and violence."[15] In a speech to an American audience, Zheng Bijian, a senior policy adviser to the Chinese leadership, emphasized the difficult challenges at home, including what he called "a series of paradoxes in the process of economic and social development, such as uneven development between the coastal areas and the hinterland, the contradiction between fairness and economic returns, rural–urban disparity, the wealth gap, and the tension between reform and stability."[16]

Facing difficult challenges at home, China has cautiously kept a low profile in international affairs while making an effort to "cultivate good relations with the outside world" in order to create a favorable international environment for its modernization programs.[17] Aware that "the U.S. strategic goal is to maintain and perpetuate its primacy in the world, protect and expand its strategic and economic interests around the world, and keep on exporting American values and political system,"[18] Chinese leaders have tried to avoid confrontation and enhance cooperation with the U.S.A. For this purpose, Beijing abandoned the old position against the superpower hegemony and proposed to build "constructive strategic partnerships" with the U.S.A. as well as with many other major powers. Holding that its relationship with Washington is the most important bilateral relationship, Beijing has envisioned the China–U.S. relationship as within a framework of strategic partnerships with a group of great powers to balance against one another in a multipolar world that it has perceived and promoted in order to prevent any potential U.S.-led coalitions to contain China.[19]

In response to the China policy debate in the U.S.A., some Chinese political and intellectual elites have called for a tougher position against the U.S.A. and are forcefully pressing for China's rising power status. However, Beijing's leaders have taken a pragmatic position to maintain a cooperative relationship because they realize that China's continuing rise rests on the maintenance of a favorable international environment, the most important element of which is a cooperative relationship with the U.S.A., the unwieldy superpower holding the key to China's rise. Articulating a strategy of peaceful development and insisting that China's rise will not be a threat to the U.S.A., Chinese leaders have welcomed Zeollick's invitation for China to become a "responsible stakeholder" in the international system. A *China Daily* commentary suggests that the invitation indicates that the Bush administration, just as the previous six U.S. administrations, has come to see China as a "strategic partner." Chinese leaders particularly welcome Zoellick's remarks that the "China of today is simply not the Soviet Union of the late 1940s: it does not seek to spread radical, anti-American ideologies; it does not see itself in a twilight conflict against democracy around the globe. It does not see itself in a death struggle with capitalism; it does not seek to overturn the fundamental order of the international system."[20]

From a pragmatic perspective, Chinese leaders believe that: "In the long term, the decline of U.S. primacy and the subsequent transition to a multi-polar world are inevitable, but in the short term, Washington's power is unlikely to decline, and its position in world affairs is unlikely to change." Admitting that: "The Chinese–U.S. relationship remains beset by more profound differences than any other bilateral relationships between major powers in the world today," and that there exists a gap between the two countries in national power,[21] China has set a policy priority to prevent U.S. actions from harming China's vital national interests. Taking advantage of its increasing strategic and economic assets as a rising power, China has tried to defend its interests by both cooperative and coercive means. As one Chinese scholar indicates, while China has utilized its strategic assets to cooperate with the U.S.A. on issues of mutual interest, thereby exchanging benefits and altering the U.S.A.'s negative impression on China, it has also utilized its strategic assets to thwart U.S. objectives, including using or threatening to use force, forming alliances to curb U.S. power and voting against proposals favorable to the U.S.A. in international organizations. In the meantime, China has used its economic resources, such as market access, not only to meet the economic needs of the U.S.A. but also to undermine U.S. economic well-being through trade embargoes, trade barriers, etc.[22]

It is revealing to see that the Chinese foreign minister joined foreign ministers of India and Russia two years in a row to discuss how to build a "more democratic multi-polar world" in 2006 and 2007. Their formal agenda at the 2007 meeting covered issues ranging from Iran, Iraq, Afghanistan, the Middle East, and North Korea to energy security, nuclear nonproliferation, and trade. An observer commented that the subtext of the conference agenda was: "how to use their growing economic and political muscle to prevent Washington from tackling such issues alone." These three countries account for 40 percent of the world's population, a fifth of its economy, and more than half of its nuclear warheads. According to this observer, although it is premature to talk about a strategic axis between the world's largest country and the two most populous nations because they still have more in common with the West than with each other, "they appear to be forming a partnership to challenge the U.S.-dominated world order that has prevailed since the end of the Cold War."[23]

In this case, the U.S.–China relationship has become extremely complicated and difficult to manage during this period of China's rise. In retrospect, the U.S.–China relationship has never been an easy one. Harry Harding called it a "fragile relationship" in the 1980s and David M. Lampton used "same bed different dreams" to characterize the relationship in the 1990s.[24] The U.S.A. and China in the recent decade have cooperated more and more often on many fronts but have also found themselves in sharp disagreement over many contentious issues, such as how to deal with the Taiwan independence, China's military modernization, the U.S. unilateralism, energy security, the trade deficit, and the Korean nuclear crisis. China's rise in the twenty-first century has brought about a new dimension of mutual suspicion about each power's long-term strategic intentions. Concerned that rapid increase in economic and military capacities may produce inflated Chinese ambitions and lead to more conflicting rather than cooperative behavior, some Americans have become anxious about China's rise. Equally, many Chinese have been concerned about the implications for China in a world dominated by the U.S.A. and that the U.S.A. might overreact to perceived threat from China's rise and try to keep China down by taking preemptive actions to preserve its supremacy. These mutual suspicions have given rise to perceptions of a "China threat" in the U.S.A. and a perception of a "U.S. threat" in China.

The perpetuation of suspicion about each other's long-term intentions is dangerous because it could lead to the conclusion that a U.S.–China conflict is inevitable. In a discussion of U.S.–China relations, Joseph S. Nye reminds us of Thucydides' warning more than two millennia ago that "belief in the inevitability of conflict can become one of its main causes. Each side, believing it will end up at war with the other, makes reasonable military preparations which then are read by the other side as confirmation of its worst fears."[25]

Consequently, it is crucially important that leaders in both Beijing and Washington do not let mutual suspicion dictate their policy. A dangerous confrontation is neither in the interest of China nor the U.S.A. Aaron Friedberg, a former senior adviser to U.S. vice president Dick Cheney, indicates that "whether for good or ill, the most significant bilateral international relationship over the course of next several decades is likely to be that between the U.S. and the PRC."[26] As far reaching as it is, the transformation of the U.S.–China relationship has profound implications for the world of the twenty-first century. A cover-page article in the January 2007 issue of *Time* magazine described China's rise as the "dawn of a new dynasty" and called the twenty-first century "the China century," but it concluded that "China's rise to global prominence doesn't have to lead to the sort of horror that accompanied the emerging power of Germany or Japan. There need be no wars between China and the U.S., no catastrophes, no economic competition that gets out of hand."[27] For this purpose, leaders in both Washington and Beijing have to demonstrate their wisdom by helping to overcome the pervasive mutual suspicions and use their political skill to communicate with each other on sensitive issues in order to assure that China's growing power produces cooperation instead of confrontation in the years to come.

In this case, it becomes profoundly important to understand how foreign-policy analysts in both countries have perceived the transformation of U.S.–China relations. This book serves this purpose by presenting views and assessments of foreign policy specialists from both countries. It does not seek to confirm either an alarmist or optimistic position but to demonstrate that the transformation has provided opportunities for both confrontation and cooperation, with the hope that leaders in Washington and Beijing will make positive adjustments toward cooperation and avoiding confrontation.

The structure of this book

This book is composed of three parts. Part I includes two overview chapters. Following this introductory chapter, Chapter 2 examines China's geo-strategic thrust and diplomatic engagement in the light of China's rise. It addresses some important concerns of many Americans: How has China defined its national security objectives? What role has China played on the global stage and in the Asia-Pacific region? Has it sought to advance interests that undermine the global economic and security system or help to promote peace and prosperity around the world? Has China used its rising influence in ways that are compatible with U.S. interests? Is China rising to become a "responsible stakeholder" or a vicious challenger to the established international system? The author finds that in setting economic modernization and political stability as overarching goals while worrying about potential ideological and structural conflict with the U.S.A. and resource vulnerability, Beijing has developed a pragmatic engagement strategy to promote multipolarization at the same time that China recognizing the reality of a unipolar world dominated by the U.S.A. Developing strategic partnerships with all major powers, China has set other foreign policy priorities for pursuing China's national interests, including searching for energy security, diffusing tension along its immediate borders, and working within the framework of multilateralism.

Perspectives of Chinese scholars

Part II presents five Chinese scholar's views on the changing strategic relationship between China and the U.S.A. Chapter 3 by Qingguo Jia, a leading foreign-policy scholar in Beijing, analyzes China's efforts to adapt to the post-Cold War world and the underlying factors that have shaped such efforts. Jia characterizes China's behavior as "learning to live with the hegemon," i.e., adapting and adjusting policy to the U.S. dominance in the international system. He attributes the behavior to the following three factors. First, gradually accepting the post-Cold War international reality, the Chinese government has decided that it is not in China's interests to challenge the most powerful country unless China's own core national interests are involved. Second, facing a whole array of tough domestic challenges to its political stability brought about by modernization, systemic transformation from a central planned economy to a market economy, and leadership transition from a generation of charismatic leaders to one of techno-bureaucrats, China badly needs a peaceful international environment to maintain political stability. Since relations with the U.S.A. are critical in order for China to manage these in an international environment, the Chinese government naturally does all it can to seek improvement of its relations with the U.S.A. Third, as China's influence continues to grow, the Chinese government has begun to appreciate the fact that China's rise will have serious implications for other countries, and China is likely to confront growing suspicion and even resistance on the part of some countries, especially the U.S.A. Under the circumstances, China needs to do all it can to alleviate such concerns through cultivating understanding and trust between China and other countries.

Chapter 4 by Dongxiao Chen, a Shanghai based foreign-policy analyst, makes a case for long-term Sino-U.S. cooperation by examining the structural transformation of Sino-U.S. relations in the following three aspects: mutual perceptions, interest-based interactions, and institutionalized management. According to Chen, the transition of mutual perception has led both Chinese and American governments to reorganize bilateral relations for constructive cooperation. Globalization and interdependence have increased efforts by both countries to pursue their mutual interests. In particular, the common threat about terrorism has weakened or diverted U.S. concern about "China's geo-strategic challenge." Dialogues for building regional and global orders have become an important aspect of bilateral relations. In the meantime, the institutionalization of Sino-U.S. relations has involved building crisis management mechanisms and regional and global multilateral mechanisms. These complex mechanisms have provided a certain degree of institutional guarantee to the health and stability of these relations, helping the two countries build up confidence, dispel suspicion, and prevent and manage crises. Specifically, these mechanisms have served to reduce and avoid trivial disputes that might divert from the overall development of bilateral relations.

While Chen is optimistic about the transformation of Sino-U.S. relations, Chapter 5 by Jian Xu, a Beijing based government think-tank analyst, takes a more pessimist position due to his concern over the consequences of U.S. unilateralism. Xu starts from China's new concept of cooperative security, which, according to him, advocates mutual trust, mutual benefit, equality and cooperation among nations because it places emphasis not only on China's comprehensive security but also on cooperative security as against the Cold War mindset of a zero-sum game. In comparison, Xu criticizes U.S. neo-conservative security concepts of "preemptive" war, unilateralism, and "neo-interventionism." He argues that a "preventive" war like the Iraq War is illegitimate and may damage the existing international security system since the use of military force in international relations by any country has to be in accordance with international law and with the authorization of the United Nations. The new-interventionist rhetoric of "human rights above sovereignty" is misleading because protection of human rights must facilitate the comprehensive and coordinated development of all economic, social, cultural, civil, and political rights; this is only possible when state sovereignty is respected and intact. In spite of his criticism of U.S. security attitudes, Xu agrees with the pragmatic position of the Chinese leadership in building a cooperative relationship with the U.S.A. He claims that there are no fundamental conflicts between the two countries since China does not have the political will nor the capability to challenge the paramount objective of U.S. foreign policy, i.e. maintaining the dominant role in the world and various regions. In addition, China does not seek to challenge the current international system. The common "stake" of the two sides covers a wide range, including cooperation in economic and cultural fields, anti-terrorism, upholding international non-proliferation regimes, and the management of certain regional hot spots, such as the nuclear issues in Iran and on the Korean Peninsula.

Chapter 6 by Baohui Zhang, a Hong Kong based Chinese scholar, examines U.S.–China relations in the context of China's modernization of its nuclear capability and evolving related doctrines. Zhang indicates that due to the concern about the ability of its small nuclear force to withstand a first strike in the event of a military confrontation with the U.S.A. over Taiwan, China has been modernizing and enlarging its nuclear arsenal. China's nuclear modernization will lead to a secure second-strike capability in the next decade. Although it is unlikely that China will change its "No First Use" doctrine, the U.S.A. should not discount the possibility of China exercising nuclear deterrence in the Taiwan Strait. Zhang argues that although the growing Chinese nuclear capability may open up a new front for Sino-U.S. competition, it will also bring greater stability to the strategic relationship between the two countries as it will generate important incentives for bilateral strategic cooperation. In particular, a more robust Chinese nuclear deterrence will make it less likely for the two sides to mishandle a crisis situation in the Taiwan Strait because a nuclear showdown would force the decision makers on both sides to exercise maximum caution. Without sufficient mutual deterrence, the current situation in the Taiwan Strait has the potential to drag the two countries into a major powers' war that is in neither side's interest. From this perspective, he urges the U.S.A. to welcome a more robust Chinese nuclear deterrent and suggests that China engage the U.S.A. in strategic dialogues for assurance purposes.

In addition to security issues, China's rise has also transformed U.S.–China economic relations and brought about trade and other economic disputes with important political implications. Chapter 7 by Wei Li, a Beijing based economist, analyzes the complex U.S.–China economic relations, focusing on the trade imbalance issue. Li acknowledges that the U.S. trade deficit with China has become a prominent problem in the bilateral relationship because some U.S. politicians complain that the huge deficit threatens the U.S. economy and has robbed the U.S.A. of job opportunities. Li, however, disagrees with the view that attributes the trade deficit to unfair trade practices by China, such as exchange rate policy and market access obstacles. Instead, Li attributes to variables such as the difference in economic structure and trade structure between the two countries; the large inflow of FDI to China; and China's special processing trade feature in which China is only used as an assembly platform while the overseas investors or contractors get the bulk of the money and China's trade surplus is expanded. From a Chinese position, Li argues that the trade deficit is only a parameter in a statistical sense and does not fully reflect the actual benefits to both countries achieved through trade. From an economic perspective, a trade deficit might not be too big a problem. The current uproar on this issue in the U.S.A. is based to a great extent on political considerations.

Perspectives of U.S. based scholars

Part III of the book includes six chapters by U.S. based scholars. Chapter 8 by Phillip C. Saunders, a Washington based foreign-policy analyst, explores a range of U.S. concerns that may give rise to cooperation but are more likely to cause tensions and potential conflicts. These issues include China's domestic developments, Taiwan, China's nuclear modernization, Chinese influence in Asia, and China's potential to become a strategic rival. Depending on the issue, he proposes four different instruments for U.S. involvement with China. One is cooperation in the areas with shared interests such as maintaining stability in the Asia-Pacific region, fostering a global system that supports trade and economic development, pursuing a denuclearized Korean peninsula, and counter-terrorism. The second is engagement to alter Chinese thinking about interests and priorities, producing changes in Chinese behavior and creating a basis for longer-term, cooperation in the areas where common interests may exist but not be recognized or when the two countries may have differing priorities. These issues include nonproliferation, protection of intellectual property rights, human rights, the Chinese role in multilateral institutions, economic policy, and environmental protection. The third instrument is deterrence for dealing with immediate challenges and to prevent China from undertaking certain actions such as invading or attacking Taiwan or using force to pursue Chinese claims in territorial and resource disputes. The fourth is discussion to deal with future conflicts of interest by shaping China's strategic choices in either a narrow technical sense, such as efforts to discourage China from developing anti-satellite weapons, or in a broader strategic sense, such as efforts to discourage China from challenging the U.S. global position. Some of these are compatible with the U.S. hedging strategy, especially those that work indirectly by influencing the costs and benefits of Chinese strategic choices. All these activities are taking place within a broader context where the U.S.A. is attempting to influence China's political evolution and long-term strategic choices in positive directions. This complexity does not mean that the two countries are fated to be enemies, but it does mean that a degree of ambivalence and tension is unavoidable.

How well the U.S.A. copes with both cooperative and competitive dimensions of relations with China depends to a great extent on whether domestic consensus can be built in response to China's rise. Chapter 9 by Jean A. Garrison, a university professor in Wyoming, outlines the parameters of domestic politics with regard to U.S. policy toward China. According to her, the U.S. domestic debate over China policy since Tiananmen Square has undermined U.S. bipartisan engagement policy and made it difficult for presidents to forge a China policy consensus. Single interests with an axe to grind with China have flourished and the domestic debate emphasizing China's many threats to U.S. prosperity continues to recapture the China policy agenda. Congress has gained a great degree of direct influence over Sino-American relations to the extent that coalitions of unlikely allies from the political left and right continue to challenge presidential prerogatives in China policy-making. As a consequence, China policy appears more volatile than stable. Although engagement remains the default policy orientation, this concept represents a convergence around a broad range of discrete policy choices rather than a coherent policy consensus. The last three presidents have all oversold the opportunities in their engagement policy and painted a rosy future for U.S.–China relations in order to overcome their domestic critics. Part of the problem is that U.S. engagement policy rests on the notion that placing China into a web of interdependency will lead to liberal reforms, an unrealistic view that assumes the U.S.A. will maintain the top position in the relationship thus having the means to influence it directly. China's rise and U.S. dependence on its economy should belie this belief. Domestically this situation has led to a deep gap between American expectations and the reality of what can be accomplished in the relationship. The sooner the U.S.A. closes the gap between its rhetoric and its expectations for China policy to fit the pragmatic political reality, the sooner a truly "normal" relationship that openly acknowledges areas of shared interest and disagreement can flourish.

Chapter 10 by Bernard D. Cole, a Washington based scholar, examines China's military modernization in the context of its search for energy security and the implications for U.S.–China relations. He defines "energy security" as including three primary elements: energy availability, affordability, and military capability to secure the required energy supplies. Focusing on the third element, Cole finds that Beijing faces two major problems in securing the energy supplies: locating and procuring those supplies and then distributing them throughout the enormous Chinese hinterland. To resolve these problems, China has made a huge investment in energy exploration and production overseas and become concerned about its reliance on the sea lanes for importing petroleum supplies. Therefore, the People's Liberation Army Navy (PLAN) is entrusted to defend China's search for energy security through its mission of securing sea lanes and ocean bed energy fields, the latter of which the U.S.A. views as the most likely threat. In this context, Cole explores China's military modernization program with a focus on the modernization of the PLAN. Cole concludes that although Chinese leaders view energy issues and maritime interests as vital elements in their nation's economic health and their own political legitimacy, China's concern for the security of its overseas energy supplies does not dominate its national security policy process. The most important aspects of energy security for Beijing are economic and political, not military. In this case, Beijing's energy security concerns will not necessarily lead to an armed conflict with the U.S.A.

Chapter 11 by June Teufel Dreyer, a university based scholar, agrees with Cole that the conflict between the U.S.A. and China over energy supplies is not imminent because the two countries face serious common challenges that include increasing dependence on foreign sources, higher energy costs, and intensifying environmental impacts. Since the U.S.A. is a leader in many fields of energy research and technology, and China has achievements of its own in such fields as high-energy physics, coal sequestration, and next-generation nuclear reactors, the energy security of both countries can be enhanced through cooperation. A policy of active engagement between China and the U.S.A. can prevent harm to common economic interests. For the U.S.A., it can also diminish China's incentive to take bilateral relations with energy suppliers to the level of security relationships, which would challenge American military superiority. Cooperative efforts include the establishment of extensive bilateral energy dialogues at both policy and working levels. The two sides have worked together on "smart buildings." There are proposals for joint hydrogen development. Potential for further progress exists in these and other areas, including air pollution and control, water treatment, solid waste treatment and disposal, renewable energy, pollution control, and energy efficiency equipment. Nonetheless, sovereignty issues remain, and both sides continue to desire energy independence.

Chapter 12 by Pieter Bottelier, a U.S.-based European scholar, focuses on the economic implications of China's rise. Presenting a complex picture of bilateral economic interaction, Bottelier urges the U.S.A. and China to resolve disputes using economic rather than political logic. He finds that the bilateral disputes over economic issues have been caused by the difference in economic growth patterns of these two countries. China's growth is primarily investment-driven, promoting investment to create jobs. In contrast, the U.S.A. relies more on consumption growth to protect employment. Consequently, while the latter has spent more than it earned for many years, China typically has a current account surplus and even financed part of the U.S. current account deficit. As China becomes competitive in a wide range of industries and is rapidly moving up the value chain, China's economic growth and influence on global markets have unavoidably affected the U.S.A. and other countries linked through trade. According to Bottelier, the reasons for China's current competitiveness go well beyond low wages and an undervalued currency as some U.S. officials have suggested. Analyzing U.S.–China economic disputes over China's WTO compliance, trade unbalance, U.S. job loss and related Chinese currency value, Bottelier argues that these issues are more complicated than many American politicians have recognised.

Although China is aspiring to become a global power, its greatest influence largely focuses on the Asia-Pacific, a region where China's most important economic and political interests are located. As a result, the implications of China's rise for U.S.–China relations in this region are one of the focused concerns of many observers. To address this concern, Chapter 13 by Elizabeth Economy, a New York based think-tank analyst, examines the implications of China's rising influence in Southeast Asia for the reconfiguration of regional power relations in the Asia-Pacific. She points out that China's aggressive engagement with Asia-Pacific countries contrasts starkly with a policy of relative neglect by the U.S.A. While U.S. relations with Southeast Asia, as with most of the world, seemed to develop common purpose in the wake of the September 11 terrorist attacks, over time, much of this shared sense of purpose has dissipated. The Bush administration's doctrine of preemption, unilateralism, and the invasion of Iraq led to a precipitous decline in the U.S.A.'s reputation among much of the public in Southeast Asia. Moreover, President Bush's singular focus on security issues, such as the war on terror and the North Korea nuclear threat, did little to persuade many regional leaders that the U.S.A. understood the region's priorities of domestic economic development and political stability. In this context, Economy presents three scenarios to help understand the long-term implications of China's rise in the region. The best case scenario is that a more active China will share leadership with the U.S.A. and Japan, helping forge consensus within a more active and integrated region to address its political, security, and economic challenges. This scenario is likely to have a better chance of either pressuring or inducing change in some of the more recalcitrant actors in the region and also provide an opportunity for regional actors to relieve the U.S.A. some of the burden of leadership by assuming a more proactive role in responding to regional crises.

The second scenario, less attractive from the U.S. perspective, suggests a traditional balancing act, in which the nations of Asia use China to ignore the U.S.A. on selective issues, developing alternative approaches to security, political and economic affairs in ways that perhaps more directly serve their domestic interests. The worst case scenario is that as China assumes a more dominant economic, political, and even security role in the region, the U.S.A. will confront an Asia less likely to respond favorably to U.S. security initiatives, less dependent on U.S. economic leadership and U.S.-run financial institutions, and potentially less open to the full range of U.S. diplomatic initiatives on issues such as human rights and terrorism. She concludes that although China is in no position to displace either the U.S.A. or Japan in the near future, China's greater presence and activism suggest at the very least that the U.S.A. and Japan cannot remain complacent about the status quo that has governed political, economic and security relations for the past few decades. Shared leadership within Southeast Asia will likely include China in the near future, with all the potential benefits and challenges that such leadership will entail.

Notes

1 There is a rich literature on power transition in international relations. Among them, see R. J. L. Tammen and J. Kugler, eds, *Power Transition: Strategies for the 21st Century*, New York: Deven Bridge Press, 2000; J. Kugler and D. Lemke, *Parity and War: Evaluations and Extensions of the War Ledges*, Ann Arbor, MI: University of Michigan Press, 1996; and B. Bueno de Mesquita and D. Lalman, *War and Reason: Domestic and International Imperatives*, New Haven, CT: Yale University Press, 1992.

2 The Chicago Council on Global Affairs and the Asia Society, *The U.S.A. and the Rise of China and India: Results of a 2006 Mutination Survey of Public Opinion*, Chicago, IL: 2006, p. 15.

3 Banning Garrett, "US–China Relations in the Era of Globalization and Terror: A Framework for Analysis," *Journal of Contemporary China*, vol. 15, no. 48, August 2006, pp. 389–416.

4 David, M. Lampton, "The Faces of Chinese Power," *Foreign Affairs*, vol. 86, no. 1, January/February 2007, p. 117.

5 Zhiqun Zhu, *US–China Relations in the 21st Century: Power Transition and Peace*, London: Routledge, 2006, p. 173.

6 Yan Xuetong, "The Rise of China and Its Power Status," *The Chinese Journal of International Politics*, vol. 1, no. 2006, p. 13.

7 Eric A. Posner and John Yoo, "International Law and the Rise of China," *Chicago Public Law and Legal Theory Working Paper*, no. 127, The Law School, the University of Chicago, May 2006, pp. 2, 5.

8 David M. Lampton, "Paradigm Lost: The Demise of 'weak China'," *National Interest*, Fall 2005, pp. 67–74.

9 U.S. Department of Defense, *Quadrennial Defense Report*, September 30, 2001, http://www.defenselink.mil/pubs/qdr2001.pdf

10 U.S. Department of Defense, *Quadrennial Defense Report*, February 6, 2006, p. 29, http://www.qr.hq.af.mil/pdf/2006%20QDR%20Report.pdf

11 U.S. Department of Defense, *Quadrennial Defense Report*, February 6, 2006, p. 29, http://www.qr.hq.af.mil/pdf/2006%20QDR%20Report.pdf

12 Kenneth Lieberthal, "Why the US Malaise over China?" *YaleBlobale Online*, January 19, 2006, http://yaleblobal.yale.edu/display.article?id=6842

13 Robert B. Zoellick, "Whither China: From Membership to Responsibility?" *NBR Analysis*, vol. 16, no. 4, December 2005. pp. 5–14.

14 Dan Blumenthal, "America and Japan Approach a Rising China," *Asian Outlook*, No. 4, December 2006, p. 1.

15 Michael Elliott, "The Chinese Century," *Time*, January 22, 2007, p. 35.

16 Zheng Bijian, "Zhongguo Heping Jueqi xingdaolu yu zhongmei guanxi" (China's new road of peaceful rise and Sino-US relations), *Zhongguo Zhanlue Guancha* (China strategic review), July, 2005, p. 4.

17 Jia Qingguo, "China's New Leadership and Strategic Relations with the U.S.A.," paper presented at International Conference on Challenge to China: Foreign Policy and the Implications to Macao," Macao, May 28–29, 2006, p. 3.

18 Yang Jiemian, "International Environment and Sino-US Interactions," *China International Studies*, Winter 2005, p. 63.

19 Suisheng Zhao, "Beijing's Perception of International System and Foreign Policy

Adjustment after the Tiananmen Incident," in Suisheng Zhao, ed., *Chinese Foreign Policy, Pragmatism and Strategic Behavior*, Armonk, NY: M. E. Sharpe, 2003, pp. 140–150.

20 Xue Fukang, "Hedging Strategy Won't Do Relationship Good," *China Daily*, November 21, 2005, p. 4.

21 Wang Jisi, "China's Search for Stability with America," *Foreign Affairs*, vol. 84, no. 5, September/October, 2005, pp. 40, 46.

22 Sun Xuefeng, "The Efficiency of China's Policy towards the U.S.A.," *Chinese Journal of Internaitonal Politics*, vol. 1, no. 1, 2006, p. 59.

23 Jermy Page, "Giants Meet to Counter US Power," *The Times*, February 15, 2007.

24 Harry Harding, *A Fragile Relationship: the U.S.A. and China since 1972*, Washington D.C., Brookings Institution, 1992; David M. Lampton, *Sam Bed Different Dreams: Managing US–China Relations, 1989–2000*, Berkeley, CA: University of California Press, 2001.

25 Joseph S. Nye, Jr., "The Future of US–China Relations," PacNet, 10, March 16, 2006.

26 Aaron L. Friedberg, "The Future of US–China Relations, Is Conflict Inevitable," *International Security*, Nov. 30, no. 2, Fall 2005, p. 8.

27 Michael Elliott, "The Chinese Century," *Time*, January 22, 2007, p. 42.

2 China rising

Geo-strategic thrust and diplomatic engagement

Suisheng Zhao

For some time since the end of the Cold War, two often contradictory self-images of a great power and a developing country constantly tested China's foreign-policy makers.[1] While they cherished a rising power status and wanted to play a role accordingly, China kept a low profile in international affairs and played down its pretense to being a global power because of its concern that "the existing gap between China and the developed countries, and the U.S.A. in particular, is enormous in terms of national wealth, standard of living, education, and science and technology."[2] In this case, although China's great power aspiration sparked anxieties and hot debate in almost all world capitals, the topic remained delicate in China's media at least until a 12-part TV series with an explicit title, *The Rise of Great Powers*, was broadcast twice by China's Central Television during the last two months of 2006. The series looks closely at the ascendance of nine great powers – including Britain, Germany, Japan, and the U.S.A. – and the lessons that China can draw from their rise. The message is that "China is on the verge of the same historic rise."[3] Whether or not the broadcast signaled that the dual-identity syndrome of great power versus poor country finally diminished along with the rapid growth of China's national power, it was interpreted as meaning that Chinese people were encouraged "to discuss what it means to be a major world power" and the Chinese leadership "has largely stopped denying that China intends to become one soon."[4] This observation was supported by a 2006 Chicago Council on Global Affairs and the Asia Society survey, which found that 87 percent of Chinese respondents thought that China should take a greater role in world affairs. Most Chinese believed that China's global influence would match that of the U.S.A. within a decade.[5] Consequently, a Western reporter observed that although the Chinese leaders still coyly insist that China is merely a developing country, "a growing number of Chinese scholars and commentators are discarding the old bashfulness and beginning to talk openly of China's rising power."[6]

China's rise to great power status has prompted politicians in some Western capitals and its Asian neighbors to wonder whether an increasingly strong and assertive China would become a rational, peaceful, and pragmatic power or an irrational, bellicose, and expansionist state. In a speech on U.S.–China relations, Robert Zoellick, former U.S. deputy secretary of state, raised the question he considered essential for the U.S.A. and the world – how will China use its influence? Uncertain himself about an answer, he urged China to become a "responsible stakeholder" in the international system.[7] Is China rising to be a "responsible stakeholder" or a vicious challenger to the established international system? This chapter seeks answers to this question by examining China's national security objectives and its geo-strategic engagement in recent years.

National security objectives

In the debate about the prospects and implications of China's rise as a great power, a perception gap has often existed between Chinese officials and many Western observers. As Robert Zoellick indicated, while many Americans are anxious about China's rise, "the overwhelming priority of China's senior officials is to develop and modernize a China that still faces enormous internal challenges. ... Therefore, China clearly needs a benign international environment for its work at home."[8] Indeed, Chinese leaders have set economic modernization and political stability as the twin overarching national objectives and pursued them enthusiastically since China decided to open up to the outside world in the late 1970s. At the 16th Chinese Communist Party (CCP) Congress in October 2002, the Hu Jintao leadership reconfirmed these objectives by presenting the goal of quadrupling the 2000 GDP by 2020 and transforming China into a *xiaokang* society, where the Chinese people would enjoy a much more abundant and comfortable life. Pursing these objectives, China has boasted the world's fastest-growing economy in recent decades. An OECD country survey said that China's rapid economic growth over the past two decades "represents one of the most sustained and rapid economic transformations seen in the world economy in the past 50 years."[9]

After two decades of phenomenal growth, China is recognized as a rising global power and certainly feels more secure and confident in the international arena. Other than the dispute over the status of Taiwan, it has not seen any issues that might result in an imminent conflict with foreign powers directly threatening China's sovereignty, territorial integrity, and independence. It has also generally dismissed the possibility of a new Cold War against China, especially after the terrorist attacks on September 11, 2001, which prompted the U.S.A. to engage China in its global war on terrorism rather than pick a fight with her.

However, China does have a peculiar and persisting sense of insecurity or vulnerability, driven mostly by the following three factors. First, Chinese political leaders are very concerned about the possible threat to China's modernization program as a result of a potential ideological conflict between China and the Western powers, particularly the U.S.A. Since the collapse of the communist regimes in Europe, China has been left as one of very few "communist" countries in the post-Cold War world. Given the growing problems of political legitimacy and governance in an increasingly pluralistic society, the Chinese leadership has a fear of domestic unrest supported by foreign forces that would threaten China's political system and the survival of the CCP regime. Consequently, Chinese leaders have a deeply rooted sense of political insecurity and concern for the regime's survival.

Second, many Chinese analysts have talked about a structural conflict between China as a rising power and the U.S.A. as the sole superpower in the post-Cold War world. Although China enjoys the status of a rising power, a persistent sense of frustration and even victimization still colors the feelings of many Chinese elites in relations with Western powers, particularly the U.S.A. and Japan. They worry that the U.S.A. has a hidden agenda to prevent China from rising as a peer power and feel the anxiety of unsatisfied nationalistic aspirations. They have called for completing the historical "mission" of national unification, restoring past glory, and making contributions to the peace and prosperity of the world. Paradoxically this aspiration has led many Chinese elites to feel less powerful and secure when they see many of China's aspirations are increasingly scrutinized by the Western powers, particularly the U.S.A.[10] This frustration was revealed by a Chinese analyst, Pan Zhengqiang, at a forum held by a foreign affairs magazine in Beijing: "Although China is developing rapidly, its development prospects remain uncertain. China has been making large efforts to merge into the international community, but it has still not been fully accepted by the international system dominated by the Western countries."[11]

Third, rapid economic growth has brought China to an unprecedented resource vulnerability that could threaten China's sustainable development. Zheng Bijian, a senior adviser to Chinese president Hu Jintao, listed the shortage of resources, particularly energy, as the first of three fundamental challenges to China's rise in the twenty-first century. According to him, China's per capita water resources are a quarter of the world average, and its per capita areas of cultivatable farmland are 40 percent of the world average. China's natural gas, copper, and aluminum resources in per capital terms are around 8.3 percent, 4.1 percent, 25.5 percent, and 9.7 percent of the world average respectively.[12] China overtook Japan as the second largest oil consumer next to the U.S.A. in 2003 and overtook the U.S.A. as the world's biggest consumer of grain, meat, coal, and steel in 2004. This massive appetite for resources, however, has met with what China has perceived as "unfair" competitive pressure from the U.S.A. Chinese scholars often cite the example of China having had to abandon an $18.5 billion takeover bid for California-based oil firm Unocal Corp in early 2005 because of unusual political intervention from the U.S. Congress.

This sense of insecurity has sustained the frustration among the Chinese people and their leaders at a time when the nation is rapidly rising. At the popular level this frustration was revealed by outbursts of public feeling – from the numerous best-selling anti-American tabloids published in the mid-1990s to the stoning of the American Embassy by college students avenging the U.S. bombing of the Chinese Embassy in Belgrade in 1999. It was a shock to many in the West to witness more than 20 million Chinese signatures gathered on the Internet in early 2005 to oppose Japan's bid to join the United Nations Security Council, and thousands of Chinese protesters marched through major Chinese cities, shouting slogans and throwing rocks, bottles, and eggs at the Japanese consulates, protesting against Japan's approval of history textbooks – which they say whitewashed Japanese wartime atrocities – and Japan's pledge to help the U.S.A. defend Taiwan in the event of an attack by Beijing. A rather broadly based nationalist sentiment, longing for a greater China, is on the rise. While the Chinese public have eagerly sought stature, acceptance, honor, and respect on the world stage, serious Chinese scholars have openly argued for a more assertive and more demanding Chinese foreign policy.[13] Holding high expectations for the government to fulfil its promise to safeguard China's national interests, popular nationalists have routinely charged the Chinese government as being "too chummy" with Japan and "soft" in dealing with the U.S.A. in recent years.

At the state level, Chinese leaders have taken a pragmatic position regarding the popular nationalist outburst. On the one hand, they have tolerated and encouraged the popular expression of nationalism to make their own policy positions more credible to the U.S.A. and Japan on issues involving China's vital interests. On the other hand, pragmatic leaders have been very cautious to prevent the nationalist sentiment of Chinese people from getting out of hand and cause a backlash in both domestic and foreign affairs. Although there is a popular call for the government to take a hard line against what they perceive as provocations from the U.S.A. and Japan, leaders are aware that China's economic success depends heavily upon integration with the outside world and, particularly, upon cooperative relations with advanced Western countries. Chinese leaders have emphasized the principles of peaceful co-existence, peaceful orientation, peaceful rise, and peaceful development as China rises to the status of a great power.

In response to perceived insecurity and vulnerability, China's foreign policy objectives have been set to create and maintain a stable and favorable international environment, staying alert to any threats at home and abroad that could subvert its modernization program. Chinese leaders believe that although the U.S.A. needs cooperation with China in its war against terrorism, it still sees China as a "potential threat" to its ultimate strategic objective of world hegemony. To avoid confrontation with the U.S.A. while China is still in a weaker position, Chinese leaders have made a preemptive effort to build an image of a rising China as a peace-loving and responsible power by promoting the new concepts of "peaceful rise/development" and "a world of harmony."

The concept of "China's peaceful rise" was put forward saliently for the first time by Zheng Bijian at the April 2003 Boao Forum – an annual high level gathering of political and business leaders from Asia-Pacific countries on China's Hainan Island. Premier Wen Jiabao endorsed this concept in his New York City speech in December 2003. Since then, however, many Chinese scholars and officials have expressed their concerns that using the word "rise" might intimidate some of China's Asian neighbors since "the word 'rise' implies attaining superpower status."[14] As an alternative, President Hu Jintao used the words "peaceful development" in his speech at the 2004 Boao Forum. In a way to reconcile "rise" and "development," Zheng Bijian in his 2005 Boao forum speech explained that "China has chosen a strategy to develop by taking advantage of the peaceful international environment, and at the same time to maintain world peace through its development. This is a strategy of peaceful rise, namely, a strategy of peaceful development."[15] Whether using the term "peaceful rise" or "peaceful development," Chinese officials have attempted to assure China's neighbors and other major powers that China's rise as a global power will bring opportunities and benefits instead of threats to peace and stability. In other words, China's rise is not a zero-sum game. The ultimate message in this concept is that China is seeking an accommodating rather than a confrontational approach toward the U.S.A. and other powers in the process of its rise.[16]

The concept of the "world of harmony" was presented to the international community by President Hu Jintao in his September 15, 2005 speech at the U.N. General Assembly. The concept was derived from traditional Chinese thinking that "harmony" was at the core of dealing with everything from state affairs to neighborly relations. According to a discussion among Chinese foreign affairs specialists, the world of harmony signifies first of all the importance of the co-existence of diversified civilizations as a very powerful driving force for the progress of the human race. Tolerance, which is free of restrictions by any ideologies and social systems, plays a role of paramount importance in bringing about the peaceful co-existence of different civilizations. Applying this concept to international politics means consultation among all countries involved, not unilateralism driven by hegemonic ambitions. Major powers can play a key role in building the world of harmony in the same way that they waged fully fledged wars and the Cold War in the twentith century. Chinese analysts see major powers as possibly alternately encountering times of strained relations and enjoying relaxed exchanges in the twenty-first century. Although the possibility of a deterioration in relations should not be ruled out, major power relations are poised to develop in a benign direction. The international community should help make this happen because the nature of relations between the leading global powers will determine war and peace on the world stage and the smooth running of world affairs and upheavals.[17]

Arguing for China's peaceful rise and the world of harmony, China has identified many new threats to its national security in recent years. An *Outlook Weekly* article indicated that

> along with the development of new technology and the acceleration of globalization, the national security issues have become more and more complicated. In addition to traditional military security, many non-traditional security issues, including economic security, financial security, information security, and organized transnational crime, international terrorism, etc. have threatened the international community.[18]

Therefore, Chinese leaders have proposed a new security concept stressing the development of China's comprehensive national strength (*zhonghe guoli*), composed of international competitiveness, an efficient and flexible diplomacy, and a compatible military capability. The emphasis on comprehensive national strength is a major departure from its previous perception of national security, which was based on military security of survival from external attacks. To enhance the "comprehensive national strength," Chinese leaders have emphasized "the integrity of national sovereignty and territory, the intactness of its political institutions, social stability, the capability to resist internal or external revolts, and the safety of its economic prosperity and natural resources."[19]

Seeing that its comprehensive national strength is not strong enough to confront the U.S.A., Beijing has adopted a *"tiaoguang yanghui"* (hide brightness and nourish obscurity) policy designed by Deng Xiaoping in the early 1990s. This policy emphasizes that China keep a low profile in international affairs, bide its time, never take a lead, and build up its capabilities. Increasingly awareness of China's rising power status in recent years, has resulted in a debate among Chinese foreign-policy elite about whether China should still follow a passive foreign policy. Some Chinese elites have begun to explore a "new thinking" (*xinsiwei*) and argued for abandoning a passive posture in favor of a more active response to international challenges. There has been a noticeable relief in Beijing that the U.S.A. is less likely to carry out a containment policy against China while Washington is heavily preoccupied with the fighting in Iraq after the September 11 terrorist attacks. As Wang Jisi, a policy scholar in Beijing, elaborated,

> The U.S.A. now needs China's help on issues such as counterterrorism, nonproliferation, the reconstruction of Iraq, and the maintenance of stability in the Middle East. More and more, Washington has also started to seek China's cooperation in fields such as trade and finance, despite increased friction over currency exchange rates, intellectual property rights, and the textile trade.[20]

Enjoying the best international environment since the founding of the PRC, many PRC analysts have urged China to take a "great power" (*daguo*) responsibility in the world stage to ensure a "just and rational" new security order.

A pragmatic engagement strategy

Debating its role in the world, Beijing has developed a pragmatic engagement strategy. Pragmatism by definition is behavior disciplined neither by a set of values nor established principles. Pragmatist strategy is therefore ideologically agnostic, having nothing, or very little, to do with either communist ideology or liberal ideals. It is a firmly goal-fulfilling and national interest-driven strategic behavior conditioned substantially by China's historical experiences and geostrategic interests. In the early years of the PRC, Chinese foreign policy was justified mostly by communist ideology and some moral principles. Pragmatic calculation of power and interests was often relegated to a secondary position.

These ideology/morality-driven foreign policies, however, caused more harm than good to the communist regime. After the inception of Deng's market-oriented economic reform, the emphasis on economic modernization has propelled China's foreign policy toward pragmatism motivated by geo-politics and economic interest. Pragmatic strategy is flexible in tactics and avoids appearing confrontational, but it is uncompromising on the issues that involve China's vital national interest or that trigger historical sensitivities.

One scholarly reflection on the turning tide of China's strategic thinking toward pragmatism was the publication of Yan Xuetong's *Guanyu Zhongguo de Guojia Liyi Fenxi* [Analysis of China's national interests] in 1996. Yan's book is "designed to clarify the confusing concept of national interest, provide an analysis of China's national interest after the Cold War and propose some strategic suggestions for realizing national interest."[21] This serious scholarly book gained unusual popularity because Yan argues that China is facing a competitive international environment. It is therefore crucial that China's leaders place emphasis on its economic, political, and security interests. Yan suggests that while China should avoid military conflict with other powers, particularly the U.S.A., it should be assertive in defending China's national interest against any external erosion. Yan's argument has found strong supporters among Chinese strategic analysts and foreign-policy makers calling for a more pragmatic approach toward international affairs in line with Deng Xiaoping's position that "national interests" should be the "overriding consideration" in foreign-policy making.

Pursuing a pragmatic strategy comes partially from the realization that China has increasingly become a part of a larger international environment that provides opportunities for as well as constraints on its policy options. As a result, Beijing's leaders have been particularly sensitive to China's position in the evolving international system, which Beijing has only a limited role in shaping. Chinese scholars and officials often start their analysis of international relations from *liliang duibi* (balance of forces) in the world, a Chinese term similar to the conception of distribution of power in Western literature on international relations. Policy makers in Beijing have tried to adjust foreign policy according to *liliang duibi* since they understood the dynamics of international politics as a change of power distribution across the world. As Wang Jisi indicated, "Without a study of *liliang duibi*, policy makers in Beijing presumably would not be able to adjust foreign policy accordingly."[22]

Chinese leaders have envisioned different patterns of power distribution and tried to adapt to them in different periods of PRC history. Mao Zedong saw two camps in the 1950s and decided to lean toward one side. In the early 1970s, Mao perceived a hierarchical structure of three worlds, and developed a strategy to cooperate with the developing countries of the Third World as well as developed Japan and Western Europe – which constituted Mao's second world – in an attempt to counter the alleged hegemonism of the two superpowers that constituted the First World. After the U.S.A. extended diplomatic recognition to Beijing in 1979, post-Mao leaders worked very hard to shape a strategic triangle in which China played a crucial role maneuvering between the two superpowers, the U.S.A. and the Soviet Union. Since the end of the Cold War, Beijing's foreign-policy makers have tried to resist the formation and persistence of a unipolar world that is perceived not in China's favor. To find an alternative, China has envisioned and promoted a multipolar world in which China is on the upward trajectory and plays a balancing role. That is why, Beijing's foreign-policy analysts suggested, "The world has undergone a transition to multipolar-ization (*duojihua*) since the end of the Cold War. A relative balance of power has resulted in an effective check on all global powers."[23]

Three possible types of multipolar system have been presented. One is a tripolar world, in which Europe constitutes one pole; North America forms the second pole; and Asia-Pacific is rising as the third pole. The second is a five-polar structure, which consists of the U.S.A., Germany, Russia, China, and Japan. The third is a pattern of "one superpower and many big powers" (*yi chao duo qiang*). The one superpower refers to the U.S.A. and the big powers to the European Union, Japan, Russia, China, and perhaps India. Bilateral relations differ between these powers. Some are diametrically opposed on the ideological; some are in sharp political conflict; some have serious economic conflicts; some are political allies but full of economic contradictions; some have different social systems but complement each other economically, and some have normal political ties but are rather cool in their economic relations. The most frequently mentioned pattern in Chinese literature of strategic studies has been the "one superpower and many big powers."[24]

Although Beijing's perception of multipolarity stands against the speculation that a unipolar world characterized by U.S. hegemony was emerging from the ashes of the Cold War, Chinese leaders admit that the U.S.A. has remained the sole superpower because of its comprehensive national strength, whether in terms of its economy, scientific and technological strength, military might, or foreign influence. As Wang Jisi said, "The United States is currently the only country with the capacity and the ambition to exercise global primacy, and it will remain so for a long time to come. This means that the U.S.A. is the country that can exert the greatest strategic pressure on China."[25] As the sole superpower the U.S.A. has strong security interests and competed energetically for its dominant position in the world. In particular, the Bush administration's articula-tion of ambitious goals has given a whole dimension to the unipolar world order that the U.S.A. has sought to maintain.

In this case, although China has emphasized the desirability and likely emer-gence of a multipolar world of sovereign states mutually respecting the principle of noninterference and has tried to retain its independent power aspirations by building a united front with other states against the U.S. hegemony, Chinese leaders have made pragmatic accommodations to the unipolar world. In spite of frustrations in the ups and downs of relationships with the U.S.A., China's leaders have taken the Sino-U.S. relationship as the most important in all of China's foreign relations and have hoped to establish and maintain a friendly and cooperative relationship with the unwieldy superpower holding the key to China's future of economic modernization. They have concluded that the failure of the Soviet Union was largely due to its strategy of confrontation with the U.S.A. in a competition for the position of world superpower that exhausted its economic and military capacity. As a Chinese scholar suggested, as one of the weaker poles in the multipolar world, China should not become the second "Mr. No" after the former Soviet Union to confront the U.S.A. and exhaust itself. Instead, China should defend its national interest by conducting a shrewd diplomacy, which "requires rationality and calmness."[26]

Liu Ji, a senior aide to former Chinese president Jiang Zemin, made an explicit call for political leaders in both countries to make pragmatic decisions based on strategic interests rather than ideological and moral grounds in handling the Sino-U.S. relationship. Liu argued that ideological and cultural differences between China and the U.S.A. should not become the cause of conflict because these two countries could establish a cooperative relationship supported by strategic interests.[27] Liu's argument for strategic interests to a great extent explains China's steadfast effort to maintain a cooperative relationship with the U.S.A. in recent decades. It is a testimony to the pragmatism of Chinese leaders that China did not make a sharp reaction to President Bush's initial negative attitude toward China and steadfastly worked to build a cooperative relationship after Bush came to office. This pragmatic policy paid off as the Sino-U.S. relationship quickly returned to a "strategic partnership" in the second term of the Bush administration.

Avoiding confrontation with the U.S.A., pragmatic engagement strategy also holds that the U.S.A. has failed to enact an effective strategy for controlling the globe unilaterally. The U.S. government is not only subject to strong domestic resistance to foreign military intervention due to the American public's concern with their domestic problems and the runaway costs of the war in Iraq but also faces the reality that the traditional control of its allies has become more difficult as other major powers have adopted more independent policies. One major feature of global politics after the end of the Cold War is that a growing number of major powers have become bold enough to say no to the sole superpower. To manage its relations with major powers while actively pushing for a multipolar world, China has designed a new network of strategic partnerships mostly on bilateral basis, since the mid-1990s. This network of partnerships practically covers all the major powers and regional organizations, including Russia, France, the U.S.A., the U.K., the Association of Southeast Asian Nations (ASEAN), the European Union (EU), South Africa, Canada, Brazil, India, Mexico, and Japan.

Promotion of strategic partnerships with a growing number of countries reflects China's attempt to find its right place as a rising power in international strategic relations. The network of strategic partnerships is an instrument for China to secure a multipolar world in which the major powers will establish relationships based on equality to provide a better guarantee of regional and global power balance and stability. Within the framework of partnership, Chinese leaders have appealed to their counterparts to abandon the Cold War mentality and actively identify common interests, with the hope that differences and contradictions in political systems and values would not affect the healthy development of state-to-state relations. As Zheng Bijian wrote,

> In pursuing the goal of peaceful rise, the Chinese leadership has strived to improve China's relations with all the nations of the world. Despite the ups and downs in U.S.–China relations over the years, as well as other dramatic changes in international politics, such as the collapse of the Soviet Union, Beijing has stuck to the belief that there are more opportunities than challenges for China in today's international environment.[28]

The idea of partnership is in accord with China's strategic objectives of maintaining a peaceful international environment in which China can concentrate on economic development and maintain political stability. The concept is vague enough to allow China to encourage countries to adopt a more independent foreign-policy line while avoiding the perception of a confrontation or anti-U.S. alignment.

Pursuing this strategy of pragmatic engagement, China has increased what Phillip C. Saunders called "global activism," driven mostly by two forces. One is perceived international threats and opportunities and China's changing role in the global balance of power. The other is economic development needs and China's changing role in the world economy.[29] The top priority of China's engagement strategy is to protect China's vital national interests against the possible U.S. containment policy and to develop strategic partnerships with all major powers. In addition, pragmatic engagement strategy has gradually unveiled many other policy priorities, including the search for energy security; diffusing tension along its immediate borders; and striving for resolution of international problems through mutilateral cooperation. As a result of implementing the pragmatic engagement strategy, Beijing has deepened its political relations with energy producing nations around the world; sought better relations with, and greater influence on, neighboring Asia-Pacific countries; and taken a more cooperative approach to multilateral activities. The remainder of this chapter will elaborate on the pragmatic engagement strategy in the above three aspects.

Search for energy security on the global stage

Energy security has become one of the top foreign policy priorities as China's dependence on overseas energy supplies has increased steadily after it turned into a net petroleum import country in 1993. While China's rapid economic growth has produced hungry basic industries, and the mushrooming middle class has consumed growing quantities of heating oil and gasoline, China's domestic oil production can meet only about two-thirds of the country's crude oil needs today. The Chinese government estimates that China's need for crude will be more than triple its expected output of oil by 2020. As a result, China's oil imports will account for 77 percent of the country's estimated demand then.[30]

China's pursuit of a stable energy supply, therefore, is all about maintaining the nation's strong economic growth, a linchpin to social stability and the regime legitimacy of the CCP as well as the foundation for China's rising power aspirations.

The Chinese government has initiated numerous policies to cope with its increasing energy consumption, including intensive reorganization of the energy sector to coordinate energy production and consumption, stepping up exploration activities within its own borders, developing alternative fuels, promoting energy conservation, improving energy efficiency, and encouraging investment into energy-friendly technologies such as hydrogen-powered fuel cells and coal gasification. In addition, the Chinese government has begun building a 90-day strategic reserve of crude oil, based on U.S. and European models, which will protect China's industries and military against sudden disruption of oil supplies. This strategic reserve, located in Zhejiang province, near the East China Sea, south of Shanghai, is expected to be ready by 2009.

In the meantime, Chinese leaders have actively sought energy supplies around the world as China's future political stability depends more and more on continued economic growth fueled by readily available, affordable energy supplies from foreign sources. Soon after taking office in 2002, President Hu Jintao and Premier Wen Jiabao decided that securing reliable supplies of petroleum and other scarce resources was not only crucial to sustained economic development, but also integral to China's national security. While China's ninth five year plan (1995–2000) called for, among other things, improving energy efficiency by 5 percent annually, in part by acquiring modern technology, the tenth five year plan (2001–2005) added a call for seeking international sources of oil and gas. As one indicator of this new strategic move, China's state-owned energy corporations have been transformed into multinational companies by overseas acquisitions and direct investments with a goal to emulate the Exxon-Mobil model, with overseas production accounting for 60–70 percent of profits.

As a major policy initiative, China has intensified its efforts to invest in and deepen political relationships with energy producing countries around the world. In particular, China has become an active player in the Middle East, a region Beijing used to consider remote to China's strategic interests. As the Middle East accounts for the majority of China's oil imports, China has made a great effort to forge ties with oil-rich Middle East countries, making deals in transportation and technology, showcasing its consumer goods and shoring up agreements to meet its enormous energy needs. While the trade volume between China and the six countries of the Gulf Cooperation Council – the United Arab Emirates, Saudi Arabia, Bahrain, Kuwait, Qatar and Oman – has increased steadily, China has started talks since the summer of 2004 to strike a free trade agreement with the Gulf Cooperation Council countries.[31] The surge in trade and other economic interactions have come largely through China's selling military equipment and technology and investing in industries and energy infrastructure in the gulf nations pairing up to get oil and natural gas to China. In addition to Saudi Arabia, Iran is the largest Middle East oil supplier to China. Growing

Sino-Iranian relations have undermined U.S. sanctions against Iran as China has opposed bringing the controversy over Iran's uranium enrichment program before the U.N. Security Council and has even threatened to veto any resolution that is brought against Iran. The Bush administration has sanctioned Chinese companies many times for violating U.S. or international controls on the transfer of weapons technology to Iran and other states.

Concerning America's military and political dominance in the region, China has embarked to ensure energy security by diversifying supplies beyond the Middle East after the Iraq War broke out in 2003. Before the war, China's view of the global energy map focused mostly on the Middle East. Iraq was regarded as one well-supplied country. To develop some of Iraq's reserves, Beijing advocated lifting the United Nations sanctions that prevented investment in Iraq's oil patch and limited sales of its production. China had been waiting for the end of sanctions to begin working on the Al-Ahdab field in central Iraq under a $1.3 billion contract signed in 1997 by its largest state-owned firm, China National Petroleum Corporation (CNPC). The field's production potential was estimated at 90,000 barrels a day. China was also pursuing rights to a far bigger prize – the Halfayah field, which could produce 300,000 barrels a day. Together, those two fields might have delivered quantities equivalent to 13 percent of China's current domestic production. Then the U.S.A. went to war in Iraq in 2003. The war not only wiped out China's stakes in Iraq but also reshaped China's basic conception of the geopolitics of oil. To avoid the zero-sum contest for Middle East energy supplies with the U.S.A., Beijing has to lessen dependence on Middle East supplies and intensify its search for new stocks in other parts of the world, including Africa, Latin America, and neighboring Asian countries.

This new strategy encourages Chinese state-owned oil corporations to secure investment agreements involving energy exploration, pipelines, and refinery facilities with all states around the world that produce oil, gas, and other resources. China has successfully expanded its relations with many oil-rich countries in Africa, such as Nigeria, Angola, Chad, and Sudan. China currently imports a quarter of its total imports from Africa. In some cases of expanding relations with African countries, China has come to confront U.S. interests. For example, it started oil investments in Sudan, a country accused by the U.S.A. of genocide in its Western region of Darfur, in the mid-1990s. Sudanese oil began pumping in 1999 and has become China's first successful overseas effort to produce significant output. Sudanese output now accounts for the majority of CNPC production. China also purchased crude oil from Libya, another country that has been under U.S. sanction.

A relative newcomer to Latin America, China has moved quickly to become an important trade partner with many countries in the region. Chinese president Jiang Zemin made a landmark visit to the region in 2001. This visit sparked a wave of subsequent visits by senior officials and business leaders between China and Latin American countries. President Hu Jintao traveled to Argentina, Brazil, Chile, and Cuba in 2004 and visited Mexico in 2005. Chinese Vice-President

Zheng Qinghong also made a historical tour of three Latin American countries and signed multibillion agreements for investment in oil, gas, and other projects in January 2005. One of the major outcomes of this tour was a series of oil exploration and purchase agreements with Venezuela led by anti-American president Hugo Chavez, who has made no secret of his concern about his country's dependence on oil exports to the U.S.A. and built his popularity at home by tapping into anti-American sentiment.[32] With the largest oil reserves outside the Middle East, and a president who says that his country needs to diversify its energy business beyond the U.S.A., Venezuela has emerged as an obvious contender for Beijing's attention. The Sino-Venezuelan agreements commit CNPC to develop Venezuelan oil and gas reserves and thus divert oil from the U.S.A. to China.

Implementation of the diversification strategy has borne fruit. China's Middle East oil imports were reduced from 50.9 percent of total imports in 2004 to 45 percent in 2005. China's energy diversification strategy is also welcomed by some developing countries as it allows them to exploit as yet untapped resources and gain leverage to negotiate better deals with other oil-importing countries. However, this strategy has stepped on the toes of the U.S.A., the world's largest energy consumer, and raised concerns among some in the U.S.A. that China is not only potentially challenging the U.S.A.'s historic dominance in Africa, Latin America, and Asia but also undermining Western efforts to promote transparency and human rights in these developing countries, damaging U.S. interests and values. The U.S.A. is particularly concerned that China has pursued deals with countries that are off-limits to Western companies because of sanctions, security concerns, or the threat of bad publicity. China's pragmatic, nonideological approach to energy security has provided these countries with an alternative to dependence on the U.S.A., thereby reducing the effectiveness of U.S. policy. Some observers have worried that China's active quest to secure energy supplies in Africa and Latin America may have fueled an energy Cold War.

A good neighbor policy

China's pragmatic engagement strategy has paid special attention to the Asia-Pacific region "where China exerts greatest influence and where its most important foreign policy interest are located."[33] China often calls its Asian neighbors "periphery countries" (zhoubian guojia). For a long time in the early years of the PRC, China was a regional power without a regional policy.[34] The tensions with many of its neighboring countries became an important source of threat to China's national security. Beijing was in constant alert against possible invasions of hostile powers via its neighboring countries and fought several wars with neighbors, or with hostile powers in neighboring countries, to defuse the threat. China's recent resurgence to the status of a global power has given rise to the speculation about a "China threat" among China's weak neighbors. They have worried that, after China becomes modernized, Beijing would like to have East Asia as its exclusive sphere of influence, a modern equivalent of the traditional tributary system. Beijing has denied this speculation and offered repeated assurance that "China will never seek hegemony."[35] However, this assurance has not eased the fear of China's weaker neighbors.

It is, therefore, crucially important for China to have a coherent regional policy to address its security concerns in the periphery and the concerns of its neighbors over China's rise. As a matter of fact, after China launched market-oriented economic reform, opening up to the outside world in the early 1980s, Chinese leaders have determined to create a favorable peripheral environment for economic modernization. As a result, Beijing has made a deliberated effort to devise an integrated *"zhoubian zhengce"* [periphery policy], known as *"mulin zhengce"* (good neighbor policy) to cope with the changes that challenged China's relations with neighboring countries. A study by two Chinese scholars pointed to three developments in Asia that led Chinese leaders to pay a special attention to its periphery.[36] The first was the prospect of a "pacific century," which Beijing embraced with the hope that fast economic growth in the Asia-Pacific region could offer new opportunities for China's economic prosperity. The second was the emergence of "new Asianism," which claimed that the success of Asian modernization was based on its unique values. This concept resonated in the hearts of many Chinese leaders, reformers and conservatives alike, because it challenged Western ideological and economic centrality. The third was the development of regional or subregional blocs. Beijing decided to take advantage of the collectivism that might provide new mechanisms useful for China to face the West.

In light of these developments, Beijing's leaders began to devise a regional policy aimed at exploring the common ground with Asian countries in both economic and security arenas and conveying the image of a responsible power willing to contribute to stability and cooperation in the region. Working with the region for its economic modernization program, Beijing's periphery policy has two security goals. The first is to reassure Asian neighbors that in spite of its rising power status, China is settling border disputes "through consultations and negotiations." The second is to develop strategic relationships and find common ground with Asian countries to resist pressures on market penetration and human rights issues from Western powers. Implementing this policy, China improved its relations with most of its periphery countries in roughly two chronological stages: the late Cold War period of the 1980s and the post-Cold War period after the 1990s.

The first stage started in the early 1980s with two policy shifts. The first was to abandon ideology as the policy guide and to develop friendly relations with neighbors regardless of their ideological tendencies and political systems (*buyi yishi xingtai he shehui zhidu lun qingsu*). The second was to change the practice of defining China's relations with its neighbors in terms of their relations with either the Soviet Union or the U.S.A. (*yimei huaxian, yisu huaxian*). China would develop normal relations with neighboring countries regardless of their relations with the superpowers. These policy changes resulted in an improvement of China's relations with some periphery countries previously in tension.

One example was the normalization of its relationship with Mongolia, which had long been perceived as a Soviet satellite on China's northern frontier. A border agreement between the two countries was signed in November 1988. Another example was China's effort to improve its relationship with India. This effort resulted in the ice-breaking visit of the Indian prime minister, Rajive Gandhi, to Beijing in December 1988, the first such visit after the Sino-India border war in 1962. Maintaining a good relationship with North Korea and, at the same time, improving its relationship with South Korea at the end of the 1980s was a third example.

The Tiananmen Massacre in 1989 and the subsequent end of the Cold War started the second stage of improvement of China's relations with periphery countries. The massacre led to economic sanctions by Western countries. However, it had little negative impact on China's relations with its Asian neighbors as the human rights records in most of these countries were not better than that in China. To improve China's international environment after Tiananmen, Beijing decided to further reduce the role of ideological factors in China's foreign relations and stop drawing lines according to a country's social-political system or attitudes toward China. As a result, it was really ironic that while China's relations with Western countries soured, its relations with Asian-Pacific neighbors improved in the 1990s.

China normalized diplomatic relations with several influential Southeast Asian countries during this period: Indonesia (August 8, 1990), Singapore (October 3, 1990), Brunei (September 30, 1991), and Vietnam (November 1991). China was invited to attend the ASEAN post-Ministerial Conference in 1991 and became a member of the ASEAN Regional Forum (ARF) in 1994 and ASEAN's comprehensive dialogue partner in 1996. Since then, China has actively participated in what they called "*shanhui jizhi*" [three meeting mechanism]: the ASEAN Foreign Ministerial Meeting, the Enlarged ASEAN Foreign Ministerial Meeting, and ARF.[37] The Asian financial crisis in 1997 provided a good opportunity for China to further improve its relations with Southeast Asian countries. Although China was not immune from its effect, it withstood the crisis better than many of its neighbors. Sending several billion dollars in aid to afflicted Southeast Asian economies, the Chinese government kept its promise to maintain a stable currency. A Chinese devaluation would have set off competitive devaluation across the region. The Indian Ocean tsunami that hit the coast of some Southeast Asian countries in December 2004 provided another opportunity for China to show its good faith. The Chinese government provided more than US$87 million in humanitarian assistance, the biggest emergency package that China has ever offered to foreign countries in PRC history. These policy actions have helped establish a good neighbor and mutual-trust partnership between China and ASEAN, oriented towards the 21st century.

In addition, China has also significantly improved relations with its neighbors in the north and northwest. A formal diplomatic relationship with South Korea was established on August 24, 1992, that marked the success of China's policy to secure a balanced relationship with both Koreas. Following the disintegration of the Soviet Union, China secured a good start with the newly independent Central Asian states of Kazakhstan, Tajikistan, Kyrgyzstan, Uzbekistan, and Turkmenistan in 1992. Three of the five Central Asian states share borders of more than 3,000 kilometers with China. Securing its relations with these countries is crucially important to ensure China's border area stability and energy supplies, the twin pillars of its future economic growth. China shares with these countries the concern that radical Islam would stir ethnic and popular revolt and fears the possibility of fundamentalist fervor erupting in that region since China's westernmost region is inhabited by Turkic-speaking Muslim Uyghur. Russia has been bogged down in guerrilla wars with Muslim nationalists in Chechnya. Tajikistan, Kyrgyzstan, and Uzbekistan have cast militant Islam as their main enemy. This common concern led these countries to work with China to contain ethnic fundamentalism. Eager to prevent Islamic militancy from fueling separatism in Xinjiang, China has dispatched waves of senior politicians and military delegations to Central Asia. It gave parachutes, medicine, and other supplies to airborne forces and border guards in Tajikistan, which has been convulsed by civil war. It also pledged military aid to Uzbekistan, which has been raided annually by an opposition group called the Islamic Movement of Uzbekistan.

While China's initial consideration was border area security, energy security quickly became an important issue on the agenda for China's relations with the Central Asian states as these countries, particularly Kazakhstan, could be an excellent source for China's energy supplies. Oil from the Caspian was traditionally exported to Russia and more recently to Western markets via the Black Sea. Kazakhstan's economy has grown strongly in recent years due to foreign investment in oil and gas production around the Caspian Sea. It is now looking for new markets for expanding production. The vast and growing energy market in China is attractive. Beijing is aware of this and has cultivated economic ties with Central Asia. As a *Beijing Review* article stated, "The large oil market in China is no doubt a big magnet to Central Asian countries that are placing priority in energy industry development."[38] China has invested heavily in several oil and gas fields in Central Asia. Most important are the oilfields that the China National Petroleum Company (CNPC) has invested in Kazakhstan for some US$5 billion. Exporting oil to the east, rather than the west, requires a 3,000 km pipeline across the plains of central Kazakhstan. Through a landmark agreement with Kazakhstan, Beijing completed the construction of a major pipeline linking the western province of Xinjiang to Caspian energy development in 2005. This pipeline is able to deliver up to 20 million tons of Caspian Sea crude to western China annually.

China's arrival as a big player in the great game of Central Asia, however, has caused some concerns. Local rivalries have been uneasy at Beijing's growing power and sharply boosted defense outlays. China is constantly accused of expansionist aims in the area. In addition, "Russia is wary of China muscling into parts of Central Asia it has long viewed as its own turf."[39] To maintain good relations with Russia and Central Asian states, Chinese president Jiang Zemin took a lead in putting together a "Treaty of Enhancing Military Mutual Trust in the Border Areas" signed by China, Russia, Kazakhstan, Tajikistan, and Kyrgyzstan in Shanghai in April 1996. This group was then known as the "Shanghai Five," designed as a talking shop on minor issues of borders and territory among China and its Central Asian neighbors. Yet in a few short years, the group began to address political and military questions. The five countries signed a "Treaty of Mutual Reduction of Military Forces in the Border Areas" in April 1997. At its June 2001 meeting in Beijing, the Shanghai Five accepted a new member, Uzbekistan, and began to meet under a new name, the Shanghai Cooperation Organization (SCO). Since the terrorist attack on the U.S.A. on September 11, 2001, the SCO has increasingly focused on security issues. These six countries have agreed on political, military, and intelligence cooperation for the purpose of "cracking down on terrorism, separatism, extremism" and to maintain "regional security" and established an anti-terrorism center in Bishkek, Kyrgyzstan, with a secretariat in Beijing. The SCO represents Beijing's most significant effort at securing its border security and energy resources through a multilateral security mechanism. A Western observer believed that: "Together, the Shanghai Pact countries have a population of 1.5 billion; they control thousands of strategic and tactical nuclear weapons, and their combined conventional military forces number 3.6 million."[40] It was from this perspective that an Australian newspaper report stated that: "The newly formed Shanghai Co-operation Organization, bracketing China, Russia and four Central Asian republics, is poised to emerge as a potent force against U.S.A. influence and a rising tide of Islamic militancy in the region."[41]

Beijing's relationship with Russia has also improved spectacularly in the recent decade. Together with the relationship with the U.S.A., China's strategic relationship with Russia is the most significant as these two important bilateral relationships may be an extension and reshaping of the Cold War strategic triangle in the new international environment. Following Boris Yeltsin's first official visit to China in December 1992, Beijing and Moscow institutionalized a twice-a-year summit meeting system at president and premier levels. The Sino-Russian Relationship was first defined as a "constructive partnership" in 1994 and "strategic" was added in the Sino-Russian Joined Communiqué published on April 25, 1996. This relationship was finalized as a "strategic cooperative partnership oriented towards the 21st Century" in 1997. After the retirement of Yeltsin, Chinese leaders continued the partnership with President Vladimir Putin. At the July 2001 summit in Moscow, the presidents of the two countries signed the Good Neighborly Treaty of Friendship and Cooperation to defend mutual interests and boost trade. This Sino-Russian strategic/cooperative partnership has thus become the most developed partnership, with well-established operational mechanisms. Chinese leaders highly value this partnership because it is the only relationship with possible leverage to pose a credible alternative to the lone superpower, the U.S.A., and an entry ticket back to what Chinese strategists have recently often called a "great power strategy" (*da guo zhanlue*). The partnership represents not only a stable and meaningful commitment to bilateral relations but also the attempt by two large and precarious multiethnic continental empires to form a mutual help relationship that would be uniquely useful to them in a volatile international environment.

As a result of successfully implementing the periphery policy, China's security along its borders has been substantially improved. China not only became more confident in its security environment but also advanced its influence in Asia. As suggested by Robert Sutter,

> China is clearly more popular and the target of less suspicion than in the past among many Asian governments, elites and popular opinion, and its economic importance as an engine of Asian growth has increased . . . there is no question that an image of China's rising influence has been important, particularly in Southeast Asia and Korea, where Chinese relations have improved markedly.[42]

Learning to work within the framework of multilateralism

A new priority of China's pragmatic engagement strategy is to work within the framework of multilateralism. For a long time in PRC history, Beijing's leaders stressed the importance of bilateralism and were reluctant to endorse multilateralism because of China's concern over possible erosion of national sovereignty. As a Chinese scholar indicates, the contradiction between multilateralism and bilateralism is a contradiction that has constantly tested China's foreign-policy makers. The open-door policy requires China to be fully integrated into international society, but the strong concern over sovereignty makes it difficult for Beijing to embrace some mainstream values. Beijing has long been accustomed to dealing with others in bilateral settings, but the post-Cold War era is witnessing a rise of mulilateralism in international politics that is putting more and more pressure on China's traditional diplomacy. This contradiction has given rise to a dichotomy in China's foreign-policy behavior. While China seeks to integrate its economy into the international system, it stands vigilant on the sovereignty issue and rejects any interference into its internal affairs. While Beijing expresses enthusiasm about multilateralism, it still feels more comfortable with bilateralism.[43]

This contradiction certainly becomes less important in constraining China's foreign-policy behavior as China rises to the status of a great power and becomes integrated into regional and global economic and security communities. With enhanced confidence in securing its national security and territorial integrity, China has learned to take a more flexible attitude toward the issue of sovereignty, growing more reflective of the new reality in an interdependent world. Consequently, China has become more experienced and confident with multilateral activities, has found less tension between bilateralism and multilateralism, and feels comfortable conducting both types of activities in its diplomacy. This development has helped narrow the gap between China's accorded status and expected status and hence has strengthened the pragmatic strategy for pursuing China's national interests.

As China's rising international status and increasing involvement in multi-lateral organizations and cooperation challenged China's preference for bilateralism and its over-commitment to national sovereignty, Chinese leaders have become more confident working within the framework of multilateralism. While adhering to many bilateral partnerships, Beijing has gradually developed enthusiasm toward global and regional multilateralism. Chinese leaders began to play an active rule in multilateral activities at regional levels in the early 1990s. China, one of the founding members of the Asian Pacific Economic Cooperation in 1993, began to participate in the ASEAN Regional Forum in 1994, and took a lead in establishing the SCO in 1996. China's involvement in multilateralism at the time was mostly aimed at promoting "multipolarization" in an attempt to counter U.S. preponderance rather than adopting multilateralism per se. "Multipolarity" implies a world order where countries balance against the prevailing power; whereas the notion of multilateralism means a kind of foreign policy that may be carried out even in a world dominated by a single power. In recent years, the Hu Jintao leadership has made a subtle yet significant move toward embracing multilateralism on its own terms as China has taken a more sophisticated multilateral approach and worked hard within the multilateral framework seeking China's legitimate interests. Under a policy line of multilateralism, Beijing has not only become increasingly involved in regional multilateral activities but has also taken a more active rule in international regimes/institutions at the global scale.[44]

Taking a pragmatic approach, China has accepted many prevailing international norms beneficial to its foreign policy objectives and gained access to some international regimes in light of its calculation of their impacts upon its national interests while rejecting others it deems in conflict with these. The evolution of China's nonproliferation policy clearly demonstrates how China calculates its national interests to selectively endorse international norms and regimes. China changed its position on nonproliferation from one of dismissal in the 1970s–1980s to one of selected support to serve its national interests in the 1990s when Beijing began undertaking serious efforts to integrate itself into the formal international nonproliferation regime through accession to key treaties and conventions and by active participation in multilateral negotiations, particularly in such forums as the Conference on Disarmament in Geneva. Adhering to international treaties and conventions, Beijing not only demonstrated its commitment to nonproliferation principles, but also placed itself, to some extent, under international legal constraints. There are many explanations regarding the evolution of Chinese nonproliferation policies, but the core of these explanations is based on national interest. China has gradually realized that proliferation of weapons of mass destruction (WMD) and delivery systems can negatively affect its security interests. The existing international nonproliferation regimes, such as the Treaty on the Nonproliferation of Nuclear Weapons (NPT), offer tangible benefits for China, not the least of which would be the prohibition of Japan, the Koreas, and Taiwan to acquire nuclear weapons. While the Comprehensive Test Ban Treaty (CTBT) imposes constraints on China's own nuclear weapons modernization programs, Beijing is willing to pay the price if such mechanisms would prevent countries such as Japan from joining the nuclear club. In addition, with its rising power status, China does not want to be seen as an outcast or impediment to international nonproliferation efforts, which would damage its efforts to establish its image as a responsible power.[45]

In addition to a more active role in multilateral arms control regimes, China has greatly increased its participation in U.N. peacekeeping operations such as those in Haiti and East Timor. It has also tried to engage with the E.U. and NATO, and even began to promote initiatives on security and economic issues in multilateral forums where the U.S.A. has played a dominant role. This is a departure from the previous practice of criticizing American-led alliances. One powerful expression of the serious commitment to multilateralism is Hu Jintao's acceptance of the invitation by the G7 to attend the summit in 2003. Hu became the first Chinese leader at a G7 summit and continued his presence since then. In addition, Beijing played a key role in the six-party talks of the U.S.A., China, Japan, Russia, South Korea, and North Korea over Pyongyang's nuclear program since August 2003. Beijing cajoled both the U.S.A. and North Korea to continue meeting each other despite repeated threats by both sides to discontinue negotiations. After four rounds of talks, China's draft of accord was accepted by all six parties in September 2005. Although this accord was not implemented and North Korea tested its first nuclear device in October 2006, China once again played a leading role in bringing Pyongyang back to the Six Party talks and reaching a new agreement in February 2007. These agreements are milestones in establishing China's strategic importance as a rising power in multilateral diplomatic negotiations involving major powers. Although the implementation of these agreements remained problematic, Chinese analysts in numerous articles and interviews have expressed their safisfaction in searching for a solution to international problems within the framework of mutilateralism. They praised China as an ardent supporter of multilateralism and criticized the U.S.A. for its insistence on unilateralism. A Chinese statement after the 2005 agreeement was reached described the agreement as a big victory for China as it "convinced the U.S. to retreat [from] its long-standing unilateral demands and agree that is beneficial to allow in multilateral interests, even if the results meant more arduous and difficult negotiations lie ahead."[46] A Western report also wrote, after China helped broker the second agreement in February 2007, that: "The six party talks has [sic] shown China in a new light, highlighting its new-found global power in the realm of international diplomacy."[47]

Conclusion

Setting economic modernization and political stability as the overarching object-ives of China's diplomatic thrust, China has benefited greatly from the estab-lished international system and, therefore, has a growing stake in the system. As a rising power, although China has a peculiar sense of insecurity and is not satis-fied with its international status, it has followed a pragmatic diplomatic strategy to pursue its national security objectives of maintaining a peaceful international environment that allows China to realize its dream of becoming a rich and powerful country. Carrying out this pragmatic diplomatic strategy, China has made impressive strides in advancing national security objectives and fulfilling its aspiration to become a great power. In this process, China has expanded its influence in Asia-Pacific and many other parts of the world. As China is still far away from a position of matching the U.S. ability to deliver security or even economic benefits to the countries in its periphery, let alone the other parts of the world, China's geo-strategic thrust has not aimed at challenging the U.S. superpower status and the existing international system. China has tried to fit more comfortably into the established international system. Promoting a multi-polar world, China has made unprecedented efforts to align its interests closely with the U.S.A. in great power diplomacy. As a "system maintainer" not a "system destroyer," China has acted prudently, like most other countries, in light of the opportunities and constraints provided in the current international system although not without frictions and mishaps.

Notes

1 Wu Xinbo, "Four Contradictions Constraining China's Foreign Policy Behavior," *Journal of Contemporary China*, vol. 10, no. 27, May 2001, p. 293.
2 Wang Jisi, *China's Changing Role in Asia*, The Atlantic Council of The U.S.A., January 2004, p. 2.
3 Geoffrey York, "Self-confident China Sees its Own Star Rising," *Global and Mail*, December 5, 2006.
4 Josph Kahn, "China, Shy Giant, Shows Signs of Shedding Its False Modesty," *New York Times*, December 12, 2006.
5 The Chicago Council on Global Affairs and the Asia Society, *The U.S.A. and the Rise of China and India: Results of a 2006 Multination Survey of Public Opinion*, Chicago, IL: 2006, p. 33.
6 Geoffrey York, "Self-confident China Sees its Own Star Rising," *Global and Mail*, December 5, 2006.
7 Robert B. Zoellick, "Whither China: From Membership to Responsibility?" *NBR Analysis*, vol. 16, no. 4, December 2005, p. 7.
8 *Ibid*, p. 8.
9 OECD, "Economic Survey of China 2005: Key challenges for the Chinese economy,"; http://www.oecd.org/document/7/0,2340,en_2649_201185_35343687_1_1_1_1,00.html
10 Fei-ling Wang, "Preservation, Prosperity and Power, What Motivates China's Foreign Policy," *Journal of Contemporary China*, vol. 14, no. 45, November 2005, pp. 678–679.
11 Luntan, Zhongguo shi qiangguo me [forum: is China a major power?], *Shijie Zhishi* [the world affairs], January 1, 2007, p. 18.
12 Zheng Bijian, "China's Peaceful Rise to Great Power Status," *Foreign Affairs*, vol. 84, no. 5, September/October 2005, p. 19.
13 Suisheng Zhao, *A Nation-state by Construction: Dynamics of Modern Chinese Nationalism*, Stanford, CA: Stanford University Press, 2004, pp. 9–15.
14 Yan Xuetong, "The Rise of China and Its Power Status," *The Chinese Journal of International Politics*, vol. 1, no. 1, 2006, p. 12.
15 Cheng Bijian, "China's Peaceful Rise and New Role of Asia," *China Forum*, Autumn, 2005, p. 3.

16 Xiaoxiong Yi, "Chinese Foreign Policy in Transition: Understanding China's Peaceful Development," *The Journal of East Asian Studies*, vol. XIX, no. 1, Spring/Summer 2005, pp. 85–86.

17 Lun Tan, "China's dream of harmonious existence," *China Daily*, November 11, 2005, p. 4.

18 "Shiliuda tebiebaodao, yiqizhouguo shishannian" [The 16th Party Congress Special Report: walk through 13 years together], *Liaowang Zhoukan* [outlook weekly], no. 44, November 4, 2002, p. 31.

19 Wu Baiyi, "The Chinese Security Concept and its Historical Evolution," *Journal of Contemporary China*, vol. 10, no. 27, May 2001, p. 279.

20 Wang Jisi, "China's Search for Stability with America," *Foreign Affairs*, vol. 84, no. 5, September/October 2005, p. 39.

21 Yan Xuetong', *Guanyu Zhongguo de Guojia Liyi Fenxi* [Analysis of China's national interests], Tianjin: Tianjin Renmin Chuban She, 1996, p. 1.

22 Wang Jisi, "International Relations Theory and Study of Chinese Foreign Policy: A Chinese Perspective," in Thomas W. Robinson and David Shambaugh, eds, *Chinese Foreign Policy: Theory and Practice*, Oxford, UK: Clarendon Press, 1995, p. 489.

23 Feng Lidong, "An Interview with Yang Chengxu, Director of International Studies Institute," *Banyuetan* [Bimonthly talk], January 10, 1995, p. 67.

24 Suisheng Zhao, "Beijing's Perception of International System and Foreign Policy Adjustment After the Tiananmen Incident," *Chinese Foreign Policy: Pragmatism and Strategic Behavior*, Armonk, NY: M. E. Sharpe, 2004, pp. 141–144.

25 Wang Jisi, "China's Search for Stability with America," *Foreign Affairs*, vol. 84, no. 5, September/October 2005, p. 39.

26 Shen Jiru, *Zhongguo Budang Bu Xiansheng: Dangdai Zhongguo de Guoji Zhanlue Wenti* [China does not want to be Mr. No: problems of international strategy for today's China], Beijing: Jinri Zhongguo Chubanshe, 1998, p. 62.

27 Liu Ji, "Making the Right Choice in Twenty-First Century Sino-American Relations," *Journal of Contemporary China*, vol. 7, no. 17, 1998, pp. 89–102.

28 Chen Bijian, "China's Peaceful Rise to Great Power Status," *Foreign Affairs*, September/October 2005, p. 21.

29 Phillip C. Saunders, "China's Global Activism: Strategy, Drivers, and Tools," Washington D.C., National Defense University Press, 2006, p. 1.

30 Xu Tao, "Major Central Asia Players: What Does a Rising China Mean Politically, Economically, and Security Wise to Central Asia?" *Beijing Review*, vol. 47, no. 5, February 5, 2004, p. 43.

31 Borzou Daragahi, "China Goes Beyond Oil in Forging Ties to Persian Gulf," *New York Times*, January 13, 2005

32 Drew Thompson, "China's Global Strategy For Energy, Security, And Diplomacy," *China Brief*, Jamestown Foundation, Volume 5, Issue 7, March 29, 2005.

33 Robert Sutter, *China's Rise in Asia: Promises and Perils*, Lanham, MD: Rowman & Little Field Publishers, 2005, p. 2.

34 Steven I. Levine, "China in Asia: The PRC as a Regional Power," in Harry Harding, ed., *China's Foreign Relations in the 1980s*, New Haven, CT: Yale University Press, 1982, p. 107. Denny Roy, in a book of 1998, still believed that "China has no apparent 'Asian policy.'" Denny Roy, *China's Foreign Relations*, Lanham, MD: Rowman & Littlefield Publishers, 1998, p. 8.

35 Jiang Zemin's report to the 15th Party National Congress of the CCP, Beijing *Xinhua*, October 16, 1997.

36 You Ji and Jia Qingguo, "China's Re-emergence and Its Foreign Policy Strategy," in Joseph Y. S. Cheng, ed., *China Review, 1998*, Hong Kong: Chinese University Press, 1998, p. 128.

37 Yan Xuetong, *Zhongguo de Jueqi, Guoji Huanjing pinggu* [The rise of China: an

evaluation of the international environment], Tianjin, China: Tianjin Renmin Chuban She, 1998, p. 287.

38 Xu Tao, "Major Central Asia Players: What Does a Rising China mean politically, economically, and security wise to Central Asia?" *Beijing Review*, vol. 47, no. 5, February 5, 2004, p. 43.

39 Andrew Higgins and Charles Hutzler, "China Sees Key Role for Central Asia in Ensuring Energy Supplies' Stability," *The Wall Street Journal*, June 14, 2001.

40 Constantine C. Menges, "Russia, China and What's Really on the Table," *Washington Post*, July 29, 2001, p. B2.

41 John Schauble, "Russia–China alliance emerges as a foil to US," *The Sydney Morning Herald*, June 16, 2001.

42 Robert Sutter, *China's Rise in Asia: Promises and Perils*, Lanham, MD: Rowman & Little Field Publishers, 2005, p. 10.

43 Wu Xinbo, "Four Contradictions Constraining China's Foreign Policy Behavior," *Journal of Contemporary China*, vol. 10, no. 27, May 2001, pp. 293–302.

44 Xiaoxiong Yi, "Chinese Foreign Policy in Transition: Understanding China's Peaceful Development," *The Journal of East Asian Studies*, vol. XIX, no. 1, Spring/Summer 2005, pp. 91–92.

45 Jing-dong Yuan, "The Evolution of China's Nonproliferation Policy Since the 1990s: Progress, Problems, and Prospects," *Journal of Contemporary China*, vol. 11, no. 31, May 2002, 209–234.

46 Antoaneta Bezlova, "China Crows Over N. Korea 'Diplomatic Coup,'" Inter Press Service, September 27, 2005.

47 Katheen E. McLaughlin, "North Korea Deal Lifts China's Stock in World Diplomacy," *Chronicle Foreign Service*, February 17, 2007.

Part II

Perspectives of Chinese scholars

3 Learning to live with the hegemon

China's policy toward the U.S.A. since the end of the Cold War

Qingguo Jia

A peacefully rising China has to learn to live with the sole superpower in the post-Cold War World, the U.S.A. This chapter reviews China's efforts to adapt to a world dominated by the U.S.A. and analyzes the underlying factors that have shaped such efforts. It attempts to make three points: (1) the adaptation process has been an eventful and difficult one; (2) China's gradual appreciation of the new international reality, the daunting domestic challenges China faces, and China's growing awareness of the implications of its rise for its developmental prospects have helped shape its efforts of adaptation; and (3) if the U.S.A. does not treat China as an enemy and if the two countries can effectively manage the Taiwan problem, China is likely to continue its efforts to accommodate and cooperate with the U.S.A.

Difficult adaptation

The collapse of the Soviet Union in 1991 left the U.S.A. the only superpower in the world. Moreover, contrary to the pessimistic predictions about the U.S. economy at the beginning of the 1990s, the U.S.A. went through a long period of sustained economic growth during the better part of the 1990s. As a result, by the turn of the century, the U.S.A. was not only the only superpower in the world but also a beefed up and rising one. This new international reality has broad implications for international relations. With unrivaled power, the U.S.A. found unprecedented opportunities to shape the world. Confronted with the huge gap in power between the U.S.A. and other major powers, China, like other countries, did not have much choice but to make necessary policy adjustments in its own search for security and prosperity.

In retrospect, China's adaptation to this post-Cold War reality has gone through three phases: (1) seek to restore the damaged official relations with the U.S.A. – June 4, 1989 and June 1994; (2) try to sustain the relationship – June 1994–September 11, 2001; and (3) seize new opportunities to expand and deepen the relationship – September 11, 2001–date).

Seeking restoration of the damaged official relationship

The unexpected outbreak of the June 4th Incident (Tiananmen) in 1989 left China internationally isolated and friendless. Led by the U.S.A., the Western community harshly condemned the Chinese government for its rough handling of the incident and quickly imposed a series of sanctions against China. Among other things, it discontinued high-level official contacts with the Chinese government. It also publicly demanded that the Chinese government release the people arrested for organizing the Tiananmen demonstrations and give in to domestic pressures for political liberalization and democratization.

Confronted with the acute domestic crisis and harsh international pressures, the Chinese government realized that it was facing a critical historical moment. Whatever it did would have serious impact on the fate of the Chinese Communist Party and China's future. After careful analysis of the situation, the Chinese leadership decided that it could not accept Western demands. Surrender meant nothing short of political suicide. The only thing it could do was to step up efforts to stabilize the situation at home and resist the pressures for political liberalization from abroad. Accordingly, it publicly and vehemently rejected Western demands while defending its handling of the Tiananmen incident.

Rejecting Western demands, however, did not mean that the Chinese government did not wish to maintain and develop relations with the West. On the contrary, it was keenly aware of the fact that it badly needed a peaceful international environment for domestic reforms and development. In its efforts to secure such an environment, the Chinese government decided that it should take a low-key posture on international affairs so as to minimize external attention on China and interference with China's developmental and reform process. Specifically, Deng Xiaoping proposed three principles for China's foreign policy: *Lengjing guancha* [carefully assess the situation]; *Wenzhu zhenjiao* [consolidate China's positions]; and *Chenzhuo yingfu* [calmly cope with the challenges].[1]

In line with the three principles, the Chinese government took a moderate and low-key approach in conducting its external relations. It used every opportunity to explain to the world how important political stability was for China and how determined China was to adhere to its policy of reforms and opening up to the outside world. In the meantime, it moderated its efforts to punish people involved in the demonstrations and released most of the people detained for organizing the Tiananmen demonstrations. It even privately cut a deal with the U.S. government to allow Fang Lizhi, an opinion leader of the demonstrations who had sought refuge in the U.S. embassy in Beijing following the June 4th Incident, to leave China for the U.S.A.

Given the paramount influence of the U.S.A. in the world, the Chinese leaders realized that the key to change its difficult international environment was the U.S.A. Despite the official rhetoric about the allegedly pernicious role of the U.S. government in the outbreak of the June 4th Incident, the Chinese leaders privately urged the Bush administration to take steps to rescue the rapidly sinking relationship between the two countries. In his meeting with former president Richard Nixon in October 1989, Deng Xiaoping asked him to convey to President Bush that he hoped the latter would take the initiative to restore the relationship. In his talk with President Bush's special envoy and National Security Advisor Brent Scowcroft on December 10, Deng Xiaoping also made a personal appeal to President Bush, urging the latter to take measures to improve relations between the two countries. He said that despite the current problems, China and the U.S.A. must improve their relationship because world peace and stability demanded it.[2] The Chinese government expected that the U.S.A. would eventually realize that it was not just in China's interests but also in U.S. interests to restore official relations with China.

The opportunity to restore official relations finally came when Iraq invaded Kuwait on August 2, 1990. Immediately after the invasion, the Bush administration denounced it and decided to use force to get the Iraqis out of Kuwait. In order to rally international and domestic support for such an effort, it believed that it needed a resolution from the U.N. Security Council to authorize the use of force against Iraq. Because China is a permanent member of the U.N. Security Council and had long rejected the use of force in international affairs, it was speculated that China would veto the resolution. In order to secure China's cooperation, the Bush administration decided to lift the sanctions prohibiting high-level official contacts with China imposed in the wake of the June 4th Incident and invited Chinese Foreign Minister Qian Qichen to visit Washington.[3]

The resumption of high-level contacts between China and the U.S.A. represented an important step in restoring official relations between the two countries. However, it did not make the relationship smoother. The collapse of the Soviet Union had produced much confidence among Americans for changing the rest of the world into democracies. To many Americans, the Chinese government stood in the way of such efforts and the U.S.A. should do its best to bring it to its knees. Against this backdrop, Bush's pragmatism in dealing with China became an object of public ridicule and condemnation in the U.S.A. During the presidential election campaign, the Democratic presidential candidate Bill Clinton condemned President Bush for "cuddling" the dictators in Beijing. He promised that he would get tough with China if he were to take over the White House. The subsequent Democratic victory gave little comfort to China about its relationship with the U.S.A.

One of the first things Clinton did upon coming into office was to follow up his campaign promises by taking a heavy-handed approach to demand that China improve its human rights record. On May 28, the White House came up with a list of demands and threatened to revoke China's most favored nation status (now called "normal trade nation status" since such a status does not actually accord any privilege to concerned countries) if China failed to meet his demands. Confronted with Clinton's public threats, the Chinese government felt cornered. The Clinton administration was essentially asking the Chinese government to tell the world as well as the Chinese people that its efforts to restore political order at home were wrong and, even worse than that, that the U.S. government had a better idea as to how to govern China. No viable government would accept such demands. Accordingly, the Chinese government did what it deemed politically necessary: it publicly rejected Clinton's demands.

On May 29th, in reaction to Clinton's decision to attach conditions to the renewal of China's MFN status in the following year, the Chinese Ministry of Foreign Affairs issued an official statement. In the statement, the Chinese government protested against the U.S. decision on the grounds that it had violated the three communiqués and trade agreements between the two countries and that it constituted a serious interference in China's internal affairs. It pointed out that politicization of the trade issue, especially attaching conditions to the renewal of China's MFN status, was an unacceptable practice, claiming that such a practice could only seriously damage economic and trade cooperation between the two countries. Ultimately it would also hurt important interests of the U.S.A. itself. Accordingly, it urged the Clinton administration to revoke the decision in the best interests of the two countries.[4]

China's fierce resistance, coupled with Clinton administration's realization of the futility of its efforts to link trade with human rights, eventually led the Clinton administration to abandon the linkage policy. President Clinton publicly acknowledged that his policy of linking trade and human rights issues had not achieved its purpose and that he had ceased to believe that suspending China's MFN status would facilitate American objectives and interests. Accordingly, he said that his administration would discontinue the linkage policy from then on. In an article explaining his decision, Clinton wrote that the linkage policy had reached its logical end. The annual debate on the renewal of China's MFN status might hinder necessary progress on security and economic questions and it was unlikely to lead to any significant progress, including ameliorating the human rights situation in China. The administration believed that the best way to promote human rights in China was to increase contacts, promote trade, enhance international cooperation, and seek extensive and frequent dialogues on the question of human rights. As pragmatism prevailed in the Clinton administration's efforts to deal with China, the seriously damaged official relationship between the two countries was fully restored.

Sustaining the relationship

The restoration of normal official relations between China and the U.S.A. turned out to be fragile at best. American media continued to churn out bloody images or references to the Tiananmen suppression in almost every piece of news about China. Influenced by the media, the American public had little idea about what was going on in China, let alone the development and progress China had made since the June 4th Incident. Therefore it took an increasingly negative view of China. Taking advantage of this situation to advance their causes and interests, some American politicians stepped up their efforts to condemn China with every excuse they could think of. As a result, one heard many largely unsubstantiated accusations against China in those years: proliferation of nuclear and missile technologies to Pakistan and North Korea, selling banned chemicals abroad, systematic murder of handicapped orphans, massive trade of prisoners' organs, stealing top secret weapon information from American labs, making illegal campaign contributions to the Democratic Party, etc.

Confronted with this situation, the Chinese government did all it could to prevent these issues from destroying its efforts to consolidate and improve its relationship with the Clinton administration. It tried to explain to the latter that it had done none of the above. It agreed to take serious steps to tighten its control over arms sales and to ban proliferation of technologies of weapons of mass destruction and delivery systems.[5] On top of all this, it repeatedly expressed willingness to develop closer ties with the U.S.A.

The Chinese efforts to improve relations with the Clinton administration, however, met with a serious challenge from the Taiwan authorities. Headed by Lee Teng-hui, the Taiwan authorities changed their previous policy stance on national reunification and opted for an independence course. They began to push aggressively for the idea of a separate and sovereign status for Taiwan in international society. Through careful political maneuvers, buttressed with a promise of sizable financial contributions, they managed to get Cornell University to invite Lee Teng-hui to visit the university and get the U.S. Congress to pass a resolution to pressure the Clinton administration to give permission for Lee's visit. After initial resistance, the Clinton administration reversed its previous position and decided to approve Lee's visit in an unofficial capacity. This about-face damaged China's perceived core national interests and led to a crisis in the Taiwan Strait and in the relationship between the two countries. Eventually, after missiles were fired and U.S. aircraft carrier groups were dispatched to the Taiwan Strait, both governments managed to emerge from the crisis. With efforts by both sides, Chinese President Jiang Zemin and President Clinton exchanged visits in 1997 and 1998. The leaders of the two countries stressed the importance of developing good relations with each other and vowed to build toward a constructive strategic partnership. Official relations between the two countries assumed a positive momentum.

However, the Taiwan Strait crises of 1995 and 1996 highlighted the potential for military conflicts between the two countries and helped enhance the claim that China was the next challenger to U.S. power and influence in the world. A group of American strategists of a realist persuasion had taken notice of China's rapid economic development and increasing national capabilities. Proceeding from the realist assumption that interests of the rising power and the established power inevitably collide, they argued that the U.S.A. should start to contain China rather than facilitate its development. This group was known as "the blue team." Following the Taiwan Strait crisis, they stepped up efforts to publicize their views and publicly condemned the Clinton administration's China policy.[6]

The Chinese public outrage with the U.S. bombing of the Chinese Embassy in Belgrade in 1999 provided fresh ammunition for the blue team to advance their views. The strong anti-U.S. feelings held by the Chinese public, they argued, demonstrated that the Clinton administration's policy of engagement was doomed to fail. Given their respective positions and interests, China and the

U.S.A. could not be friends. The U.S.A. should abandon the illusion that it could make a friend out of a strong China, democratic or not.[7] Although the Clinton administration resisted the blue team's ideas, such ideas gradually found ways to influence U.S. government policy considerations.

With the change of guard in the White House in the year 2001, the blue team's ideas on China found more sympathetic ears in the U.S. official deliberations on China policy. During the presidential election campaign, George W. Bush vehemently denounced Clinton's engagement policy. He argued that, given China's ideological preference and ill-conceived ambitions, it was inappropriate for the U.S.A. to regard it as a strategic partner. Rather, China should be labeled as a strategic competitor to the U.S.A. Bush lashed out at an alleged Clinton administration's preference for dealing with China than with Japan, the most important ally of the U.S.A. in Asia, claiming that such a practice compromised American security interests in Asia. He also announced that the policy of strategic ambiguity with regard to Taiwan was out of date. If he were elected, he would clarify the policy so that the U.S.A. would be more effective in helping Taiwan defend itself.[8]

Upon entering the White House, President Bush honored his campaign promise by assuming a tougher position on China than his predecessor. He "telephoned every major world leader but Chinese President Jiang Zemin." His administration reportedly planned to "target more U.S. missiles against China." It gave serious consideration to "prioritizing preparation for conventional war in East Asia against China and has promoted enhanced strategic cooperation with India and Japan." It "encouraged Japan to loosen its restraints on a more active regional military presence" and "proposed development with U.S. allies South Korea, Japan and Australia of a 'regional' dialogue." It "stressed cooperation with Russia on missile defense seemingly at the expense of China." It decided to bar Chinese-made products and essentially stopped contacts between the Pentagon and the Chinese military. It "reversed a twenty-year U.S. policy by agreeing to sell submarines to Taiwan" and "allowed high-profile visits to the U.S.A. by Taiwanese President Chen Shui-Bian and the Dalai Lama." On top of all this, the administration did not appoint "a specialist on China to any senior position in the government."[9]

Confronted with the new unfriendly administration, the Chinese government decided to make the best of the difficult situation by making strenuous efforts to keep the relationship on the right track. Soon after Bush came to the White House, the Chinese government sent a stream of officials including Vice Premier Qian Qichen to meet the Bush team in Washington,. Chinese leaders also made other gestures to demonstrate their willingness to work with the Bush administration to develop relations between the two countries. While they protested against the administration's rough handling of the Taiwan problem, they did nothing else beyond making statements. The Chinese government hoped that with the passage of time, the Bush administration would come to realize the importance of the relationship as the Clinton administration had done previously and the two countries would find good reasons to cooperate with each other again.

China's hope of improving relations with the Bush administration diminished over time as the latter refused to moderate its position on China. The rough interactions between Beijing and Washington in the wake of the E-P3 Incident in April 2001 highlighted the intensity of the mistrust and tension. In the wake of the incident, both sides raised voices and went public with blame for the other side for the collision. Popular emotions in both countries ran high. To many in Washington, China's objection to U.S. spy missions along the Chinese coast constituted an early warning of China's international strategic orientation: As it grows in power, it will expand its security perimeters and deny American access to an ever larger area in the Asia-Pacific region. To many in Beijing, the incident showed that the U.S.A. harbored ill intentions towards China and showed how unreasonable it could be when it came to getting its way.

However, Beijing suppressed its frustration and managed to reach a compromise with Washington. It decided not only to return the captured American intruders but also the reconnaissance plane to the U.S.A. In the mean-time, it asked the Chinese people to calm down and focus on building their country stronger to avoid such humiliation in the future. The eventual resolution of the problem did not help produce any good feelings on either side. Even the successful July visit on the part of U.S. Secretary of State General Powell did not fundamentally change the situation.[10] Confronted with an administration that regarded China largely as a potential threat, the Chinese government braced itself for the worst, even though it still wanted to develop good relations with the U.S.A. out of consideration for its own national interests.

Seizing and enlarging the new opportunities

Ironically, it was the outbreak of 9/11 that brought fresh hope for a better relationship between the two countries. In the wake of the terrorist attacks on the U.S.A., the Chinese government expressed its condolence for the casualties and offered support to the U.S.A. in its fight against terror. The Chinese government told the Bush administration that it was willing to help out. It not only said so but also did it. Among other things, it voted in favor of anti-terrorism resolutions in the U.N. Security Council, supported Pakistan's efforts to cooperate with the U.S.A. to oppose Bin Laden and the Taliban regime of Afghanistan, and provided the U.S. intelligence with information it had on terrorist networks and activities in the region. It also agreed to freeze accounts of terrorist suspects in Chinese banks at the request of the U.S. government and to let the U.S.A. use the Shanghai APEC Summit platform to promote the anti-terrorist cause.[11] Contrary to the expectations of some Americans hostile to China, China did all this without attaching any conditions.

These and other cooperative efforts on the part of China eventually evoked favorable reactions from the Bush administration. Secretary of State Colin Powell said in Shanghai in October 2001 that the U.S.A. had been encouraged by the support of the Chinese government. He said that despite the problems of the E-P3 incident earlier in the year, Sino-American relations were back on track.[12] In his meeting with President Jiang Zemin in Shanghai in October 2001, President Bush thanked China for its speedy reaction in expressing its clear and firm support for the U.S.A. and for its efforts to cooperate in the war against terror. He stressed that his administration attached high importance to U.S.–China relations. He also said that China is a great country and was by no means an enemy. On the contrary, he viewed China as a friend, and his administration was committed to developing candid, cooperative, and constructive relations with China.[13] "The Chinese share our resolve to shut down the global terror network linked to Osama bin Laden," said Gen. Frank Taylor, the State Department's ambassador at large for counter-terrorism after his retirement from the Air Force. "We're pleased with the cooperation we have received from China since September 11."[14]

The Chinese government did not simply stop at helping out in the war against terror. It also tried to help out on other issues. Among other things, it tried to enhance its efforts at combating the proliferation of weapons of mass destruction and missile technologies. In addition, China made many efforts to seek a peaceful resolution of the Korean nuclear crisis. Furthermore, in response to U.S. domestic pressures on the Bush administration to address the trade deficit problem with China, the Chinese government sent several delegations to make significant purchases of U.S. airplanes, cars, and agricultural produce and made significant concessions in the recent negotiations on phasing out tax benefits to computer chip makers in China.

On top of all this, the Chinese government has tried to limit the damage to Sino-American relations on issues when the two countries do have significant conflicts of interests and views. Among other things, it did not react strongly to the U.S. withdrawal from the ABM treaty; it did not make a strong protest about the U.S. bugging of President Jiang's plane; it did not take a strong stand against the U.S. invasion of Iraq; and it has not let the U.S. arms sales to Taiwan, or even the increasing contacts between the U.S. and Taiwan militaries, to seriously affect its cooperation with the U.S.A. on other issues.

Primarily because of these and other Chinese efforts to cooperate with the U.S.A. and manage its relationship with the latter the Bush administration found the relationship between the two countries in its best shape since the normalizations of relations between the two countries.[15] Even the leadership transition in China, the widening trade imbalances between the two countries, and the continued rapid rise of China have not changed the positive course of the relationship.

Explaining Chinese behavior

Reviewing Chinese efforts to improve relations with the U.S.A., one cannot avoid asking the question: Why has China behaved like this? Given that the Chinese government was known to raise voices in conducting relations with the U.S.A., and the fact that the Bush administration was by no means friendly to China, this is a legitimate question. Analysis shows that at least the following three factors have been significant in shaping China's behavior: acceptance of the post-Cold War power reality; the need to focus on domestic challenges; increasing appreciation of the implications of the rise of China.

Gradual acceptance of the power reality

To begin with, despite initial resistance, the Chinese government gradually accepted the post-Cold War international reality and decided that it was not in China's interests to challenge the most powerful country in the world unless China's own core national interests were involved. Until the early 1990s, the Chinese government still found it difficult to appreciate the fact that the U.S.A. had become the only superpower in the world. Chinese think-tanks were debating whether U.S. power was on the rise or in decline.[16] Chinese officials and foreign-policy experts were wondering aloud whether the world was unipolar or multipolar or something else. Against this background, the Chinese government was not entirely clear about what kind of world it was to face during the early 1990s. It did what it did because of its concern for political survival.

However, since the mid-1990s, it became clear to the Chinese government that U.S. power was on the rise and that the world was unipolar. As the Chinese government increasingly saw the world as a unipolar one, it became increasingly reluctant to have head-on conflicts with the U.S.A. This is the case especially when it sees other major powers competing to curry favors with the U.S.A. This could be seen on a whole range of issues, including arms trade, arms control, Iraq, Korea, etc. China might have different ideas about how these issues should be handled and might even openly express its reservation about the way the U.S.A. dealt with these. However, the Chinese government has chosen to minimize and if possible avoid conflicts with the U.S.A. on these issues as demonstrated in the previous passages.

The need to focus on domestic challenges

As a country undergoing rapid economic changes and fundamental reforms, China is facing a whole array of tough domestic challenges. Broadly speaking, over the past 20 years, China has been undergoing three historical transitions namely, modernization, systemic transformation from a central planned economy to a market economy, and leadership transition from a generation of charismatic leaders to one of techno-bureaucrats. All of these transformations are drastic and fundamental. And they have been generating tremendous challenges to China's political stability.

By nature, modernization is a very destabilizing process. According to Ted Gurr, as the economy takes off in a country, people's expectations tend to grow much faster than what can actually be obtained in reality. As a result, they tend to develop a strong sense of deprivation and become restless and often rebellious in their behavior.[17] The fundamental changes in social structures and value orientation in the process of modernization make the situation even more unsettling, providing the fertile ground for social unrest and political rebellions.

Compared with modernization, systemic transformation is no less psychologically traumatic and politically destabilizing. During such transformation, a central planned economy and a market economy exist side by side. Consequently, people are confronted with two sets of very different distribution principles and codes of moral conduct. Whereas many in the state sector complain about the "obscenely" high incomes people in the private sector get and deplore the moral corruption associated with the market economy, many in the market sectors complain about the "unearned" privileges (job tenure, free or subsidized housing, free medical care, as well as power) people in the state sectors enjoy and ridicule the mores of the old days. As a result, literally everyone feels frustrated and unhappy. In addition, as the reforms deepen, official corruption worsens, the gap between the rich and the poor widens, and increasing numbers of people in the state sector lose their jobs. All this has led to escalating frustration and resentment of the government and its policies.

If modernization and systemic transformation generate increasing social frustration and political tension, the leadership transition undermines the authority of the government to meet the challenges. Charismatic leaders derive power from either ancestry or their legendary feats in founding the state. They are the creators of the institutions rather than the other way around. Under a charismatic leadership, individuals in leadership positions are strong and institutions weak. A techno-bureaucratic leadership, on the other hand, represents a different relationship between individual leaders and institutions. Having been promoted into leadership positions through various institutional channels, techno-bureaucrats derive their power from the institutions. In contrast to the case with charismatic leadership, institutions create individual leaders. Accordingly, under a techno-bureaucratic leadership, individuals are weak and institutions strong. Political stability is possible under either type of leadership. However, this is not the case when they are in transition from one to the other. This is because when charismatic leaders depart, they leave behind them a set of weak institutions. Since techno-bureaucratic leaders are weak by nature and depend on institutions for power, their authority and powers are very vulnerable to political challenges.

Both from a comparative and a historical perspective, any one of these three transitions poses a serious threat to political stability and has the potential to cause political collapse. China has been undergoing all three simultaneously. It is precisely because of this that the Chinese government has attached high importance to political stability. Successive Chinese leaders – Deng Xiaoping, Hu Yaobang, Zhao Ziyang, Jiang Zemin, and Hu Jintao – all have repeatedly stressed the need for maintaining political stability. They argue that political stability is the most important condition for China's development and reforms. Without political stability, China would not be able to accomplish anything, certainly not economic development, let alone make social and political progress.[18]

These and other domestic challenges require China's full attention. To do so,

China badly needs a peaceful international environment. Since the U.S.A. is the country that is critical for China in obtaining such an international environment, the Chinese government naturally did all it could to seek improvement of its relations with the U.S.A. If the Chinese government did not have much of a chance to do so before 9/11 because the strong U.S. pressures undermined its legitimacy, it began to be able to do so after 9/11. This also explains why China became so accommodating to the U.S.A. after 9/11.

Increasing appreciation of the implications of the rise of China

By 1994, China's rapid economic development had caught the world's attention. Many outside China began to reverse their previous assessment that China would disintegrate or collapse. Instead they began to argue that China was rising and its rise would have profound implications for world affairs. Some even claimed that China was going to challenge U.S. power and privileges.

At the beginning, the Chinese government dismissed the idea as pure fantasy. More than anyone else it knew how backward many parts of China still were and how many difficult problems China was facing. It publicly expressed doubts about the motivations of those behind the idea of the rise of China. Some Chinese even speculated that the real reason that those people advocated the rise of China was because they wanted to disqualify China as a recipient of soft loans from the World Bank.

However, as China's economy continued to grow at a high rate, and as the world showed more respect for China because of its perceived achievement and influence, the Chinese government began to realize that China was indeed rising. Moreover, it gradually began to appreciate the fact that China's rise would have serious implications for other countries, especially the U.S.A. And as it rises, China is likely to confront growing suspicion and even resistance on the part of some countries, especially the U.S.A. Under the circumstances, China needs to do all it can to alleviate such concerns through cultivating understanding and trust between China and other countries. It is with such an understanding that some Chinese, like Zheng Bijian, former executive vice president of the CCP Central Committee Party School, proposed the idea of the peaceful rise of China. The idea received official endorsement later.

Although the idea is still being debated, it is already an important component of foreign-policy deliberations by the Chinese government. The peaceful rise of China among other things requires seeking understanding from and cooperation with the U.S.A. so as to avoid confrontation between the two countries as predicted by some realists in Washington. This idea also underlines China's efforts to enhance cooperation and minimize conflicts with the U.S.A. in recent years. A peaceful rise, however, does not mean that China would sacrifice its core national interests, nor does it suggest that China will abandon efforts to enhance its defense capabilities. It rests on the assumption that it is possible and desirable to develop cooperation through efforts to facilitate understanding and cooperation. However, it also demands precautionary measures such as enhancing military capabilities to defend China's core national interests should such efforts for various reasons fail to achieve the desired results.

Conclusion

Since the end of the Cold War, China's policy toward the U.S.A. has been evolving toward more accommodation and cooperation. While it wished to develop good relations with the U.S.A. all the time in consideration of its own national interests, its policy has shifted from one of securing political survival, to brinkmanship in the mid-1990s, to actively promoting the relationship since the latter part of the 1990s. China's appreciation of the post-Cold War international reality, pressing domestic challenges, and a growing awareness of the implications of its rise for its developmental opportunities have underlined such changes.

How likely is China going to adhere to its policy of accommodation with the U.S.A.? Given that the three underlying factors are not going to change soon, the probability of China continuing this policy remains quite high. However, two factors may seriously affect or even change this process. One is the Taiwan problem. If the Taiwan authorities continue to push for independence, it could make it politically necessary for the Chinese government to use force to defend China's territorial integrity and sovereignty. And this may lead to U.S. intervention and even a Sino-U.S. military confrontation.

The other factor would be a significant change in U.S. policy toward China. Should the U.S.A. revert to a policy that treats China as an enemy or potential enemy as it practiced during the initial period of the Bush administration, this might force China to regard the U.S.A. similarly. Of the two factors, the Taiwan problem is more likely to affect China's policy toward the U.S.A. in the immediate future.

Notes

1 Deng Xiaoping, *Deng Xiaoping Wenxuan* [Selected works of Deng Xiaoping], Beijing: Renmin Publishing House, 1993, p. 321.
2 Hong Shi, "China's Political Development After Tiananmen: Tranquility by Default," *Asian Survey*, December 1990, pp. 1206–1351.
3 Richard Solomon, former assistant secretary for East Asian and Pacific Affairs in the State Department, said in an interview: "After the Iraqi invasion of Kuwait [August 1990], it was evident that if we were going to have a UN coalition, or at least the UN sanction of some collective effort to deal with Saddam [Hussein]'s aggression, we would have to work with the Chinese, given their veto position on the Security Council." Nancy Tucker ed., *China Confidential: American Diplomats and Sino-American Relations 1945–1996*, New York: Columbia University Press, 2001, p. 453.
4 Jia Qingguo, "Shilun kelindun zhizheng yilai de zhongmei guanxi" [On Sino-American relations since Clinton assumed office], *Liang Shoude et al, Mianxiang 21 shiji de zhongguo guoji zhanlue* [China's international strategy facing the 21st century], Beijing: Zhongguo Shehui Kexue Publishing House, 1998, p. 121.
5 In an interview, Winston Lord, the assistant secretary of state for East Asian and Pacific Affairs in the Clinton Administration, gave a list of the actions the Chinese

government took in this regard. Nancy Tucker, ed., *China Confidential: American Diplomats and Sino-American Relations 1945–1996*, New York: Columbia University Press, 2001, p. 469.

6 For a discussion of the blue team and its views on China, J. Michael Waller, "Blue Team Takes on Red China," http://www.insightmag.com/archive/200106047.shtml

7 John Mearsheimer, *The Tragedy of Great Power Politics*, New York: W. W. Norton & Company, 2001, p. 4.

8 James Conachy, "Bush Visit to Japan Cements Closer Ties Against China," March 1, 2002, http://www.wsws.org/articles/2002/mar2002/jap-m01.shtml.

9 Robert S. Ross, "The Stability of Deterrence in the Taiwan Strait," *The National Interest*, Fall: 2001, pp. 67–68.

10 Bates Gill, "Powell's Asia Visit: A Chance to Shape American Thinking Toward the Region," *Newsweek Korea*, July 25, 2001, http://www.brook.edu/views/op-ed/gill/20010725.htm.

11 Bonnie S. Glaser, "Northeast Asia After Sept. 11: Testimony on U.S.–Chinese Relations and the Taiwan Strait," FDCH congressional Testimony, 11/15/2001, Record: 1, 32y401591370920011115.

12 "Baowei'er cheng 911 hou mei dui laizi zhongguo de zhichi gandao guwu" [Powell said that the U.S.A. was encouraged by the support from China], www.peopledaily.com.cn, October 19, 2001.

13 Xiang Xun, "Jiang Zemin zhuxi yu bushi zongtong juxing huitan" [Detailed report: President Jiang Zemin and President Bush held talks], October 19, 2001, www.peopledaily.com.cn

14 Erik Eckholm, "Official Praises China for Its Cooperation in Rooting Out bin Laden's Terror Network," *New York Times*, December 7, 2007.

15 Many Chinese scholars and foreign policy experts do not share such a view because of the U.S. handling of the Taiwan problem.

16 Wang Jisi, "Gaochu bu sheng han" [It is cold at the height], Zhao Baoxu ed., *Kua Shiji de Zhongmei Guanxi* [Sino-American relations at the turn of the century], Beijing: Dongfang Publishing House, 1999, pp. 18–19.

17 Ted Robert Gurr, *Why Men Rebel?*, Princeton, NJ: Princeton University Press, 1970.

18 Jiang Zemin, "Gaoju dengxiaoping lilun weida qizhi, ba jianshe you zhongguo tese de shehuizhuyi shiye quanmian tuixiang qianjin" [Uphold the great banner of the Deng Xiaoping theory and carry forward the course of building socialism with Chinese characteristics into the twenty-first century], *Shiwuda baogao duben* [Collected reports of the Fifteenth Party Congress], Beijing: Renmin Publishing House, 1998, p. 18.

4 Complexity and transformational structure of China–U.S. relations

Dongxiao Chen

The Sino-U.S. relationship in the last years of the Bush administration is seen as one of "complexity," reflected in the three aspects of mutual perceptions, interest-based interactions and institutionalized management. Both countries have recognized the multidimensions and the importance of bilateral relations and have tried to maintain a constructive cooperation. While mutual interdependence has played an increasingly important role in countries' policy-making, regional and global interdependence as well as competition have made dialogues and frictions around building regional and global orders an important issue in bilateral relations. The institutionalization of Sino-U.S. relations has moved forward as mechanisms of the complex bilateral and multilateral management have taken initial shape to provide a certain degree of institutional guarantee in building up confidence, dispelling suspicion, and preventing and managing crises.

Transition in the mutual perceptions

The core of Sino-U.S. mutual perception is how they assess the nature of their bilateral relations in three aspects: the importance of bilateral relations to each other's general interest (important, less important, or ordinary), the basic status of the bilateral relations (hostility, alliance, partnerships, or a mix of these), and the connotations of the bilateral relations (rivalry and competitive relations, or cooperation and win-win relations, hegemony and bandwagon, or a mixture of the above). Sino-U.S. mutual perception has transformed in recent years though this transformation is nonlinear and fraught with distortions. The two countries have come to recognize the importance of bilateral relations and turning from regarding the basic character and connotation of bilateral relations in a rather singular way to a more comprehensive way.

Since the end of the Cold War, China and the U.S.A. have had a large gulf in their perceptions over the importance of bilateral relations. For a period after the June 4th event in 1989, the U.S. government and the public thought that bilateral relations were no longer of global/strategic interest. Therefore, China lost its importance on Washington's foreign-policy agenda. This situation did not end until the spring of 1996 when the Clinton administration conducted an inter-agency review of Chinese policy that ended with the decision to refurbish the seriously outdated Sino-U.S. relations. The U.S.A. thus came to a more realistic perception about China and Sino-U.S. relations, and China's importance on the U.S. foreign-policy agenda remarkably increased. President Clinton stressed that relations with China were most important to America, and regarded expansion of relations with China as one of the three targets of the U.S. Asia-Pacific strategy. Following President Bush taking office in 2001, the U.S. assessment of the importance of Sino-U.S. relations has experienced similar ups and downs. At the beginning of the Bush administration, the U.S.A.–Japan alliance was stressed as the main focus for U.S. Asia-Pacific interests, thus downgrading and weakening Sino-U.S. relations. The U.S.A. also rediscovered India's ideology and strategic values in an attempt to balance China's influence. The 9/11 event altered the Bush administration's assessment of security threats, emphasizing the importance of a "concert of powers" to deal with various new types of threat,[1] and providing an opportunity to reassess and improve Sino-U.S. relations. China has played a considerable or even primary role in a range of issues, such as counterterrorism, post-war reconstruction of conflict areas, preventing proliferation of WMD, and pressing ahead with a peaceful solution to the Korean nuclear issue.[2]

China's sustained growth of comprehensive national strength is another and more important factor that has changed the U.S. assessment. China's increasing influence on regional and global affairs provides the Sino-American interaction with greater regional and global significance. In order to maintain its strategic dominance, Washington has been increasingly concerned about the impacts of China's rise on U.S. regional and global interests and, therefore, regards the maintenance of candid, constructive, and cooperative Sino-U.S. relations as one of the most important on the U.S. foreign-policy agenda. The heated debate over China policy since 2005 demonstrates the weight of Sino-U.S. relations in U.S. foreign strategy. Leading American politicians of the U.S.A., including President Bush, have made speeches on multidimensional aspects of the China policy and Sino-U.S. relations and both Houses have held a range of hearings on China policy since 2005. In addition, major media such as *Newsweek*, the *Atlantic Monthly, Washington Post,* the *New York Times, Wall Street Journal* have also made long and in depth reports on China's development and its influence and authoritative academic journals, such as *Foreign Affairs, Foreign Policy*, and *International Security* have also given space to or even published special issues discussing America's China policy and Sino-U.S. relations.

In contrast, China has been relatively stable in recognizing the importance of the U.S.A. and Sino-U.S. relations. Although Chinese academics followed the international discussions about whether "the U.S. is declining" in the late 1980s and early 1990s, the Chinese public generally admitted that the U.S.A. was the only superpower in the world, and that no power or group of powers could challenge the U.S. hegemony.[3] In the post-Cold War era, China's leadership and academic elites deemed Sino-U.S. relations as the top priority of China's foreign relations.[4] Although some people pointed out that U.S. importance to China was "declining comprehensively,"[5] this view did not represent the major view of the elite.

Although their different strategic priorities produced the gap between their perceptions of importance in their bilateral relations, China and the U.S.A. have come closer in their perceptions of each other's importance and regard the bilateral relationship as affecting each country's vital interests and overall foreign policy, and even regional and global orders in the new millennium. It is predicted that Sino-U.S. relations will become the most important set of bilateral relations in the international political arena for the coming decades.[6] The Chinese leadership from Deng Xiaoping onward has maintained considerable continuity in defining the basic characteristics of the bilateral relations.[7] They have all insisted that Sino-U.S. relations are nonhostile and are committed to building "a constructive and cooperative relationship." They have called for cooperation, coordination, and benign competition to be the bedrock of Sino-U.S. relations.

In contrast, U.S. assessment of the relationship has been chaotic and unstable. It is due in part to the change in the geo-political landscape after the collapse of the Soviet Union who, along with the U.S. government, also largely lost the strategic rationale guiding its China policy, America's unique domestic political system has also compounded the difficulties in its China policy-making.[8] During the Clinton administration, the U.S.A. was severely biased towards China. The notion of "ideologically hostile relations" was followed by various "China threat perceptions" and breaking events that caused bilateral crises. As a result, the "constructive strategic partnership" established in the second term of the Clinton administration failed to be carried out effectively.

With President George W. Bush, Washington has undertaken a fairly large adjustment in its perception of Sino-U.S. relations. The Bush administration in its early term highlighted the so-called geo-strategic competition and rivalry between the two countries. Condoleezza Rice wrote in 2000 before she was appointed National Security Advisor that China was a rising power and would inevitably be involved in a zero-sum geo-political game regionally and globally with the U.S.A., the "status quo" power. She urged enhancement of U.S.–Japanese cooperation as a means of downgrading the status of Sino-U.S. relations in Asia-Pacific region. She refuted the constructive strategic partnership reached by the Clinton administration and replaced it with "strategic competitors."[9] The Quadrennial Defense Review Report in 2001 strongly implied that the U.S.A. was extremely concerned about China's challenge to U.S. leadership in Asia and urged the U.S.A. to strengthen ties with its military allies, to keep an advantageous regional balance, and to deter potential enemies.

After the midair plane collision over the South China Sea and the shock of 9/11, the Bush administration gradually redefined the Sino-U.S. relations as "constructive, cooperative and candid." President Bush claimed on May 31, 2005 that "Americans ought to view relationship with China as a very complex relationship." The four "C"s then become the major framework underlying Washington's view of the bilateral relationship. For the U.S.A., cooperation can come about because China and the U.S.A. share many common and similar interests in regional and global issues, such as international counter-terrorism, post-war reconstruction and recovering order, non-proliferation of WMD, regional prosperity and stability. "Candid and constructive" suggests that China and the U.S.A. will not avoid disagreement, though they should deal with contradictions and differences through various bilateral and multilateral dialogues, consultation mechanisms, while maintaining constructive communication and policy coordination.[10] "Complex" indicates that Sino-U.S. relations involve not only special issues but also comprehensive realms. As China's national power and influence grows, the multilateral and global influence of the bilateral interaction also expands. China and the U.S.A. have not only common interests that require cooperation, but there is also contradiction and conflict, which are dynamic rather than static. So a simple definition is hardly adequate.[11]

Although the 4 "Cs" perceptional frameworks have been fairly positive, they fail to define the "China Image" explicitly, nor do they clarify the pattern of Sino-U.S. relations. In the face of various "China threat perceptions," it's hard to say whether Sino-U.S. relations are mainly cooperative or in conflict. Consequently, the divergence and debates within the U.S. administration on how to balance approaches for "engagement," "integration," "deterrence" or "containment" are far from over. The "hedge" and "hedged integration" have become the core words in recent U.S. domestic debates, fueling suspicions and creating difficulties for a U.S.A.–China policy. Sino-U.S. relations have developed to the point that the U.S. administration needs to clearly outline its "China Image" and further define bilateral relations.

Robert B. Zoellick, former deputy secretary of state, made a speech on September 21, 2005 and systematically outlined the Bush administration's new vision of its China strategy. Three points are noticeable in Zoellick's speech. First, China was identified as a "stakeholder," which demonstrates that the Bush administration has developed a more objective and clearer judgment about the important status and sometimes even crucial role of China in maintaining and constructing the current U.S.-dominated international system and the process of realizing U.S. interests. On the one hand, the Bush administration believed that "China is big, it is growing, and it will influence the world in the years ahead."[12] Thus, the U.S.A. will think about Chinese strategy based on the perception of a "strong China paradigm."[13] On the other hand, just as the U.S. State Department put it, only primary powers can fundamentally support and undermine the international system and are eligible to be called by U.S. as "stakeholder in the international system."[14] Bush has stressed the identification of China's new role within this context, demonstrating that Washington not only recognizes China as an important member of the international system but also upgrades its importance.

Second, in contrast to the post-war U.S. perception of China and its then definition of the basic shape of Sino-U.S. relations, the "stakeholder" identification has enriched the connotations of the Sino-U.S. interaction. "Stakeholder" is apparently different from "strategic rivalry," for the latter highlights the zero-sum relationship. Just as the U.S. administration continually claimed in recent years that the U.S.A. welcomed a confident, peaceful, and prosperous China,

"China of today is simply not the Soviet Union of the late 1940s;" "it does not seek to spread radical, anti-American ideologies;" "the Cold War analogy does not apply to China, neither does the balance-of-power politics of 19th Century Europe."[15] Conversely, the word "stakeholder" highlights shared interests between China and the U.S.A., and especially underlines their shared stakes in the process of maintaining and constructing the international system. "Stakeholder" is however, distinct from "partnership". "Partnership" indicates the degree of closeness of interstate cooperation, but not the degree of importance. "Stakeholder" implies that China's behavior (in either a positive or negative sense) creates valuable and even vital impacts on the normal operation of the U.S.-dominated international system.[16] The connotation and substance of "stakeholder" is also richer than "strategic rivalry" and "partnership." On the one hand, the Bush administration insists that Sino-U.S. relations are based on a vital interest in maintaining and constructing an international system since both sides share profound cooperative dynamics. On the other hand, both are beneficiaries of the present international system, but "stakeholders" do not necessarily or automatically become partners. The Bush administration is well aware that the criteria of the two countries regarding the operational institutions of international subsystems, norms of behavior, responsibilities, rights, distribution of benefit, and so on, do not entirely overlap. Therefore, with cooperation as its mainstay, the bilateral interaction must involve dialogue, coordination, competition, pressure, hedge and so on. Nevertheless, it does generally reflect the Bush administration's optimism and positive attitude towards Sino-U.S. relations.

Third, the Bush administration's call for China to become a "responsible stakeholder" demonstrates that Washington wants to hold onto its dominance in claiming initiatives over the discourse of bilateral relations. It is natural that China and the U.S.A. adjust each other's image in their interactions, but the U.S. administration has time and again redefined the role of China and demonstrated the U.S. perception of China as unstable and immature. Moreover, the assumption of "responsible stakeholder" still aims at maintaining the U.S. strategic interest of primacy by requesting that China share more responsibility in maintaining the U.S.-dominated international system, and by pressing China's transition of its internal politics and social system to evolve in a direction dictated by the U.S.A. This is typical of U.S. attempts to continue its dominance over Sino-U.S. relations. It's unequal since it calls for China to take responsibility rather than taking account of China's rights, suggests that the responsibility for development of Sino-U.S. relations depends on whether or not and how much China shares common interests and values with the U.S.A.

A shifted pattern of interaction

The 9/11 events and the diversification of the global and Asian-Pacific security threats have helped to enlarge the spaces for Sino-U.S. cooperation and have weakened, or diverted, the Bush administration's concern over the so-called "China geo-strategic challenge." However, with the accelerating growth of

China's comprehensive national power, the problem of how to deal with and shape China's "peaceful rise" again came to the fore of the U.S. foreign-policy agenda in the second term of the Bush administration. The most important issue is how to understand each other's interests, motives, and evolving capability; how to expand new cooperation areas, especially those tied to vital interests, and how to manage competition and friction.

The bilateral interactions have been shifted. There is a simultaneous deepening of interdependence and competition. The impact of China's development on the U.S. economic structure and social psychology is apparently strong and complicates the U.S. perception of China's growing strength. This shift may be observed in the following two aspects. First, the traditional "ballast" of the bilateral relations and its functions are evolving and its role has become increasingly complicated. Before China's access to the WTO, China was largely "a passive acceptor/receiver" in Sino-U.S. economic and trade relations. The impacts of U.S. economic action and policy on China's economic policy, development, and its entire economic and social system have been far greater than China's reaction, to the extent that many Chinese have preferred to label globalization as "Americanization." But, the asymmetrical pattern or the unilateral impacts have been greatly altered in recent years. On the one hand, China's rapid economic growth and its enormous spillover effect on the global economy allow it to become one of the engines of global economic growth. On the other hand, the U.S.A. is increasingly concerned about China's economic growth rate, scale, and external ramifications, and its impacts on the U.S. economy. In recent years, frictions between China and the U.S.A. on trade deficits, the RMB exchange rate, textile exports, the protection of intellectual property rights, China's WTO commitments compliance, and so on, have repeatedly affected the stability of Sino-U.S. relations.

Moreover, as China has become deeply integrated into the world economic system, Americans have increasingly felt that their own economic and social system (like the ratio of investment and saving, the input-output structure of education, public health system and so on) have been remarkably influenced by the China factor. While some Americans have begun to call for a corresponding reform of U.S. institutions, a considerable number of negatively affected social strata and interest groups are calling for trade protection and even trade sanctions against China.[17] Although Sino-U.S. economic relations are still fundamentally more complementary than competitive, the previously simple stability and positive role, owing to the then great gaps in economic scale and the high degree of complementary economic structure, is now disappearing, and thus the "politicization" of economic issues is escalating in the U.S.A.

Second, changes have appeared with respect to politics, ideology, and values. On the one hand, while the U.S.A. attempts to influence and transform the Chinese political and social system with its own model, both countries will maintain their disagreements about political systems and ideological conceptions for a long period, but the differences in those aspects are not insoluble in terms of the overall relationship. They will have to address these differences on the basis of dialogue, which will allow them to find more room for compromise and accommodation.

The traditions of U.S. foreign policy and the reality of its national interests call for spreading Western democracy as an irreplaceable instrument and the goal of its foreign strategy. In the wake of 9/11, the Bush administration raised democratization to the height of its security interests. Although the U.S.A. gives priority to the Middle East in its foreign strategy and views anti-American Islamic extremism as America's imminent enemy, it has regarded "democratization" and subverting any "outpost of tyranny" as fundamental. It has pursued "regime change" and a "color revolution" in the Middle East and Central Asia via military, economic, and diplomatic instruments and involved allies, international organizations and NGOs. It has never hidden its intention to push democratic transformation in China. The U.S.A. has identified a common ideology and values as important conditions in developing relations with China's periphery countries, applauded Taiwan's "democratization process," and intervened in the political process in Hong Kong.[18] In recent years, it has been more concerned about China's "nationalism," believing that the Chinese government is exploiting nationalism in mobilizing the public to support Beijing's domestic and foreign policy. China's "authoritarian" regime only adds difficulties for Beijing in curtailing nationalism.[19]

Political and ideological contradictions between China and the U.S.A. are not unmanageable, nor have they developed into irreconcilable confrontation. Despite the differences, China, unlike the countries dominated by "Islamic extremists," does not intend to subvert U.S. core values and wipe out the American political system, nor has it attempted to impose its own ideology and political system on other countries around the world. This has been widely recognized within the U.S. government. More importantly, after 20 years of reform and opening up, China has transformed its economic and social institutions by drawing upon and learning from foreign economic, social and political systems, including America's, and made institutional reforms and innovations for a better governance. As a result, China has shared more, rather than fewer, common values with America, particularly in economic and social fields. Some scholars have also noted that China's experience of reform and opening up can even be regarded as a positive template for influencing those "evil states" alleged by the U.S.A.[20]

The mutual hedging and deterrence between both countries on military and security fronts is escalating. China harbors no intention nor has the capability to pursue military expansion and war preparation (internal balance of power strategy) or to establish regional and global anti-American military alliances (external balance of power strategy) to contend with U.S. military primacy. However, when confronted with the issues of territorial security centered on Taiwan, China has increasingly regarded how to hedge and deter the U.S.A. from threatening China's core national interest as an important aspect of its military modernization and policy adjustment.

Meanwhile, as the Bush administration shares interests with China against

Taiwan's de jour independence and on maintaining stability in the Taiwan Straits, it has conducted limited, though fruitful, cooperation with Beijing, but Washington has become increasingly alarmed by China's military modernization and has stepped up hedging and deterrence against China. The U.S. Department of Defense has submitted an annual report to Congress on *The Military Power of the People's Republic of China* in pursuit of the *2000 Fiscal Year Defense Authorization Act*. The report comprehensively assessed China's military strategy and policy, its growth of military strength, and its impacts on regional security. According to the last two reports, the U.S. thought that China was elevating capabilities in sea, land, and air ballistic missile, space, and integrated command systems and so on. The reports focused on the so-called rapid growth of China's military power. Moreover, the 2005 report claimed that China was committed to military preparations for waging a limited and high-intensity war in the Taiwan region, that the growth of China's military power "could pose a credible threat to other modern militaries operating in the region," and that "China is at a strategic crossroads."[21]

In order to deal with China's "military competition," the U.S.A. continues to pursue a combination of "dissuasion" and "deterrence" toward China. Specifically, in military and security deployment, besides stepping up its military cooperation with Taiwan and consolidating bilateral military alliances with Japan, the Bush administration has pursued a closer strategic relationship with India as one of the priorities of U.S. global and Asia-Pacific strategy. It has also strengthened military cooperation with Singapore, Vietnam, and other ASEAN nations as a balance against China's military power. In addition, it has pressured the E.U., Israel, and other nations not to provide arms to China. Although these postures of military containment and security hedging are "mainly defensive" by nature, rather than attempt at "outright confrontation" with China, the U.S.A. has obviously stepped up measures of "defensive hedging."

There is another sign of a shifting Sino-U.S. interaction. By broadening the scope of bilateral interaction and its growing global impacts, the U.S.A. is particularly sensitive as to whether and how China's growing power can challenge U.S. global and regional dominance, and is taking hedging measures to deal with it. The U.S.A. reacted strongly to China's business expansion in the world energy market. The bid by the China National Offshore Oil Corporation (CNOOC) for Unocal, the U.S.-based oil company, in the first half of 2005 caused a wave of a so-called China energy threat in the U.S.A. It even led to obstruction from the U.S. administration itself, a move which has been criticized by a U.S. scholar as "setting a bad precedent and was contrary to U.S. commitments to free markets, free trade, and upholding international rules."[22] Some U.S. congressmen have become increasingly alarmed by China's business expansion in Latin America, assuming that this will pose a potential challenge to the U.S. "Monroe doctrine" in South America.[23] Furthermore, the second term Bush administration took China's so-called structural challenge to U.S. predominance in the Asia-Pacific as an important issue in its foreign policy agenda setting. On June 7, 2005, the U.S. Senate held a hearing on China's rise and its impacts on U.S. interests in the Asia-Pacific. The core issue was how China would exploit its rising influence, and whether it would conform to the interests and stance of the U.S.A. and its allies. The U.S.A. has shown mixed feelings over the impact of China's growth on the region and on American interests.

While the U.S. government admits that "China's success in extending its political influence in Asia-Pacific is a logical evolution closely tied to its economic clout, and certainly is not a zero-sum game for the U.S.A.." On the contrary, "There is much that is complementary with China in our approach to the region and much on which we look forward to cooperating with them." On the other hand, the U.S. government claims that China is pursuing "mercantilist diplomacy," ignoring and neglecting U.S. political and security interests. The U.S.A. hopes that China, with its growth in power and influence, will join U.S. and international efforts "to enforce the norms of acceptable behavior." The U.S.A. insists that China has expanded its investment and trade with Iran, Sudan, and Myanmar, and harming U.S. political and security interests because these nations are either hostile toward U.S. security policy or adopt political systems that are inconsistent with U.S. values.[24] To cite an American scholar, China "needs to steadily increase resources, so that China's further economic growth will follow its responsibility and commitment to the development and humanitarianism in the region."[25] While increasingly feeling that U.S. supremacy is being challenged by Chinese influence or its periphery, especially in the Asia-Pacific region, the U.S.A. equally embraces a paradoxical attitude about China's "economic diplomacy" in Asia. Although the U.S.A. welcomes China's economic growth, it alleges that China is committed to enhancing its political and diplomatic clout as well as weakening U.S. political and security influence in the region. Thus, in the second term of the Bush administration, the U.S.A. has not only strengthened its dialogues with China on the core strategic concerns of both countries, but also on how to reduce strategic misunderstandings and promote policy coordination. In addition, the U.S.A. has expanded its political and economic participation in Asian development in order to maintain its predominant position in the region.

Changes in the regional situation and order also provide China and the U.S.A. with new opportunities and challenges for policy coordination in the following three aspects. First, subregional interdependence is strengthening, advancing intra-regional collaborations. Second, the rapid rise of newly emerging powers, especially China, complicates the relations of major powers in the region. Third, regional and subregional multilateral regimes are booming, promoting regional cooperation in all aspects.

There are roughly two major types of regional cooperation in the Asia-Pacific. The first is over transnational and multilateral issues associated with globalization, including "soft threats" such as ecological erosion, public health (epidemics), organized crime, drug trafficking, humanitarian disasters, natural disasters, etc., as well as "hard threats" such as international terrorism and the proliferation of WMD. Global issues often pose direct threats to the entire international system and even human security, which involve the vital interests of both China and the U.S.A. The two countries are expanding and deepening dialogues and cooperation in these areas. They also made progress in preventing the spread of avian influenza in 2005. In terms of energy, China and the U.S.A. have moved from initial suspicion and rivalry to dialogue and consultation, and have reached a consensus on diversification of the international energy supply, clean energy technology, nuclear cooperation, strategic reserves, the security of international energy sea lanes and so on. Successful cooperation over these global issues also helps to deepen their commitment to participate in the construction of international regimes, and to maintain stability and development of an international system.

The second type of cooperation is on strictly regional issues in the following three areas. First is the multilateral consultation around the Korean nuclear issue and a nuclear-free peninsula, and building a future Northeast Asian security order. Reassurance and confidence building are required for successful negotiations. The confidence-building measures between the U.S.A. and China are indispensable for fulfilling provisions of "commitment for commitment," and "action for action." In the long run, the cooperation of all parties aiding in economic recovery of the DPRK, encouraging its opening to the outside world and promoting its participation in regional economic integration will provide the necessary external environment for relaxing the situation in the peninsula and altering views about the DPRK on security. Although China and the U.S.A. disagree on some concrete measures regarding a nuclear-free peninsula and a peaceful solution of the Korean issue, they do share identical or similar goals. Political will and sufficient patience on the part of the Bush administration in its "peaceful coexistence" with Pyongyang are one of the crucial factors that will affect the Korean policy and process of negotiation.

The second area involves the interactions of China and the U.S.A. in the process of Asian-Pacific political and economic multilateral cooperation. U.S. Asian policy has blindly centered on "counter-terrorism and security" in recent years. This has led to U.S. "disassociation" from the process of political and economic cooperation in the region, and aggravated its groundless suspicion and criticism on the rise of Chinese influence in the region. China and the U.S.A. have to strengthen communication and policy coordination to reach win–win results for political and economic cooperation in the region.[26]

The third area is about the regional security structure (so called hub-and-spoke) led by the U.S.A. with regional bilateral alliances, i.e. U.S.-Japanese alliance, as the core. The hub-and-spoke structure has an incomplete coverage of the whole region, and is functionally incapable of dealing with the diversified and complicated security threats. At any rate, such a regional security structure is not cost-effective and its incompleteness and limitation are increasingly clear, which has become an important obstacle that impedes strategic confidence between China and the U.S.A.[27] The U.S. side sees China's initiative of a subregional security regime (Shanghai Cooperation Organization) as apparently containing the intention of balancing U.S. military influence. Nevertheless, China and the U.S.A. ought to fully take advantage of the existing multilateral security dialogues and coordination mechanisms and take intra-regional common security concerns (like energy cooperation) as a breakthrough in exploring and cultivating new regional security regimes and pushing cooperation and coordination among major regional powers.

In any event, China and the U.S.A. are contradicting as well as integrating in a range of issues involving core and vital national interests. Their contradictions, if not conflicting in the core interests, will persist, though limited in aspects. They have not come to clash with each other, thanks to the common interests emerging in the day-to-day interactions.[28] In maintaining and constructing regional and international security, political and economic orders, Sino-U.S. relations have become more complicated because of a "dualism" of contradictions and friction vs. coordination and cooperation.

Institutionalized management

The institutionalization of bilateral relations is an important guarantee to the health and stability of Sino-U.S. relations. The degree of institutionalization can be seen in three aspects. The first is the number of mechanisms of consultation and cooperation to address core and important issues with various functions. The second is the competence and efficiency of those mechanisms in addressing bilateral differences and disputes. The third is the ability of the two governments, and especially the energy the two leaderships invest in supervising the construction of the bilateral mechanisms. The more the bilateral relations are institutionalized, the more stable the relations are. Here, the institutionalization involves management mechanisms, including crisis management and bilateral interactions in regional and global multilateral mechanisms.

Since the normalization of Sino-U.S. diplomatic relations, particularly in the last decade, China and the U.S.A. have established a great number of consultative and cooperative mechanisms. The functions of the mechanisms include daily exchanges, dialogues, cooperation, as well as communication, and crisis management in case of emergencies. As for their daily interactions and exchanges, China and the U.S.A. have strengthened cooperation and consultation in addressing contradictions and differences through the joint conference system and have set up regular consultation and dialogue mechanisms, and institutions in each other's capital to advance mutual understanding in the areas of economy and trade, counter-terrorism, law enforcement, nonproliferation, human rights, military, energy and so on. Different arrangements of dialogue and consultation have different degrees of efficiency. Some are more sophisticated, such as economy and trade, while others are in their initial stages, e.g., counter-terrorism and energy issues. In addition, although China and the U.S.A. have different expectations for the roles of those consultation and dialogue mechanisms, but they have played a positive role in the exchange of information, building up policy transparence and predictability. They have also helped prevent partial and functional issues from undermining the overall bilateral relations and have become the major platform for the two countries to address the important and functional issues.

In recent years, the frequent communication and dialogues between the state leaders and the officials in charge of diplomatic, economic, and security affairs have become an important conduit to manage bilateral relations and maintain their stability. The institutionalization and growing frequency of the exchange of visits by the heads of state and their meetings in multilateral occasions started in the second term of the Clinton administration. In 2005, the two heads of state met as many as five times. Donald H. Rumsfeld, the U.S. secretary of defense, visited China the same year as well. The opening of a hotline between the two heads of state in April 1998 allowed close communication between the leaders and chief diplomats of the two countries in addressing bilateral and other important affairs. Most importantly, the hotline has been used much more frequently in recent years. The preparation period for using the hotline has been shortened from a couple of days to a couple of hours, indicating that the communication capacity between the high levels of the two governments has been greatly enhanced. The routine of direct meeting and communication between the leaders of the two countries not only is an important symbol of the development of bilateral relations but also demonstrates that the overall Sino-U.S. relations are directly controlled at high levels. In addition, the Sino-U.S. relations defined as the top priority on each country's foreign policy agenda are conducive to preventing the trivial issues from interfering.

The other important symbol and measure of the institutionalization of Sino-U.S. relations is the establishment of the regular "strategic dialogue" mechanism at a high level. The mechanism indicates the growth of China's comprehensive national power and international status and shows that China and the U.S.A. have to stabilize bilateral relations, promote "strategic mutual confidence" and expand the scope of the development. The mechanism also demonstrates that the institutionalization relations have entered a new historic stage. All major powers have built up platforms of strategic dialogues to develop and coordinate their relations and policies. Strategic dialogues have in fact outstripped the traditional "dialogue of military alliance." The start of a Sino-U.S. strategic dialogue is a new type surrounding the central issue of the "peaceful coexistence of a rising power and the sole superpower," and on the issues of how to understand each other's core interests as well as how to enhance confidence building and mitigate differences. It is an important elevation and complement to the institutionalization of bilateral relations.

Crisis management is an important aspect of Sino-U.S. relations. Since the end of the Cold War, Sino-U.S. relations have faced all kinds of tests. According to some scholars, the post-Cold War crises involving China and the U.S.A. were characterized by high frequency, a broad range of areas, "offensive U.S.A. vs. defensive China," and so on.[29] Crisis management can break down into bilateral and multilateral ones. A set of decision making systems, procedures, and norms has been set up in the process, despite considerable asymmetry between the two sides. The establishment and improvement of this mechanism is extremely significant for the development of Sino-U.S. relations. First, it can solve the casual occurrence of prominent issues and also play a long-term role in the management of special issues. For instance, the hotline and the maritime, military, and security consultation mechanism have provided mechanisms for preventing and managing similar issues from occurring in the future. Second, they allow each side to better understand the intentions and core national interests on specific issues of the other, and to cautiously pursue foreign policies on important issues that can diminish a new crisis due to mistakes in calculation and perception. Given that both are major powers, any crisis will greatly hurt both parties' interests. Ironically crises often become an important instrument for mutual understanding and serve as a push in establishing more rational and pragmatic policies. Third, since China lags relatively behind in the institutionalization of foreign-policy making, by managing bilateral and multilateral crises, China can draw on experiences by building up and improving the institutions of crisis prevention and management. Fourth, as the bilateral interactions for dealing with "multilateral crises" are growing, the joint response by China and the U.S.A. have become a stimulant that advances Sino-U.S. relations.[30]

China and the U.S.A. are not without uncertainties and difficulties in the process of expanding bilateral interaction and management mechanisms. First, the innate strategic suspicion of each other remains an obstacle, occurring time and again. For instance, insufficient strategic confidence has always been the fundamental reason behind the stagnation of Sino-U.S. military exchanges, either in terms of substantial content or institutional construction. The stagnant institutionalization of Sino-U.S. military exchange in turn aggravates the strategic suspicion and the instability underlying all relations. The absence of strategic confidence is also the fundamental reason behind the crises arising between China and the U.S.A. For instance, the deep-rooted suspicion between Beijing and Washington (particularly Beijing's doubts regarding Washington's intentions) has made crisis management of events such as the 1999 bombing of China's Embassy in Belgrade and the 2001 mid-air collision over Hainan more difficult. Therefore, those so-called accidents were more likely to be escalated into a crisis and resolutions be prolonged. Second, domestic factors increasingly interfere with otherwise normal communication between the two countries. The difficulty arises from the institutional reform of China's government, the increase of departments involving relations with the U.S.A. and the inadequate coordination between those departments. The U.S.A. is also facing contradictions in dealing with these relations; e.g., how to coordinate policies among departments involving functional issues and regional issues. After the end of the Cold War, the views of the departments in dealing with functional issues would be stronger than those dealing with regional issues, making it even harder for the U.S. government to integrate its China policy. Third, both China and the U.S.A. have a great deal of work to do in drawing on experience and lessons from history. Great differences remain in their perceptions of one another that affect the correct reading of signals sent by the other, and tend to turn into conflict when dealing with a crisis, both need to improve operational procedures and norms in addressing crises. China is in the initial phase in making laws and regulations for addressing crises and lags behind with regard to dealing with social security issues.

As China increasingly participates in various international institutions, both countries have greater interactions in global and regional multilateral institutions. New players have appeared in their interactions. In international political institutions, especially the United Nations, their differences remain on the issues of the use of international force, intervention in human rights, environment protection, arms control, and so on. They have differences about the priorities for U.N. reform. Friction over the direction of U.N. reform will persist. The U.S.A. has three objectives regarding U.N. reform. The first is to ensure that the U.S.A. continue to exercise leadership in all U.N. affairs; the second is to use the U.N. as an instrument for advancing U.S. interests; the third is to resist reform initiatives that oppose U.S. interests and values. In contrast, China sees the U.N. as the most important multilateral arena, as the major international mechanism for maintaining democratization and multipolarization of international relations, and as one important institutional guarantee for providing China's development with a durable, sustaining, peaceful, and stable international environment.[31] Nevertheless, China and the U.S.A. share similar principles and assumptions on issues such as all-dimensional and multisectional U.N. reform, priority for economic development, the establishment of the Peace-building Commission, opposition to the G4 proposal to expand the Security Council, strengthening U.N. project management, the increase in the efficiency and accountability of the Secretariat, etc. China and the U.S.A. made practical and effective cooperation in resisting the interference of the G4 proposal to the UN reform in 2005. There is still a wide gap in their policy coordination and cooperation on the issues of increasing the efficiency of U.N. institutions, boosting Peace-building Commission in international peacekeeping, enhancing U.N. dominance on a global development process, and so on.

After China became a formal member of the W.T.O., new issues have appeared in the interaction between China and the U.S.A. on the institutions of international trade, especially the W.T.O. The U.S.A. has been urging and even forcing China's commitment to W.T.O. rules, and employing W.T.O. arbitration and domestic laws in response to Chinese impacts on U.S. labor-intensive industries, but both countries are willing to seek common ground in pushing the Doha Round of W.T.O. negotiations and advancing the liberalization of international trade.

The U.S.A. as a leading global trader, though facing the pressure of protectionism at home, has pushed liberal trade in multilateral negotiations. China as a new W.T.O. member is also a beneficiary of this liberalization. Although China has actively participated and advanced the liberalization of global trade, China hopes to better reflect its own national interest and that of developing countries, and works hard to reform W.T.O. provisions that discriminate against developing countries. In the mechanisms of multilateral trade, although China and the U.S.A. have different interests and perspectives on such issues as granting special and differential treatment to developing countries, liberalizing the trade of agricultural products, their greatest common interest is to further strengthen and improve the multilateral trade system, and work hard for progress with the

Doha negotiations, which will lay down the basis for future negotiations. The progress of the W.T.O. Ministerial Conference held in Hong Kong in December 2005 reflected the efforts made by the two countries in pushing for an international system of free trade. As the role of China grows in the global economy and the global monetary system, the RMB exchange rate has become an increasingly prominent issue that impacts on international trade conditions and the financial order. The Western industrial countries led by the U.S.A. are increasingly aware of the importance of strengthening ties with China on financial issues, and have therefore, regularly invited China to join Conferences of Central Bank governors and financial ministers under the G8, which is not only good for policy coordination, but also good for the stable development of the world economy.

China and the U.S.A. have been exploring a more active role for China to play in the international financial and energy systems, though there are gaps between them regarding responsibility, rights, and respective interests. Maintaining the health and stability of international financial and energy systems is in the interest of both countries. In addition, they have been actively involved in dialogues about regional security mechanisms, e.g., six-party talks and the ARF (ASEAN Regional Forum). Although China and the U.S.A. obviously disagree on the pattern for a future regional security regime, they do agree on actively exploring it to maintain regional stability and a peaceful solution of hotspot issues.

Conclusion

"Complexity" is one of the primary features defining China–U.S. relations in the post-Cold War era, though its manifestation varies in the areas of mutual perception, interest-based interaction and institutionalized management. The driving forces underlying the complexity are multifold, involving the changing landscape of geopolitical reality and power shifting at the international level, the dynamics of domestic political, economic, and social structures of both countries as well as continuous adjustment and even transformation of strategic planning and policy-making in both capitals. The new millennium has witnessed the dynamics of this complexity. Both Washington and Beijing have come to recognize the importance of bilateral relations and are also committed to further their relations in a cooperative and constructive way. Meanwhile, interactions between the two sides are multifaceted in the "dualism" of cooperation versus conflicts. However, as the two most important and influential powers in the world, both countries have increasingly shared their interests and common concerns about maintaining the stability of the current international system and improving its efficiency. This shared stake has laid down the foundation for a more stable and cooperative interaction in the years ahead. To fully realize this potential, China and the U.S.A. need to do more to clarify their obligations as well as rights when maintaining and constructing an international system in which both sides are capable of expanding their policy coordination and cooperation. To achieve more predicable and manageable relations in the coming years, both Washington and Beijing have attached great importance to the establishment of policy communication and coordination mechanisms for managing differences, building up confidence and preventing potential crises. Of course, given the lingering strategic doubts between the two sides, the institutionalized relations in military and security areas, though extremely important, still have a long way to go.

Notes

1 As the 2002 U.S. National Security Strategy noted, the post-Cold War great powers "find themselves on the same side – united by common interests to promote global security. We are also increasingly united by common values." *The National Security Strategy of U.S.A. of America*, Washington D.C.: White House, September 2002, p. 1.
2 Aron L. Friedberg, "11 September and Future of Sino-American Relations," *Survival*, Vol. 44, No. 1, Spring 2002, pp. 33–50; David Shambaugh, "Sino-American Relations since September 11: Can the New Stability Last?" *Current History*, September 2002, Vol. 101, No. 656l; Wu Xinbo, "The Premise and Limitations of a Sino-US Partnership," *The Washington Quarterly*, Autumn 2004, pp. 115–126.
3 Wang Jisi, "China's Changing Role in Asia", in Kokubun Ryasei and Wang Jisi eds, *The Rise of China and Changing East Order*, Tokyo: Japan Center for International Exchanges, 2004, pp. 16–17.
4 Wang Jisi, "China's Search for Stability with America," *Foreign Affairs*, September/October, 2005, pp. 35–48.
5 Chu Shulong, "Declining Importance of U.S. to China," *Global Times*, July 22, 2005.
6 Aron L. Friedberg, "The Future of Sino-US Relations: Is Conflict Inevitable?" *International Security*, Vol. 30. No. 2, Fall 2005, p. 8.
7 *Selected Works of Deng Xiaoping*, Vol. III, Beijing: the People's Publishing House, 1993, p. 350.
8 I would like to thank Dr. Andrew Scobell for reminding me of some of the causes of why this contrast of perceptions exists.
9 Condoleezza Rice, "Campaign 2000: Promoting the National Interest," *Foreign Affairs* Vol. 79, no. 1, January/February 2000, pp. 45–62.
10 The testimony of James A. Kelly, assistant secretary of state for East Asian and Pacific affairs to the Senate Foreign Relations Committee on September 11, 2003. http://www.senate.gov/testimony/2003/KellyTestmony030911
11 Assistant Secretary for East Asia and the Pacific Christopher Hill's testimony before the Subcommittee of East Asian and Pacific Affairs of the Senate Committee on Foreign Relations. http://www.foreign.senate.gov/hearings/2005/hrg050607p.html
12 Robert B. Zoellick, "Whither China: From Membership to Responsibility?" Remarks to National Committee on U.S.–China Relations, September 21, 2005, http://state.gov/s/d/rem/53682.htm
13 For the notions of "strong China paradigm" and "weak China paradigm," see David Lampton, "Paradigm Lost," *National Interest*, Fall 2005, pp. 67–74.
14 Author's notes of a conversation with a senior official at the U.S. State Department Policy Planning meeting with the delegation of the Shanghai Institute for International Studies in Washington, D.C. in early December 2005.
15 Robert B. Zoellick, "Whither China: From Membership to Responsibility?" Remarks to the National Committee on U.S.–China Relations, September 21, 2005, http://state.gov/s/d/rem/53682.htm
16 Da Wei and Sun Ru: "Trend of Bush Administration's China Strategy Adjustment," *Contemporary International Relations*, No. 11, 2005, p. 11.

17 Neil C. Hughes, "A Trade War with China?" *Foreign Affairs*, July/August 2005, pp. 94–106.
18 President Bush's remarks in Kyoto on Nov. 16, 2005, http://www.whitehouse.gov/news/release/2005/11/20051116-6.htm
19 Peter Gries, *China's New Nationalism* (Berkeley, Calif.: University of California, 1994); John Pomfret, "New Nationalism Drives Beijing: Hard Line Reflects Popular Mood", *Washington Post*, April 4, 2001, p.A1; Suisheng Zhao, "China's Pragmatic Pragmatism", *Washington Quarterly*, Winter 2005–2006, pp. 131–144.
20 Wang Jisi, "American Hegemony and China's Rise," *Foreign Affairs Review*, No. 5, 2005.
21 See *Annual Report to Congress: The Military Power of the People's Republic of China* (Office of the Secretary of Defense, U.S.A., 2005).
22 Bonnie Glaser, "Sino-US Relations: Drawing Lessons from 2005," *Freeman Report*, Washington, D.C.: CSIS, January 2006.
23 Peter Hakin, "Is Washington Losing Latin America?" *Foreign Affairs*, Vol. 85, No. 1 (January/February 2006), pp. 45–47.
24 Statement by Christopher R. Hill, assistant secretary for East Asia and the Pacific, Department of State, at the hearing of the Subcommittee on East Asian and Pacific Affairs at http://foreign.senate.gov/hearings/2005/hrg050607p.html
25 Author's note from David M. Lampton's keynote speech at an international symposium: "Globalization vs. Opportunity and Challenge Confronting Chinese Foreign Policy" held in Nanchang, China, on June 7, 2005.
26 Chen Dongxiao, "Adjustment of Bush Administration's Asia-Pacific Policy," *Contemporary International Relations*, No. 19, 2005, pp. 14–20.
27 Michael Mastanduno, "Incomplete Hegemony: The U.S.A. and Security Order in Asia", in Muthiah Alagappa, ed., *Asian Security Order: Instrumental and Normative Features*, Stanford University Press, 2003, pp. 153–160; Wu Xinbo: "The End of Silver Lining: A Chinese View of US–Japan Alliance," *The Washington Quarterly* Vol. 29, No. 1, Winter 2005–2006, pp. 119–130.
28 Yang Jiemian, "Global Strategy in the Second Term of the Bush Administration and Sino-US Constructive Cooperation," in Xu Dunxin, ed., *Major Trends of the World at the Early New Century*, World Knowledge Press, 2005, pp. 258–259.
29 Wang Jisi and Xu Hui, "Comparative Analysis on Sino-US Behavior in Crisis, *American Study*, No. 2, 2005, pp. 23–33; Qiu Meirong, "Crisis Management and Sino-US Relations," *Contemporary International Relations*, No. 3, 2005, p. 2.
30 Qiu Meirong, "Crisis Management and Sino-US Relations," *Contemporary International Relations*, No. 3, 2005, p. 2.
31 Statement of Philo L. Dibble, acting assistant secretary before the House Appropriations Subcommittee at http://state.gov/p/io/rls/rm; and the Position Paper of the People's Republic of China on the United Nations Reforms at fmprc.gov.cn/chn/wjb/zzjg/gjx/gjzzyhy/1115//t205944.htm

5 Comparing security concepts of China and the U.S.A.

Jian Xu

This chapter examines Sino-U.S. relations from the perspective of the security outlooks of the two countries. It will present the features of the Chinese security concepts and outlook, then analyze the major debating points and differences between the two sides, and finally assess the prospects for Sino-U.S. relations by putting security affairs in the wider context of the increasing interdependence between China and the U.S.A.

The theoretical basis of China's security outlook

The Five Principles of Peaceful Coexistence, set forth in the mid-1950s, form the theoretical basis of China's security concepts. The Five Principles highlight mutual respect for sovereignty and territorial integrity, mutual nonaggression, noninterference in each other's internal affairs, equality and mutual benefit, and peaceful coexistence. For half a century, the Five Principles have withstood the test of international volatility and are still the theoretical basis on which China formulates its foreign policy, including security concepts.

Looking into the values embedded in the Five Principles may help in understanding how China formulates its foreign policy and security concepts.[1] The Five Principles take mutual respect for sovereignty as a core. The jurisprudential language of the Five Principles suggests that, from China's point of view, international relations are in essence legal relations rather than a balance of power. This thought is not only in conformity with the spirit of the Charter of the United Nations, but also reveals the nature of modern international systems since the Treaty of Westphalia in the seventeenth century. As a matter of fact, the evolution of international relations since then has always hinged on a fundamental issue of identifying the legal scope of applicability and a concrete mode for safeguarding the principle of sovereign equality. Prior to World War II, the application of sovereign equality was limited to relations among Western powers, who arbitrarily imposed a system of colonial hierarchy onto a vast number of developing countries. The Charter of the United Nations extends the application of sovereign equality to the widest scope, covering relations among all countries in the world.

The second point is that China rejects power politics. Indeed, the original intention of initiating the Five Principles was to defend the legitimate rights and interests of the small and weak countries in the international community via norms of international law. In addition to moral values, from China's point of view, any hegemonic international order dependent on the coercive power of a single country other than the international consensus will be shaky in the long run. Reasons for such hegemonic instability are twofold. First, the international order based on power politics is morally twisted, and is replete with contradictions, tensions, and conflicts other than harmony or stability – hence a fragile basis in nature. Second, it is inevitable that powers of the old generation will be confronted with competition and challenges from those of the new generation. When different powers struggle to replace one another, the process is apt to fuse turbulences, conflicts and even wars, destabilizing the overall international situation.

The third point worth attention is that the Five Principles call on the development of international relations to transcend ideologies, because they were set forth during the heyday of the Cold War, and were meant for relations among countries of different social systems and ideologies. In fact, China has done quite well in applying these principles to relations with countries of different social systems.

Finally, the Five Principles suggest the orientation of China as far as the future development of international order is concerned. In this respect, there is an essential question: Where should the global governance be anchored? On the exercise of power of one or two nations, or on a more multilateral international system like international law, norms, and institutions such as the United Nations? China's stand on this question is clearly in favor of the latter. For instance, in 1984, Deng Xiaoping explicitly stated, the Five Principles of Peaceful Coexistence provide the best way for handling relations between nations. Other ways, like thinking in terms of "the socialist community," "bloc politics," or "spheres of influence" lead to conflicts and tightening international tensions. Looking at the history of international relations, we find that the Five Principles of Peaceful Coexistence have a potentially wide applicability. In 1988 when he met with Indian Prime Minster Rajiv Gandhi, Deng Xiaoping proposed further that the new international economic and political order should be established with the Five Principles of Peaceful Coexistence as the norms.

China's new security concept

From China's point of view, the security environment in the world has undergone complex and profound changes in the twenty-first century. Peace and development remain the two overriding themes of the times. Factors of uncertainty and instability in international relations are on the rise, since various traditional and nontraditional security threats are intertwined. In light of the profound changes in the world since the end of the Cold War, a new concept of security has gradually come into shape in China.

The new concept of security, on the basis of inheriting the Five Principles of

Peaceful Coexistence, advocates the building of mutual trust, mutual benefit, and equality and cooperation among nations. Mutual trust is the prerequisite. It is only when mutual trust is realized, can countries, big or small, strong or weak, and different in social system, ideology, and cultural background, and level of development, respect each other, treat each other equally, and engage in sincere cooperation. Mutual benefit is the economic guarantee for maintaining peace. Dialogue conducted on the basis of equality is the right and effective means for solving disputes and preserving peace.

With the new concept of security, China's security strategy and policies in recent years has had several major characteristics.[2] First of all, it attaches importance to the concept of comprehensive security. China's perception of security has a broadened perspective, covering both traditional security and untraditional security factors. Traditional security is referring to issues of so-called high politics, such as national defense, territorial disputes, sovereignty, inter-state military posture, etc. These issues are concerned with the survival of a nation, a state, or a regime, and thus often regarded as the core of international security. Nontraditional security refers to security issues of the so-called low politics, including economic security, terrorism, environmental pollution, population explosion, drug trafficking, trans-national crimes, AIDS, etc. In old security thinking, nontraditional security problems were often put on the back burner or even beyond consideration. This kind of security thinking, however, cannot meet the demands of the current new security situation in the world. The first reason is nontraditional security threats are getting more pronounced and posing ever growing challenges to the world. The other reason is the lines between the traditional security and nontraditional security are getting more blurred, and the transformation of one type of security into the other is more likely. Therefore, the formulation of security concepts in the new era must take into account the new features of untraditional security threats. Nontraditional security is different from traditional security in terms of sources and actors. With respect to traditional security, actors and sources are both relatively clear in that they often result from conflicts of national interests and consequent disputes between states. Traditional security problems are mainly the result of actions by states or governments, reflecting typical international issues. In contrast, actors and sources of untraditional security issues are more complicated. Many nontraditional security threats are the result of nonstate actors rather than direct outcomes of actions of nation-states. Another distinction between nontraditional and traditional security lies with the fact that the former is more pronounced than the latter in terms of socialization, transnationalization, and globalization. Nontraditional security issues often relate directly to actions by individuals of certain specific social groups. With the enlargement of action areas of those specific social groups, nontraditional security problems may easily surpass various types of limitations of politics, geography, and cultures, and begin to spill over from one country or region to another, with the result that problems of certain individual countries evolve into global issues. The third feature of nontraditional security is the difficulty, the long process, and comprehensiveness concerning its management. Unlike many traditional security issues, nontraditional security problems have their roots in the social, economic, and cultural soil of different countries.

Second, China in the new security concept places emphasis on common security and thus runs counter to the Cold War mindset. The Cold War mentality is based on a zero-sum game, that maintains that security of a state can only be achieved or ensured at the expense of that of the other states. Based on this reasoning, containment, balance of power, deterrence of mutual destruction prevailed in the Cold War period. Such security conceptions and cooperation forms are obviously not appropriate for dealing with many new challenges in current international security, and especially difficult to meeting the special demands of addressing nontraditional security issues. In current circumstances of international security, no country could enjoy security, let alone absolute security, only if some other countries suffer from insecurity. Many threats in the nontraditional security field are not aimed at any specific countries but are challenges facing many states. The new features of the security environment in today's world enhance the common interests and interdependence of countries in the management of security. Against this background, the new security concept is placed on a win–win basis and attaches special importance to the value of the common security of all countries. Every country, no matter whether it is big or small, rich or poor, and strong or weak, enjoys the same equal rights for security.

Finally, China's new security concept promotes cooperative security on the basis of common security. Given the comprehensive and complex nature of security threats in the world, no single state, even the most powerful country, can cope with all the challenges alone. This situation strengthens the need for international security cooperation, on the basis of equality, in the management of security issues. In recent years, China has played a responsible role in the strengthening of the authority of the U.N. and other global institutions. China also has taken an active and constructive part in promoting regional cooperation of various frameworks based upon the conception of common security. China intends to deepen and broaden its cooperation with all countries in the world on the basis of mutual respect and equality.

Differences of security concepts between China and the U.S.A.

Security is an important dimension in Sino-U.S. relations. Bilateral relations in the security area, as in other fields, are quite complex. In the security area, China and the U.S.A. share common interests in some aspects. In others, both sides may have disagreements, but on most occasions there exists room for both sides to reach compromise.

In China, many people have reservations over the tenets of the neo-conservatism thesis over security issues.[3] Chinese criticism is especially focused on three prevailing trends in U.S. security concepts after the 9/11 events, namely the so-called preemptive strategy of U.S. defense policy, the unilateralist approach of the U.S.A. in international security cooperation, and the so called neo-interventionism thesis. From China's point of view, as far as the use of military force in international relations is concerned, every country should behave in accordance with international law and with the authorization of the United Nations. Illegitimate use of force may be convenient for a country to reach some short-term targets, but it may damage the basis of the existing international security system. If other countries followed suit, it would cause chaos or disorder in the world and eventually hurt the interests of the U.S.A. in the long run. This accounts for China's stand over the Iraq war.

For similar reasons, many Chinese also question the unilateralist approach of the U.S.A. to international security cooperation, especially over its effects on tackling nontraditional security issues. The U.S. approach puts U.S. interests at its core, relies mainly on the capability of U.S. unilateral actions, takes multilateral support of the international society as a supplement, and stresses the significance of military means for seeking rapid substantiation of objectives. From China's point of view, this approach may have the advantage of an efficient and swift response for dealing with known terrorist forces and some other international security threats. Nonetheless, when coping with unknown enemies and root causes of terrorism, it is much less effective. The negative effects of this approach on the world would become even more prominent in the longer term, if only because many aspects of this approach would not be sustainable for the U.S.A. nor acceptable for international society in the long run. In this respect, China's views share much in common with the European approach. The European approach has a preference for pan-regional and even global integrated institutions when formulating integral social, political, jurisdictional, fiscal, economic, and even cultural policies in an attempt to resolve the root causes of terrorism and other security problems. This approach is rational in the sense that it is aware of the right direction in dealing with terrorism and many other threats to international security. Of course, China also realizes the problems with the European approach. Its main problem lies with the fact that the ways it chooses for the objectives it stands for may face enormous difficulties and barriers in practice, especially for regions beyond Europe.

In terms of security concepts, many Chinese also question the neo-interventionist theory prevailing in the U.S.A. and the West in the post Cold–War period.[4] The difference between the Chinese views and the neo-interventionist school is mainly focused on the rhetoric of "human rights above sovereignty" and concerned with how to look at a diversity of cultures in a period of globalization, and how to define the correlations between domestic law and international law. From China's point of view, with regard to knowledge about human rights vis-à-vis globalization, it is misleading to claim that a globalized value system is breaking up the nation-states as bulwarks. The nation-state system was born, consolidated, and developed in keeping with the economic globalization because they were economically motivated and, in a deeper sense, because of the social and cultural forces of globalization. Culture, as an assembly of features of mental, intellectual, emotional, and material development achieved by a society or a social group, covers lifestyle, means of communications, value system, traditions, and faith as well as literature and arts. The national, geographical, and regional dimensions of culture have always been the incubator where different cultures take root and grow, and have been the motive force for the diversity of the world. Cultural nationality is formed in a long historical period with the combined forces of geography, history, tradition, and level of social and economic development, and is a social factor of the greatest stability and easiest succession not to be destroyed by globalization on any account. It does get changed and evolves as globalization deepens, but it will definitely remain effective no matter how globalization goes.

In a logical deduction, globalization will not obliterate but will enhance national cultural features, and will push for diversity in the world. The increased number of nation-states in the process of globalization provides evidence to justify this logic. Just as many people pursue individuality, instead of getting disoriented, when life becomes socialized and modernized, each nation, state, and society will also highlight its uniqueness and national appeal, voluntarily or involuntarily, by taking advantage of modernity, to avoid losing its way through globalization. The world is thus more colorful and diversified. The self-identification and self-development feature of culture provides a profound basis for the nation-states to stand on and move forward because the nation-state is a material expression of national-political culture. In another aspect, although the tide of democratization is sweeping the world, the establishment of a democratic system in a specific country should still be crafted after the national-political culture and the level of social and economic development, without using a unified model. This is the case because the mode of development including the mode of political system is not only a result of the economic, political, geopolitical, scientific, technological conditions, and the international environment of the specific country; it is also closely bound up in the cultural and historical traditions. The diversity of culture makes for diversified modes of development. Respect for, and protection of, cultural diversity entails diversification of the mode of development.

If diversity of culture is justified in the period of globalization, then globalization is even less meant to replace domestic law with international law. The nation-state system remains a staunch pillar of the world, and the relationship between domestic and international law can only be mutually complementary, not mutually repellent. On the one hand, since international law is usually a set of incomplete norms, leaving room for domestic law to supplement it, international law divorced from domestic law would be senseless. Specifically, there should be two basic factors in all complete legal norms which the objective factor prescribing what should and shouldn't be done, and the subject factor specifying who should do this or that and who shouldn't. Only when the two factors are integral can the territorial and time factors of law make sense. Norms in modern international law tend to define the object factors and leave the factors of subject, territory, and time to the domestic law, only specifying the scope of force of domestic law in this regard. As a result, though the international law provides rights and obligations for both countries and individuals, it cannot do without the domestic law for regulating the conduct of individuals. On the other hand, neither can the domestic law be separated from international law, because the latter provides a key to and a complete specification of the scope of force for the former concerning the factors of subject, territory, and time. Without international law, the concept of state and that of sovereignty would be beyond understanding. Such interdependent correlations between domestic and international laws reveals that the two are an organic unity and that any attempt to negate sovereignty or replace domestic law with international law is an attempt to isolate or twist this organic unity. There is no contradiction or sequencing between the importance of human rights protection and that of state sovereignty. Therefore, the rhetoric of "human rights above sovereignty" is theoretically absurd and cannot be maintained.

Therefore, the prevailing views in China hold that there is a universal aspect in human rights, of which the political, economic, social, and cultural contents comprise a mutually reinforcing and integrated body. The right to subsistence is a precondition to the achievement of the right to development and other cultural, civil, and political rights, while civil, political, and cultural rights help improve the right to subsistence and the right to development. For a country aiming to realize democracy, freedom, and human rights, the fundamental way is to promote economic development and the progress and stability of the society. Protection of human rights must facilitate the comprehensive and coordinated development of all economic, social, cultural, civil, and political rights, which is only possible when state sovereignty is respected and intact. It is unthinkable that without the country, individual rights could be guaranteed in a world where the nation-state system reigns. In advocating the Five Principles of Peaceful Coexistence, and promoting peace and development, the international cause of soundly promoting human rights is advanced.

China and the U.S.A: stakeholder or constructive partner?

China's criticism and reservations however, should not lead to thinking that China and the U.S.A. have little room for cooperation. Instead, in spite of their differences, the two countries share many common interests in the security field and other areas. This would become clearer if we put our evaluation of the two countries' security interests in the wider context of overall Sino-U.S. relations.

In terms of development trends, Sino-U.S. relations are in a period of strategic transformation and adjustment. It is a mutually agreed fact that relations between China and the U.S.A. feature multifaceted complexities. This situation provides much potential for both sides to mold mutual relations in the future. In other words, Sino-U.S. relations have more than one possibility in the future. In actual terms, the most likely prospects may vary in the range between *stakeholders*, a definition put forward by the U.S. side, and *constructive partners*, a definition proposed by the Chinese side. The prospects depend upon how both sides promote their common interests and handle their differences. In this sense, Sino-U.S. relations stand in a period of strategic adjustment. The following reasons account for this judgment.

Above all, in terms of the central strategic aim, there are no conflicts in the fundamental interests between China and the U.S.A. The paramount strategic objective of U.S. foreign policy is to ensure that no single state can challenge its dominant role in the world and in various regions. In theory, China may, like many other states in the world, disagree about the hegemonic elements in U.S. foreign policy. However, this does not imply that China is going to challenge the leading role of the U.S.A. Unlike the former Soviet Union, the central goal of China's foreign policy in the next two decades and even longer is to pursue a path of peaceful development for its modernization, because China's growth lies in peaceful development and a peaceful international environment. Apart from this purpose, China does not have the political will or the capability to take on this leading role in the world or even in the Asia-Pacific region. On the contrary, China is happy to see the U.S.A. take the lead in the management of international affairs as long as this is in conformity with the universally accepted norms and in the common interests of the world.

Second, from the U.S. point of view, a key factor with regard to relations with China in the future is China's attitude toward the current international order. In this respect, as suggested by China's world outlook and security concepts, the common interests and consensus the two sides can find are obviously more pronounced than any differences between them. Both the U.S.A. and China benefit enormously from the existing international system, though both sides are not quite satisfied with some of the elements of the system and wish from different angles to see the improvement in the system. For China, the emphasis of improvement should be in favor of promoting the interests of developing and poor countries. In contrast, the U.S.A. is in search of more privileges for its sole superpower status. Does this difference matter for bilateral relations? Maybe "yes" in some concrete issues. Would this difference lead to a strategic confrontation between China and the U.S.A.? The answer is "no," because the increasing interdependence and common interests of both sides in the current framework of international order would play an overwhelming role in determining the whole range of bilateral relations. It is in consideration of this observation, I believe, that the U.S. side uses the term of "stakeholder" to describe relations with China. The common "stake" of the two sides covers a wide range of areas, including cooperation in economic and cultural fields, anti-terrorism, upholding the international nonproliferation regime, and the management of certain regional hot spots, such as the nuclear issues in Iran and on the Korean Peninsula.

Even over the most sensitive factor in Sino-U.S. relations, the Taiwan question, China and the U.S.A. can reach consensus and have much potential for cooperation. China commits itself to making the strongest efforts to seek the prospect of peaceful reunification between the mainland and Taiwan, while the U.S.A. opposes the "independence" of Taiwan. The basic position of both sides converges at the point of preventing stability and peace from being upset by secessionists in Taiwan. So both sides have common interests in keeping at bay the provocation of the secessionist leadership in Taiwan.

Conclusion

Based upon above analysis, we can draw the following conclusions. First, China's security concepts and interests may have inherited its unique features from its experience in modern history. Nevertheless, with the development of China's interdependence with the external world, China's outlook and interests over security issues, as over other issues, have been under constant change and have become increasingly integrated with the common interests of the international community, including the U.S.A. China's security concepts attach growing importance to universally accepted values such as international law and multilateral cooperation. This has laid the foundation for China to deepen and expand cooperation of various forms with other countries in the future.

Second, China and the U.S.A. have common interests and a consensus over a broad range of issues in security affairs, as in affairs of other kinds, while they take different views at varying degrees on some concrete matters. However, nearly all the differences are manageable or surmountable. The complex and multifaceted nature of Sino-U.S. relations is not a barrier to strengthening mutual cooperation. On the contrary, it reveals the ever growing interdependence and common stake of the two countries in the current international system and reveals the need and enormous potential for bilateral cooperation. Both sides share great responsibilities in maintaining peace and promoting development in the world. Sino-U.S. relations may very likely find a place between "stakeholders" and "constructive partners," depending on how both sides cultivate their potential for cooperation and manage their differences.

Third, to substantiate the best prospects for Sino-U.S. relations, both sides must find the right approach. The six-point proposal put forward by Chinese President Hu Jintao during his recent visit to the U.S.A. for developing bilateral relations provides a good base for fulfilling this mission. In any case, the first step would have to stem from, quoting the words of President Hu, "increasing understanding" and "expand[ing] common ground." With growing mutual understanding and common interests, I believe that China and the U.S.A. will find ways to overcome all the difficulties between them and build stable, constructive, and cooperative bilateral relations to meet their own needs but also the entire world.

Notes

1 For a more systematic analysis of the implications and significance of the Five Principles of Peaceful Coexistence for China's foreign policy, see China Institute of International Studies, ed., *On the Five Principles of Peaceful Coexistence – Essays in Commemoration of the 50th Anniversary of the Five Principles of Peaceful Coexistence*, Beijing: World Affairs Press, 2004.

2 Xu Jian, "Facing the Challenge of Unconventional Security: The Chinese Perspective,"
   Bertrand Fort ed., *Overcoming Vulnerability – Managing New Security Challenges in
   Asia and Europe*, Marshall Cavendish Academic, 2005.
3 For prevailing Chinese observations about U.S. foreign policy, see the China Foundation for International Studies, ed., *Shijie dashi yu zhongguo de heping fazhan* [*Main
   trends in the world and China's peaceful development*], Beijing: World Affairs Press,
   2006.
4 For Chinese views on neo-interventionism, see Yang Chengxu, ed., *Xin tiaozhan-guoji
   guanxi zhong de "rendaozhuyi ganyu* " [*New challenges – 'humanitarian intervention'
   in international relations*], Beijing: China Youth Press, 2001.

6 Nuclear deterrence and the Sino-U.S. strategic relationship

Baohui Zhang

The rise of China has brought the nuclear issue to the center stage of Sino-U.S. relations. China has been pursuing a systematic modernization of its strategic nuclear forces that will lead to a secure second-strike capability versus the U.S.A. in the next 10 to 15 years. This new capability will for the first time establish a true mutual deterrence between the two countries, with important strategic consequences. Although the emerging Chinese nuclear capability may generate additional potential for bilateral competition, increased mutual vulnerability may also lend dynamics for greater strategic cooperation. Therefore, a study of the rise of China and its impact on the future direction of Sino-U.S. relations cannot be complete without examining the rise of Chinese nuclear power. As during the Cold War, nuclear mutual deterrence incorporates both competition and cooperation in great power relationships. On the one hand, nuclear deterrence reflects great powers' inherent mutual fear of each other. The resulting nuclear arms race can contribute to worsening of the security dilemma in their strategic relationship. At the same time, however, nuclear mutual deterrence provides the foundation for cooperation between great powers. A shared sense of mutual vulnerability can lead to increased strategic cooperation. Consequently, nuclear mutual deterrence became a critical stabilizing factor in the superpower relations.

Until recently, the nuclear factor did not command much attention in U.S.–China relations due to the latter's minute-sized strategic nuclear force and its passive No First Use doctrine. As a result, according to a report by the Council on Foreign Relations, there was a "tendency in Washington to dismiss China as an inconsequential nuclear power" – and this could be a big mistake.[1] Indeed, important events in recent years have shifted the attention of U.S. analysts toward the nuclear issue between the two countries. First, China successfully tested the sea-based JL-2 strategic missile in June 2005. The Type 094 strategic submarine, which will provide the platform for the JL-2 missile, was already launched in 2004. This new and important strategic weapon system signaled a breakthrough in China's long quest for a survivable second-strike capability. Then, one month later, a PLA general, when talking to a group of journalists from Hong Kong, suggested that China should use nuclear weapons to deter the U.S.A. in a future war in the Taiwan Strait. Although the Chinese government quickly denied that it was the official policy of the state, General Zhu Chenghu's remarks are not an isolated view inside China. In recent Chinese discussions of the subject, the No First Use nuclear doctrine is increasingly under criticism. Many believe that due to its vast conventional disadvantage against the U.S.A., China may have to rely more on its nuclear weapons to prevent American intervention in the Taiwan Strait. A shift toward a more offensive oriented nuclear doctrine will become especially tempting when China acquires a secure second-strike capability.

The Pentagon's 2006 report, *Military Power of the People's Republic of China*, reveals serious concerns for both potential changes in China's nuclear doctrine and its emerging strategic capabilities. It states that General Zhu's remarks "show that the circle of military and civilian security professionals discussing the values of China's current ħo first use' policy is broader than previously assessed." The Pentagon is also concerned about the imminent deployment of China's new strategic weapon systems that may impact on the choice of future Chinese deterrence doctrines. According to the Pentagon, the new Chinese Type 094 strategic nuclear submarine and its JL-2 SLBM could be deployed as early as 2007.[2]

This chapter suggests that although the growing Chinese nuclear capability may open up a new front for Sino-U.S. competition, it will also bring greater stability to the strategic relationship because it will generate important incentives for bilateral strategic cooperation. In particular, a more robust Chinese nuclear deterrence will make it less likely for the two sides to mishandle a crisis situation in the Taiwan Strait. Mutually assured destruction (MAD) in many ways prevented direct military conflicts between the two superpowers during the Cold War. Indeed, NATO continues to emphasize the importance of nuclear weapons in conflict prevention. As declared by NATO's Strategic Concept, "Nuclear weapons make a unique contribution in rendering the risks of any aggression incalculable and unacceptable. Thus, they remain essential to preserve peace."[3] In U.S.–China relations the nuclear shadow will once again force the decision makers on both sides to exercise maximum caution. Without sufficient mutual deterrence, the current situation in the Taiwan Strait has the potential to drag the two countries into a major powers' war that nobody wants.

This chapter first examines the rising instability in the Taiwan Strait that, in the absence of nuclear mutual deterrence, may cause miscalculations by both American and Chinese decision-makers. It then discusses China's recent breakthroughs with its nuclear modernization and provides a range of estimates about the future size of Chinese strategic nuclear forces. The next part of the chapter analyzes Chinese nuclear doctrine and its future trends. The next section explores whether a Chinese threat of possible first use of nuclear weapons would be able to deter U.S. military intervention in the Taiwan Strait. The last part of the chapter assesses the strategic impacts of the emerging Chinese secure second strike capability and urges that the U.S.A. and China engage each other in strategic dialogues to reach an understanding about the proper roles of nuclear deterrence in their bilateral relations.

Instability in the Taiwan Strait

The prospect of a U.S.–China war was recently discussed in the cover story of the June 2005 *Atlantic Monthly*. It was sensationally named "How We Would Fight China?"[4] The most likely cause of a war between the two countries involves the current Taiwan Strait situation. This is largely due to Taiwan's apparent efforts to change the status quo by moving toward formal independence. The Chen Shui-Bian government has pursued a variety of policies, such as the once proposed referendum on independence in the 2004 presidential election and the planned constitutional revision before 2008 to bolster Taiwan's independent identity in the world. These policies have recently even invited criticism by the Bush administration, which now sees Taiwan as a potentially greater source of threat to stability in the Taiwan Strait. A particularly dangerous threat to stability in the Strait, according to Singapore's Prime Minister Lee Hsien Loong, who visited Taiwan in July 2004 amid strong protest from Beijing, is the idea held by many Taiwanese leaders that the U.S.A. will automatically come to Taiwan's aid. As he revealed in an interview, during his discussions with Taiwan's leaders he "realized that most Taiwanese believe that once China attacks Taiwan, the U.S. will risk all to help Taiwan. I am deeply worried about this perception."[5] This widely held perception by both the Taiwanese elite and masses will likely lead to miscalculations by Taiwan and emboldens it to pursue more aggressive policies toward independence due to the belief that the world's only superpower is on its side.

Given the fact that the Taiwan Strait has become increasingly dangerous, it is ironic that nuclear deterrence between the U.S.A. and China is rarely discussed in this context. In fact, the critical roles and functions of nuclear deterrence in U.S.–China relations generally tend to be overlooked. For example, a Rand study claims that the nuclear issue is not important: "Unless Sino-U.S. relations deteriorate to Cold War-like levels, it would seem that nuclear deterrence will have little role to play in handling the types of conflict scenarios that might arise."[6] This lack of attention to the nuclear issue in U.S.–China relations is dangerous. The seemingly absent nuclear factor can only serve to destabilize U.S.–China relations in a crisis situation. The U.S.A. may perceive that it could win a conventional war against China with relative ease due to its vast technological advantage. For example, a researcher from the Rand Corporation concludes that even a modest U.S. military intervention will allow Taiwan to defeat an invasion from the mainland.[7] War is most likely when decision-makers believe that the probability of victory is high and the cost of war is low.

On the other hand, China, from a position of conventional disadvantage, may have incentives to launch a preemptive strike to level the playing field. It will include the so-called asymmetric tactics against the soft spots in the U.S. military system. Indeed, China in recent years has devoted systematic attention to exploring various tactics of asymmetric warfare, with the U.S.A. as the potential enemy. For example, a very important tactic is preemptive strikes against the U.S. space assets due to its heavy reliance on satellites for intelligence, weapon guidance, communication, and command.

This Chinese doctrine of asymmetric warfare has been discussed by a Rand expert in his testimony to the U.S. Congress. Chinese strategists believe that China must seize the initiative early in a conflict against a militarily superior enemy. As a result, the doctrine emphasizes surprise first strike in order to achieve preemption. Further, Chinese military experts emphasize the importance of weakening the fighting will of the enemy by raising the cost of conflict. These war tactics are discussed in an article by two Chinese officers at the National Defense University. They particularly emphasize the tactic of defeating the enemy by weakening his combat will through an overpowering initial strike.[8]

These Chinese war tactics, which emerged out of China's observation of the U.S. dominance of the battlefields in recent wars, sound alarmingly like the Japanese strategic calculation behind its decision to attack Pearl Harbor. This is essentially the miscalculated strategy by a conventionally weaker power to level the playing field with a stronger enemy. This strategy will bring grave instability into a potential U.S.–China crisis over Taiwan.

American experts on China also worry about a different kind of miscalculation by decision-makers which could result in a war over Taiwan. Roger Cliff and Toy Reid suggest that Chen Shui-bian's constitutional amendment to codify Taiwan's independence from Beijing could push China and the U.S.A. into a conflict since both sides may calculate that they need to stand tough in order to maintain future credibility. As they comment about the possibility of a new draft constitution by Taiwan, China could feel compelled to take action to maintain the credibility of its future warning and threats. If China's response consists of intimidating military exercises such as those conducted in 1995 and 1996, the U.S.A. could feel compelled to react with its own deployment of forces to the Western Pacific.[9]

Although Cliff and Reid do not believe that war is inevitable in this scenario, Ted Galen Carpenter takes a more pessimistic view about how miscalculation could result in a war in the Taiwan Strait. In his book about a hypothetical war over Taiwan, he argues that the president of the U.S.A. could be

> propelled towards conflict by strategic miscalculation, rather than a bold defense of a popular but geographically dispensable ally.... The president had hoped to repel China's rising bellicosity with a show of force, rather than the actual use of force. After Beijing responded by ratcheting up tensions in the Taiwan Strait, both sides feared that a subsequent climb-down would damage their global credibility and leadership.[10]

Thus, how to prevent a U.S.–China war over Taiwan has immense policy implications. There are immediate needs for mechanisms that can prevent miscalculation by both sides in a future crisis situation. Although General Zhu Chenghu's comments may sound aggressive and hawkish, this article suggests that a more robust Chinese nuclear deterrence is not only going to become an inevitable fact, it may also benefit the strategic stability of U.S.–China relations since it can reduce the chance of miscalculations by decision-makers on both sides. As Lawrence Freedman, a noted British expert on deterrence, observes about the role of nuclear weapons after the Cold War: The continued existence of nuclear weapons provide a reminder of the danger of total war. Even without an authoritative specification of the chain of events which might end in catastrophe the thought that "it just might," could introduce an immediate element of caution into any developing conflict.[11]

Moreover, a more robust Chinese nuclear deterrence will help stabilize the overall situation in the Taiwan Strait by convincing the Taiwanese leadership that it can no longer count on direct American military intervention. As mentioned earlier, this is a widely held belief among Taiwanese elites and has emboldened the more radical elements inside Taiwan to seek to change the status quo by moving toward formal independence. Recognizing the unlikelihood of direct U.S. military intervention will force Taiwanese leadership to abandon its provocative policies toward the mainland.

In essence, this article suggests that nuclear mutual deterrence, which ruled much of the Cold War era, could ironically benefit the current and future U.S.–China strategic relationship. Avery Goldstein, in a study of the rise of China, also discusses the stabilizing effect of nuclear mutual deterrence.[12] This article argues that the U.S. defense obligation to Taiwan should focus on exporting more advanced conventional weapons to the latter. The current balance of power between the mainland and Taiwan could be prolonged by at least another decade through this transfer.

China's nuclear modernization

China's limited nuclear capability grew out of its desire to acquire great power status and avoid blackmail from the superpowers. On October 16, 1964 China successfully detonated its first nuclear device and thus became the world's fifth nuclear power. However, a more challenging task for China was the development of delivery vehicles, including bombers and missiles with sufficient ranges to deter China's main rivals. China's focus was on missiles, and on October 27, 1966 it successfully delivered a nuclear warhead through a medium-range missile. This signaled the beginning of Chinese nuclear deterrence.

Through the years, China has acquired a small nuclear force that incorporates medium-range, intermediate-range, and intercontinental ballistic missiles. Moreover, China has also developed a rudimentary sea-based capability through the single Xia Class Type 092 nuclear submarine. Earlier medium- and intermediate-range missiles include the DF-3, which has a range of 2,800 kilometers, and the DF-4 with a range of 4,750 kilometers. The DF-3 is mobile while the DF-4 is placed on fixed launch sites. China has about 200 DF-3 medium-range missiles and about 40 DF-4 intermediate range missiles.

The two missiles formed an important Chinese nuclear strike force against its former enemy, the Soviet Union. However, both were liquid fueled and required hours to prepare for launch. This made them vulnerable to surprise attack from China's enemies. So in 1986, China successfully deployed a new solid fueled

DF-21 that has a range of 1,800 kilometers. The number of DF-21 missiles is guessed by the West to be between 10 and 50. The importance of the DF-21 is that it was also developed into China's first submarine-launched ballistic missile, the JL-1 with a similar range.

In the meantime, China tried to develop true intercontinental missiles that could reach the U.S.A. The result was the DF-5 with a range of 13,000 kilometers. It is armed with a single multi-megaton warhead. The missile is also liquid-fueled and launched from silos. The number of deployed DF-5 missiles is estimated at 20. This is the foundation of China's strategic nuclear force. At the moment China is undergoing rapid modernization of its nuclear forces. Two important programs involve a new generation of land-based ICBMs, more specifically the DF-31 and the DF-31A. Both are land mobile and solid-fueled. The DF-31 has a range of 8,000 kilometers while the DF-31A can travel 12,000 kilometers. The 2006 Pentagon report estimates that the DF-31 may be already in service, while the DF-31A could be deployed before 2007. It is also believed that these new missiles can be equipped with multiple and independently guided warheads.[13]

Another very important modernization program concerns China's next generation submarine-based strike capability. The program involves a new Type 094 nuclear-powered submarine that can launch the new JL-2 SLBM, which is based on the DF-31 with a similar range. The Type 094 sub was launched in 2004 in the naval shipyard of Hulu Dao and is currently going through sea trials. Additionally, in June 2005 China successfully tested the JL-2 SLBM that will equip the 094-class submarine. These recent breakthroughs surprised U.S. analysts who once believed that it would take China at least another four to five years to test and deploy these strategic nuclear weapon systems. The Pentagon has predicted that the deployment date for Type 094 and the JL-2 may be as early as 2007.

It is important to estimate the future size of China's strategic nuclear forces. The first issue is whether China will choose to focus on land- or sea-based systems. Although China will certainly deploy the road-mobile DF-31 and the longer-range DF-31A, it is likely that the future emphasis will be on sea-based systems such as the Type 094 strategic submarines and the JL-2 SLBMs for the simple reason that they can better survive an American preemptive strike. As Lieber and Press suggest, the U.S. has greatly improved its real-time intelligence, long-range targeting, and precision strike capabilities giving it unprecedented ability to launch a preemptive strike against Russian or Chinese nuclear forces.[14] Although Lieber and Press may exaggerate the U.S. offensive nuclear capability, China nonetheless must make sure that its own nuclear forces are able to survive an American preemptive strike. Sea-based forces offer China much greater chances of surviving such an attack. In fact, as demonstrated by Xu and Lewis, China had long recognized the advantages of sea-based deterrence even before it could develop the necessary technologies, such as nuclear-powered submarines and solid-propellant SLBMs.[15]

To maintain a credible nuclear deterrence, both Britain and France today operate four strategic submarines. This is considered the minimum level of force that is needed for secure second-strike capability. Subsequently, in a study of Chinese nuclear modernization by the Naval War College, Christopher McConnaughy, an active duty submariner with experience on strategic missile boats, predicts that China could deploy six Type 094s in the next decade. He suggests that "China could keep four of six SSBNs deployed continuously, the remaining two undergoing maintenance between deployments."[16] This is a very reasonable prediction for two reasons. First, with the ongoing deployment of the National Missile Defense (NMD) system by the U.S.A., the current Chinese strategic nuclear force of roughly 20 single-warhead long-range ICBMs will become ineffective. During the initial stage of its deployment, which is under-way in Alaska, the NMD will involve 200 ground-based interceptors, with 40 of them deployed by the end of 2007. A more capable space-based system remains a possibility for the NMD in the future. As a result of this emerging American defensive capability, China has to ensure that at least two of its strategic nuclear submarines can survive an American preemptive strike. This number is neces-sary to give China sufficient warheads to overcome the ballistic missile defense system of the U.S.A.

Second, with its booming economy, China certainly has the financial resources to deploy a fleet of four to six strategic nuclear submarines. Even Russia, with its dwindling national capability, is able to afford a strategic nuclear submarine force of 12 boats. In fact, Russia is currently building a new generation of strategic nuclear submarines. Three of these Borey class sub-marines will come into service around the end of the decade. Russia's goal is to maintain 208 SLBMs on its submarines by 2010.

Besides the likely number of Type 094s to be deployed by China, the number of warheads on each JL-2 SLBM is an important issue as well. It should not be a surprise that the JL-2s will carry multiple warheads. First, it is unimaginable that in the twenty-first century China would still deploy a single warhead in its SLBMs. It defeats the fundamental purpose of sea-based strategic deterrence, which rests on the assumption that a single surviving nuclear submarine can inflict unacceptable damage to an enemy. For this purpose, all major nuclear powers equip their SLBMs with multiple and independently guided warheads. Second, the JL-2s with a single warhead would simply not give China sufficient numbers to overcome an emerging American defensive capability. Imagine that only two Type 094 survive an American first strike. In this case, their 32 war-heads would not be sufficient to penetrate even a ground-based NMD system.

In fact, a 1999 study by the National Intelligence Council concluded that China has had the technical capability for multiple reentry vehicles for two decades but apparently chose not to deploy them. Bates Gill and James Mul-venon, two U.S. experts on Chinese nuclear forces, also observe that China "apparently has the ability to place multiple warheads on its missiles."[17] They argue that China may decide to do so if it perceives that American ballistic missile defense would undermine China's limited nuclear deterrence.

It is reported by several sources that in December 2002 China successfully tested a DF-21 medium-range nuclear missile with multiple warheads.[18] It was part of a Chinese experiment with technologies that can penetrate and defeat U.S. ballistic missile defense systems. If China can put multiple warheads on the DF-21, it can also do so with the significantly larger DF-31 and JL-2. Therefore, it is logical to surmise that given the new American defensive capability, China must equip its strategic missiles, especially those that are sea-based, with multiple and independently guided warheads. The only question is how many per missile. Almost all published Chinese sources mention that JL-2s are able to carry three to six warheads. Some U.S. observers predict the number is around three. Based on these different projections, this article provides a range of estimates of the future size of Chinese strategic nuclear capability.

In the case of lowest estimation, China deploys only four Type 094s and each of the sub's 16 JL-2 SLBMs carries three warheads. This will yield a total number of 192 sea-based warheads. If we further assume that China would also deploy roughly three dozen land-based DF-31s and DF-31As which are equipped with three warheads, the total number of Chinese strategic warheads could reach the 300 range. Another scenario is that China deploys six Type 094s and three warheads on each JL-2 SLBM. This will produce 288 sea-based warheads. Supplemented by land-based counterparts, the total number of Chinese strategic warheads will be close to 400. The next scenario is the possibility of four Type 094s and six warheads on JL-2s. In this case, the number of sea-based warheads alone will increase to 384 and China's total number of strategic warheads will approach 500.

In the case of highest estimation, China will deploy six Type 094s and six warheads on each JL-2 missile. This alone will result in 572 sea-based warheads. This should not be an unreasonable assumption given that even Russia manages to maintain a sea-based deterrence with 12 strategic submarines. In this case, aided by land-based systems, the total number of Chinese strategic warheads will be pushed to the range of 700. Of course, there are other possibilities since the number of warheads on China's new strategic missiles can vary between three and six. Moreover, the number of missiles carried by future Chinese strategic submarines could be more than 16. As a Taiwanese defense magazine recently reports, China is working on an improved model of Type 094 that has bigger displacement and carries 20 SLBMs.[19]

Brad Roberts has suggested that a significant increase in China's strategic capability is likely due to the U.S. deployment of ballistic missile defense (BMD) technologies.[20] He argues that the emerging U.S. defense capability is a critical factor that will define China's nuclear modernization. China will at least need to pace the BMD capabilities and deploy sufficient missiles and warheads to be able to penetrate the U.S. defensive system. However, given the increasing Chinese inability to deter American intervention in the Taiwan Strait, which is a result of the vast and expanding U.S. conventional advantages, China may adopt a bolder strategy of nuclear modernization and deploy a significantly expanded capability to deter U.S. intervention in the Strait.

Although Roberts does not offer specific predictions of the future size of

China's strategic capability, this article shares his emphasis on how the U.S. BMD capability will impact on China's nuclear modernization. This factor is not analyzed sufficiently by others and thus results in lower predictions. A published Rand study claims that "the intelligence community projects that, by 2015, China will have 75 to 100 warheads deployed on its strategic missiles."[21] A 2005 report by the *Bulletin of Atomic Scientists* argued that China is not pursuing a major expansion of its nuclear capabilities. Instead, "Chinese nuclear forces today look remarkably like they have for decades."[22]

These predictions simply will not allow China to overcome the emerging capability of NMD. Moreover, these assessments fail to take into account the latest developments with the Type 094, which has been going through sea trials since 2004, and the JL-2 SLBM, which was successfully tested in 2005. The significance of these new systems is that even a single Type 094 will be able to carry between 48 to 96 warheads. Indeed, as a recent Chinese report argues, "What needs to be emphasized is the great leap in submarine-based strategic missiles, which has allowed China's nuclear retaliatory capability to reach an all new level."[23] The Rand report, although released to the public in 2006, was actually produced in 2003 for the U.S. Department of Defense. This is why the report might have underestimated the future size of Chinese strategic deterrence. The 2005 report by the *Bulletin of Atomic Scientists* was published in May, one month before the successful test of the JL-2. In fact, it predicted that "China will likely develop and test the Jl-2 and the new sub (Type 094) later this decade."[24]

Even the aforementioned case of lowest prediction, which is quite reasonable assuming the deployment of only four Type 094s and three warheads per missile, will give China roughly 200 sea-based warheads. This alone doubles the prediction by the Rand report. Increased by several dozen new generation land-based missiles, the total number of Chinese strategic warheads could approach 300. This will be a drastic change from the 20 or so single-warhead DF-5s that have so far constituted the backbone of Chinese strategic strike capability. Thus, a recent study by the Naval War College points out that "China's nuclear forces appear to be on the threshold of a new qualitative level."[25]

Chinese nuclear doctrine and future trends

In contrast to China's rapid modernization of nuclear capabilities, its official nuclear doctrine remains minimal and conservative. This doctrine has two components. The first is the "no first use" declaration. China would only use its nuclear weapons after being attacked by them. Moreover, China will never use nuclear weapons against a nonnuclear country. Thus, the Chinese nuclear doctrine is purely retaliatory against a nuclear first strike on China. The second component of the doctrine is the limited counter-value capability of China's strategic nuclear force. China believes that even a small strategic force that targets an enemy's population center can have an enormous deterrence effect. In line with this thinking, China only needs a retaliatory force that can destroy a few large urban centers of the attacking country. As a result, China's strategic nuclear force is by choice the smallest of the five major nuclear powers.

Thus, the minimum deterrence doctrine is designed only to deter a nuclear first strike. It does not have much value in deterring a conventional war. For over two decades this presented no problems for China, since it could rely on a separate doctrine, called People's War, to handle conventional conflicts. The doctrine evolved out of Mao Zedong's military views that emphasized people's power in warfare. If China faced a full-scale invasion, it would rely on a people's war, namely guerrilla warfare, to tie down and weaken a technologically superior enemy until it was defeated by China's ill-equipped but numerically huge army.

However, the 1990s saw a major shift in China's military thinking that for the first time began to question the separation of nuclear and conventional doctrines. This shift was triggered by the 1991 Gulf War, during which the world for the first time saw the awesome capability of high tech weapons. This display of high tech warfare led Chinese experts to debate how the next war was likely to be fought. The new idea was "Limited War under High Tech Conditions." Under this doctrine, the next opponent of China will have advanced weapons and would most likely be the U.S.A. and or Japan.

The idea of Limited War under High Tech Conditions presents a critical problem for China: The next opponent will be far superior technologically and thus China can no longer confidently win a conventional war. This self-doubt began to usher in discussion of the role of nuclear weapons in future warfare. Some began to argue that a different nuclear doctrine was needed to help China deter the next war. For the first time we began to see discussions of integrating nuclear and conventional war doctrines. According to the emerging view, China does not need to match an opponent's conventional power. Instead, it can use a few hundred nuclear warheads to inflict unacceptable damages to the opponent's military forces and force the enemy to back down.

Recently this view seems to have gathered more and more strength. For example, in a conference paper titled "Revolution in Military Affairs and China's Defense Modernization," Jin Yinan, a well-known Chinese strategist teaching at the National Defense University, argues that high technology breakthroughs in the American weapon systems put China at a great disadvantage. To offset this American superiority in conventional high tech weapons, China had to develop a few "master weapons" [*shashoujian*] to level the playing field: "First of all, nuclear deterrence."[26]

An article in a Chinese military magazine argues that China needs to immediately modify its nuclear doctrine. The article ridicules the current No First Use doctrine, charging that the doctrine essentially has made China's limited number of nuclear weapons useless in deterring a potential U.S. intervention in the Taiwan Strait. It argues that China's conventional disparity against the U.S.A. needs several decades to overcome and will require massive resources. Thus the article states that China has a pressing need to adopt a new nuclear doctrine that bases its deterrence on a massive nuclear strike against the U.S.A. and Japan.[27]

Of course the most clearly stated support for a more aggressive Chinese nuclear deterrence was put forth by General Zhu Chenghu, the director of the Institute of Security Affairs, National Defense University. On July 14, 2005, General Zhu told Hong Kong journalists that China cannot win a conventional war against the U.S.A. To prevent U.S. military intervention in the Taiwan Strait, China inevitably has to use nuclear weapons. China must be ready to see all its major cities east of Xian destroyed during the nuclear exchange. Yet at the same time, the U.S.A. will also see several hundred of its largest cities destroyed by Chinese nuclear weapons.[28] The comment by General Zhu is the most explicitly stated endorsement of a new Chinese nuclear doctrine, one that intends to use the awesome destructive power of nuclear weapons to deter a stronger conventional enemy. Although the Chinese government quickly denied that it is the official policy of the government, it is noteworthy to see a prominent Chinese defense strategist boldly supporting a new and aggressive nuclear doctrine. Zhu's comment, once published in the media, quickly attracted support from military observers. For example, a military magazine published an article that argued that

> China's nuclear doctrine is the most self constraining among all nuclear powers. In fact, threatening first use of nuclear weapons is the international norm ... With the rise of its comprehensive power, China must consider changing its outdated principles. It needs to adapt to the mainstream nuclear deterrence thinking in the world.[29]

Although the Chinese government has repeatedly denied that a nuclear doctrinal change is underway, *Kanwa Defense Review*, an overseas Chinese military magazine, argues that General Zhu's statement represented a systematic change in China's strategic thinking about nuclear deterrence.[30] Recent Chinese discussions of the inadequacies of the No First Use doctrine and support for a more aggressive doctrine clearly indicate that there are growing pressures inside China for a major strategic shift. This point is acknowledged by the Pentagon's 2006 *Military Power of China* when it claims that China's internal discussion of the No first Use doctrine is broader than previously assessed.

Although China's conventional weakness and rapid nuclear modernization will make abandoning the No First Use doctrine attractive, China also faces multiple political constraints if it decides to do so. For instance, China has worried that a more robust deterrence doctrine would strengthen the conservative elements within the U.S. government and thus worsen long-term relations between the two countries. Also, China needs to consider how a new deterrence doctrine may influence the future strategic decisions by its major neighbors, such as India and Japan. As a result of these political constraints, a formal doctrinal change by China is unlikely, at least in the next decade.

Nonetheless, the U.S.A. must plan for the contingency that China might make such a shift in the future. Moreover, there is also a greater possibility that China would choose not to make any formal doctrinal change and instead maintain the option of exercising a nuclear warning as and when a crisis situation in the Taiwan Strait makes American military intervention possible or even imminent. Thus, it is important for the U.S.A. to assess the effect of Chinese nuclear deterrence in the Taiwan Strait. In particular, the U.S.A. needs to assess the effect of a Chinese version of flexible response that threatens possible first use of nuclear weapons to deter a conventional war. In the case of NATO, flexible response was used to discourage a Soviet invasion of Western Europe. In the Taiwan Strait, China may use it to deter a direct military intervention by the U.S.A. In fact, this is exactly the intention of General Zhu's comment and the subject of recent Chinese discussions of its nuclear doctrine. Although China most likely will not abandon the No First Use doctrine, it could exercise a nuclear warning if a war in the Taiwan Strait looked unavoidable or imminent.

Chinese nuclear deterrence in the Taiwan Strait

A recent Rand study on the future role of nuclear weapons indicates two critical functions of such weapons. One is to offset conventional imbalance. The other is to deter enemies from a range of actions by the threat of punishment.[31] China's flexible response strategy could perform both functions to offset the vast American conventional advantage and deter the U.S.A. from a direct military intervention in a war across the Taiwan Strait.

The flexible response doctrine was first developed by NATO to deny the Soviet Union's advantage in conventional capability. NATO's greatest worry was that a sudden and massive Soviet conventional attack might not be stoppable. Therefore, in the eyes of NATO strategy planners, nuclear weapons offered the only solution. By threatening possible first use of nuclear weapons, NATO hoped to convince the Soviet Union that a victory was impossible. For example, as the West German defense *White Paper* of 1975–76 argues, "the initial use of nuclear weapons is not intended so much to bring about a military decision as to achieve political effect. The intent is to persuade the attacker to reconsider his intentions, to desist in his aggression, and to withdraw."[32]

Moreover, through its willingness to escalate to nuclear war, NATO hoped to convince the Soviet Union that the war could get out of control and reach the highest level: a strategic nuclear war. General Rogers, NATO supreme commander, argued that through flexible response, "the Soviet Union cannot predict with certainty when or where the Alliance would resort to the first use of nuclear weapons to defend NATO territory. For them, the risks of initiating any armed conflict would be open-ended and consequences would be incalculable."[33]

China may also threaten possible first use of nuclear weapons to deter a conventional war by the U.S.A., most likely in the Taiwan Strait. On the one hand, Chinese use of tactical nuclear weapons may help offset the vast American conventional advantages. On the other hand, China's first use of battlefield nuclear weapons raises the possibility of escalation, including that of a strategic nuclear war. The prospect that a nuclear escalation might get out of control will generate a powerful deterrence effect. The effectiveness of this Chinese flexible response approach would depend on two elements: credibility and capability. China's deterrence against U.S. intervention is only effective if its threat of nuclear war is judged credible. According to deterrence theory, credibility depends largely on the importance of the stakes involved. The higher the stakes, the more credible the deterrence is. Few people questioned the vital stake of the U.S.A. in not letting the Soviet Union conquer Western Europe. Therefore, NATO's nuclear deterrence was generally considered robust and credible.

In a war over Taiwan, the stakes involved for China and the U.S.A. cannot be more different. As observed by a U.S National Defense University study, Taiwan represents a regime survival issue for the Chinese Communists. It faces the prospect of being overthrown if it loses Taiwan after a humiliating defeat by the U.S.A.[34] China still vividly remembers the humiliation it suffered at the hands of Western imperialism. Thus, Taiwan has an extremely important symbolic significance. An independent Taiwan and a humiliating defeat by the U.S.A. are simply unacceptable to both the regime and Chinese people. Since the stake involved is extremely high, China's threat of nuclear weapons to deter U.S. intervention is credible.

A 2006 Rand study of possible military conflicts over Taiwan also notes the importance of asymmetry of interests between China and the U.S.A. As it observes,

> Beijing would have much more at stake than Washington in the event of a showdown over the status of Taiwan. For Washington, Taiwan's security is undoubtedly an important U.S. interest, as reflected by the Taiwan Relations Act and subsequent statements and actions emphasizing the U.S.A.' commitment to the island's defense. For Beijing, however, Taiwan ranks as the most important security issue, and Chinese leaders have stated their willingness to þay any price' to resolve the issue on terms favorable to Beijing, or at least to prevent a change in the status quo that they would view as an unacceptable affront to Chinese interests. In a conflict over Taiwan, Beijing calculates that China's vital national interests, and perhaps, even regime survival, would be on the line.[35]

Chinese deterrence may not be so robust if the U.S.A. also has high stakes involved or if the cost of its intervention is low. Although the U.S. stake is unclear, a tactical nuclear war would make the cost unacceptable for American intervention. As pointed out by an American analyst, at least on the surface, the U.S. stake in Taiwan is not significant. Since the U.S.A. openly supports the "One China" policy, it appears to be willing to accept the strategic consequences of Taiwan's incorporation into China. Thus Taiwan has no strategic importance for the U.S.A., which only cares about the means of unification, such as peaceful means instead of military means. This lack of interest in the strategic substance of reunification and mere concern with the process weakens the real and perceived American stake in Taiwan. This means that while China's threat of nuclear war is credible, U.S. credibility in fighting a nuclear war on behalf of

Taiwan is weak. To put it another way, for the U.S.A. a horrific nuclear war does not justify the (or the lack of) strategic stakes involved.

The Chinese nuclear deterrence would also be weakened if the cost of American intervention were low. Yet this clearly is not the case in a U.S–China nuclear exchange in the Pacific. Although a tactical nuclear war would inflict huge casualties on China, it would also kill very large numbers of American troops based in the Pacific and cause tremendous loss of U.S. military assets. Moreover, a tactical nuclear war might run the risk of escalating into a general strategic nuclear war. This is an unthinkable outcome for any American president.

The effectiveness of China's flexible response deterrence, beside credibility, also depends on adequate force capability to back up its threat. As noted by the Council on Foreign Relations, most of the industrial and technological infrastructure is already in place for China to expand its nuclear force. "These are sunk costs. Increased capability would bring new but incremental costs, not an order-of-magnitude increase in the demand for scarce resources. If Beijing finds that national security requires a larger investment in strategic forces, it is likely to find a way to pay for it."[36]

China seems to have achieved rapid breakthroughs in the last two years with its latest strategic weapons systems, such as the 094 Class strategic submarine and the JL-2 SLBMs. The imminent deployment of these systems has surprised outside observers, many of whom once believed that China would have to wait until the end of this decade to test and deploy these systems. These new strategic systems will increase the number of warheads capable of striking the U.S.A. from the current 20 to 30 to a much higher level. Even a low estimation will result in roughly 300 securely deployed strategic warheads for China's forthcoming offensive capability. As shown by France and Britain, a securely deployed nuclear force of around 300–400 nuclear warheads is sufficient to deter a much more powerful opponent such as the Soviet Union. For example, France's strategic nuclear force is based on just four nuclear submarines and is deemed a highly credible deterrence.

As argued by Robert Jervis in his classical article "Why Nuclear Superiority Doesn't Matter," in the case of mutual deterrence, a numerical advantage by one country does not have any real benefit as long as both sides possess the ability to inflict unacceptable cost on the other. What is more important is the so-called balance of resolve, namely, whoever has more credibility in carrying out its nuclear threat in a given situation.[37] In the case of Taiwan, the vast asymmetry of interests between China and the U.S.A. would give the former a definite advantage in the balance of resolve.

The need for U.S.–China strategic dialogues

Chinese nuclear modernization is inevitable and imminent. American policy makers should recognize China's major nuclear power status. Any strategic calculation must incorporate this nuclear factor and the possibility of nuclear war with China. Evidence suggests that the U.S.A. is taking a new look at the rise of Chinese strategic nuclear capability. As Dan Blumenthal of the American Enterprise Institute observes, "the accelerated development of Chinese strategic nuclear forces has been one key surprise, and stood out in this year's (Pentagon) report."[38] As a specific example of the new American concern with China's possible use of nuclear weapons in the Taiwan Strait, the Institute for Defense Analysis, which performs regular consultation for the Pentagon, has conducted research to examine how the nuclear factor may impact on a U.S.–China–Taiwan standoff in the future.

If the U.S.A. can indeed give adequate attention to the nuclear issue, the emerging Chinese capability will redefine U.S.–China strategic relations in the long term. It will force both sides to adopt more realistic policies toward each other. More specifically, the U.S.A. will have to face the possibility that direct military intervention in the Taiwan Strait may no longer be a policy option. As a result, the U.S.A. needs to use other policies, such as greater efforts to reign in Taiwan's independence tendency and transfer of more advanced conventional weapons, to secure the stability of the Strait.

China's rapid nuclear modernization may be understood in the context of the National Missile Defense system that is on the verge of becoming operational. Thus the U.S. deployment of a limited NMD system and Chinese nuclear expansion offer the right context for Sino-American strategic dialogues. The two countries should establish a framework that can satisfy their mutual concerns. Specifically, through strategic dialogues, China and the U.S.A. must agree upon a proper balance between the Chinese offensive capability and the American defensive capability. This point is also raised by a Rand study on ballistic missile defense,

> the U.S.A. must be prepared for China to expand its strategic offensive arsenal, especially in weapons capable of reaching the U.S.A.. Perhaps China will expand these capabilities anyway. The U.S.A. should not be surprised or incensed to discover that the Chinese are increasing their strategic arms when the U.S. ballistic missile defense system has given them reasons to do so.[39]

A *New York Times* report in 2001 indicated that the Bush administration at the time intended to tell leaders in Beijing that it had no objections to China's plans to expand its nuclear force, in exchange for its acceptance of a limited NMD. According to the same report, the U.S.A. was willing to allow China to resume underground nuclear testing to improve its strategic strike force.[40] If the U.S.A. is willing to pursue this policy further, then it may offer important progress in achieving the necessary strategic understanding between the two countries. This understanding will be very important for preventing a future arms race between a growing defensive capability of the U.S.A. and an expanding offensive capability of China.

Averting such an arms race will be a key issue for a U.S.–China strategic relationship in the next decade. The two countries must try not to repeat the nuclear arms race of the Cold War era since it will certainly worsen the security dilemma that is bound to haunt U.S.–China relations for a long time. An escalating nuclear arms race would sharpen the perceived threat from the other side and result in dangerous misunderstanding of mutual intentions. Most importantly, the two countries should come to the understanding that China's forthcoming secure second-strike capability may allow their bilateral relations to achieve greater stability. Aaron L. Friedberg mentions nuclear weapons as a possible positive contributing factor in U.S.–China relations.[41] China's emerging nuclear capability will be particularly important in crisis situations involving Taiwan. Without the threat of nuclear war, the U.S.A. might believe that it could defeat China in a conventional war; while the latter, when perceiving war may be inevitable, might be tempted to launch a surprise attack to weaken the U.S. conventional advantage. Thus, without the shadow of nuclear war, a crisis over Taiwan could trigger a major power war and shatter world peace. A robust and credible Chinese nuclear deterrence could dissipate the possibility of such a war between the two countries.

As to Taiwan's security, the emerging Chinese nuclear capability should not become a major concern. As observed by Thomas J. Christensen, China's current policy toward Taiwan is one of accommodation.[42] The mainland is not pursuing active reunification with the island. Instead, it is content with maintaining the status quo across the Taiwan Strait, recognizing that this is the best possible outcome under the circumstance. Therefore, as long as Taiwan does not attempt to unilaterally move toward formal independence, China's increasingly potent nuclear capability should not lead to more aggressive policies toward the island. For this reason, the U.S.A. needs to consistently convince Taiwan that its pursuit of formal independence, and thus changing the status quo, is not supported by Washington. This policy will do much to eliminate possible miscalculations by Taiwan's leadership and thus ensure greater stability in the Taiwan Strait. The Bush administration since 2004 has been increasingly willing to express its displeasure with the provocative policies of the Chen Shui-bian government. Continued U.S. opposition to unilateral moves by Taiwan will no doubt serve to stabilize the Taiwan Strait situation and prevent direct confrontation between China and the U.S.A.

In conclusion, this chapter argues that the emerging nuclear mutual deterrence between China and the U.S.A. will generate greater stability in U.S.–China relations because it will force the leaders on both sides to adopt more realistic policies toward each other. One particular benefit of this mutual deterrence is increased stability across the Taiwan Strait. Furthermore, the rising Chinese offensive capability and the expanding American defensive capability should provide incentives for strategic dialogues about the proper nuclear balance of power between the two countries, since an arms race would be in the interest of no one. Therefore, while the rise of Chinese nuclear power may cause continuous tension in the most important bilateral relationship in the world, it is a stabilizing factor as well.

Notes

1 Robert A. Manning, Ronald Montaperto, and Brad Roberts, *China, Nuclear Weapons, and Arms Control: A Preliminary Assessment*, New York: Council on Foreign Relations, 2000, p. vi.
2 *Annual Report on the Military Power of the People's Republic of China*, the Department of Defense, 2006, pp. 2, 7.
3 Lawrence Freedman, "No First Use," paper for Pugwash Meeting No. 279, London, U.K., November 15–17, 2002, p. 2.
4 Robert D. Kaplan, "How We Would Fight China," the *Atlantic Monthly*, June 2005.
5 Hsien Loong's interview was reported in the Chinese newspaper *Mingbao*, July 17, 2004.
6 Abram N. Shulsky, *Deterrence Theory and Chinese Behavior*, Santa Monica, CA: Rand Corporation, 2000, p. xiii.
7 David A. Shlapak, "The Cross-Strait Balance and Its Implications for U.S. Policy," in Donald S. Zagoria, ed., *Breaking the China-Taiwan Impasse*, Westport, CT: Praeger, 2003.
8 Ning Ling and Li Shaohui, "jikui di yizhi di zuozhan mubiao xuanqu lilun" [A combat theory of defeating the enemy's will], *Guofang daxue xuebao* [*Journal of National Defense University*], June 2004. pp. 16–18.
9 Roger Cliff and Toy Reid, "Roiling the Water in the Taiwan Strait," *International Herald Tribune*, March 21, 2006.
10 Ted Galen Carpenter, "Future War: Taiwan," *National Interest*, Summer 2006. This article is based on the author's book, *America's Coming War with China: A Collision Course over Taiwan* (2006),
11 Lawrence Freedman, "No First Use," paper for Pugwash Meeting No. 279, London, U.K., November 15–17, 2002, p. 2.
12 Avery Goldstein, *Rising to the Challenge: China's Grand Strategy and International Security*, Stanford: Stanford University Press, 2005, pp. 100–101.
13 The Department of Defense, *Annual Report on the Military Power of the People's Republic of China*, Washington, D.C.: Department of Defense, 2006.
14 Keir A. Lieber and Daryl G. Press, "The Rise of U.S. Nuclear Primacy," *Foreign Affairs*, Vol. 85, No. 2, March/April 2006, pp. 42–56.
15 John Wilson Lewis and Xue Litai, *China's Strategic Sea Power. The Politics of Force Modernization in the Nuclear Age*, Stanford: Stanford University Press, 1993, pp. 237–38.
16 Christopher McConnaughy, "China's Undersea Nuclear Deterrent: Will the U.S. Navy Be Ready?" in Lyle J. Goldstein, ed., *China's Nuclear Force Modernization*, Newport, RI: Naval War College, p. 43.
17 Bates Gill and James Mulvenon, "China's Nuclear Agenda," *New York Times*, September 7, 2001.
18 This test was reported by a Taiwanese website, "China Successfully Tests Multi-Warhead Missiles" (http://taiwansecurity.org/News/2003/YS-020803.htm). The test is also discussed by the Nuclear Threat Initiatives in *China's Nuclear Policies and Programs* (http://www.nit.org/db/china/sec2.htm).
19 Lin Zongda, "Zhongguo zuixin hezi dongli feidan qianting tansuo" [Chinese newest nuclear submarine], *Defense International*, October 2006.
20 Brad Roberts, "Alternative Futures," in Paul J. Bolt and Albert S. Willner, eds, *China's Nuclear Future*, Boulder: Lynne Rienner, 2006, pp. 167–192.
21 Rand Corporation, *Chinese Response to U.S. Military Transformation and Implications for the Department of Defense*, Santa Monica, CA: Rand Corporation, 2006, p. 103.
22 Jeffrey Lewis, "The Ambiguous Arsenal," *Bulletin of Atomic Scientists*, 2005 (http://www.thebulletin.org/print.php?art-ofn=mj05lewis).

23 Gu Lu, "Beijing xin he zhanlue quebao he baofu li" [Beijing's new deterrence doctrine: guaranteed retaliatory capability], *Sun*, October 13, 2006.

24 Lewis, "The Ambiguous Arsenal," *Bulletin of Atomic Scientists*, 2005 (http://www.thebulletin.org/print.php?art-ofn=mj05lewis).

25 Lyle J. Goldstein, "Introduction," in Lyle J. Goldstein, ed., *China's Nuclear Force Modernization*, Newport, RI: Naval War College 2005, p. 2.

26 This paper was presented at the Conference on International Studies in China, June 13, 2004, Beijing. For the quote, see p. 7.

27 (no author), Zhongguo he zhanlue jixu zhuanbian" [China's nuclear doctrine needs immediate change], *Zhongguo daodan huoli [Chinese missiles]*, 2005, p. 1.

28 Meng Xuan, "Zhu Chenghu di zhong mei hewu duikang lun" [Zhu Chenghu's View on U.S.–China Nuclear War], *World Daily*, July 24, 2005.

29 Huang Dong, "Zhongguo he zhanlue xu yushi gongjin" [China's nuclear doctrine must advance with time], *Junshi wenzhai [Military digest]*, December 2005, p. 23.

30 (no author), "Zhongguo bianhuan dui mei ri weishe di shoufa" [China changing its deterrence against the U.S.A. and Japan], *Hanwa Defense Review*, October 2005, pp. 17–18.

31 Glenn C. Buchan, David Matonick, Calvin Shipbaugh, and Richard Mesic, *Future Roles of U.S. Nuclear Forces*, Santa Monica, CA: The Rand Corporation, 2003, p. 3.

32 This quote is from Ivo H. Daalder, *The Nature and Practice of Flexible Response: NATO Strategy and Theater Nuclear Forces since 1967*, New York: Columbia University Press, 1991, p. 20.

33 Ibid.

34 Jason D. Ellis and Todd M. Koca, *"China Rising: New Challenges to the U.S. Security Posture,"* *Strategic Forum*, No. 175, Arlington, VA: Institute for National Strategic Studies, National Defense University, 2000, p. 5.

35 The Rand Corporation, *Chinese Response to U.S. Military Transformation and Implication for the Department of Defense*, Santa Monica, CA: The Rand Corporation, 2006, p. 112.

36 The Council on Foreign Relations, *China, Nuclear Weapons, and Arms Control: A Preliminary Assessment*, New York: The Council on Foreign Relations, 2000, pp. 4–5.

37 Robert Jervis, "Why Nuclear Superiority Doesn't Matter," *Political Science Quarterly*, Vol, 94, No. 4, pp. 631–632.

38 Dan Blumental's comment at AEI panel discussion on China's Growing Missile Force: What It Means for the Strategic Balance in Asia, July 11, 2006. For the transcript, see http://www.aei.org/events/filter.all,eventID.1360/transcript.asp.

39 David C. Gompert and Jeffrey A. Isaacson, "Planning a Ballistic Missile Defense System of Systems: An Adaptive Strategy," *Rand Issue Paper*, 2001, p. 17.

40 David E. Sanger, "U.S. to Tell China It Will Not Object to Missile Buildup," *New York Times*, September 2, 2001.

41 Aaron L. Friedberg, "The Future of U.S.–China Relations: Is Conflict Inevitable?" *International Security*, Vol. 30, No. 2, Fall 2005, p. 28.

42 Thomas J. Christensen, "Will China Become a Responsible Statekholder'? The Six Party Talks, Taiwan Arms Sale, and Sino-Japanese Relations," *China Leadership Monitor*, No. 16, Fall 2005.

7 China–U.S. economic relations and the trade imbalance issue

Wei Li

This chapter examines the dramatic development of the bilateral economic relationship between China and the U.S.A. By 2006, the U.S.A. had become China's second largest trading partner, its largest export market and the sixth largest source of imports, and China has become the second largest trading partner of the U.S.A., its fourth largest export market, and the second largest source of imports. In addition, China has become the tenth largest U.S. services export market since 2004.

Although there is a statistical difference in the trade volume, the bilateral trade has witnessed great development. According to China's statistics, the bilateral trade amounted to $262.7 billion in 2006, 6.1 times as much as that in 1996, and U.S. statistics demonstrate that the bilateral trade totaled $343.0 billion, 5.4 times bigger than that in 1996. Since 2001 when China joined the WTO, U.S. exports to China have increased by 187.11 percent, the fastest growth among the U.S. top 15 export markets (see Tables 7.1 and 7.2).

Table 7.1 Bilateral trade between China and the U.S.A. ($ billion)

	U.S.A. statistics				China statistics			
	Export to China	Growth %	Import from China	Growth %	Export to the U.S.A.	Growth %	Import from the U.S.A.	Growth %
1996	11.98	2.0	51.50	13.0	26.69	7.9	16.16	0.2
1997	12.81	6.9	62.55	21.5	32.70	22.5	16.30	0.8
1998	14.26	11.3	71.16	13.8	37.98	16.1	16.96	4.0
1999	13.12	–8.0	81.79	14.9	41.95	10.5	19.48	15.4
2000	16.25	23.9	100.06	22.4	52.10	24.2	22.36	14.8
2001	19.24	18.4	102.28	2.2	54.28	4.2	26.20	17.2
2002	22.05	14.7	125.17	22.4	69.95	28.9	27.23	3.9
2003	28.42	28.9	152.38	21.7	92.47	32.2	33.86	24.3
2004	34.72	22.2	196.70	29.1	124.95	35.1	44.68	31.9
2005	41.84	20.5	243.46	23.8	162.90	30.4	48.73	9.1
2006	55.22	32.0	287.77	18.2	203.47	24.9	59.21	21.8

Source: U.S. Department of Commerce, China Customs.

Table 7.2 U.S. export growth among its top 15 export markets 2001–2006

Export market	Export ($ billion)		Growth rate (%)
	2001	2006	2001–2006
1 Canada	163.72	230.26	40.64
2 Mexico	101.51	134.17	32.17
3 Japan	57.64	59.65	3.49
4 China	19.23	55.22	187.11
5 U.K.	40.80	45.39	11.26
6 Germany	30.11	41.32	37.21
7 Korea	22.20	32.46	46.22
8 Netherlands	19.52	31.10	59.29
9 Singapore	17.69	24.68	39.52
10 France	19.90	24.22	21.72
11 Taiwan	18.15	23.02	26.84
12 Belgium	13.52	21.35	57.85
13 Brazil	15.93	19.23	20.71
14 Australia	10.94	17.78	62.47
15 Hong Kong	14.07	17.78	26.34

Source: U.S. Department of Commerce.

U.S.–China trade deficit dispute

With the increasing trade volume, the trade imbalance has become a prominent problem in recent years. Even if there is a gap in the trade imbalance value, it is a fact that the U.S.A. has a trade deficit with China. According to China's statistics, the U.S. trade deficit with China first appeared in 1993, at $6.3 billion, and amounted to $144 billion in 2006. On the other hand, U.S. statistics showed that its trade deficit with China first appeared in 1983 (with a value of $300 million) and reached $233 billion in 2006. U.S. statistics also revealed that China had become the second largest source of the U.S. trade deficit, next only to Japan since 1991, but the largest since 2000. The U.S. trade deficit with China in 2006 accounted for about 28 percent of the total U.S. trade deficit. What's more, the trade deficit with China is about 2.6 times as big as that with Japan, the second largest source of the U.S. trade deficit, with a value of $144 billion higher (see Table 7.3).

No matter whether the precise deficit has any economic meaning, the huge value has made some U.S. politicians uneasy. They have assumed that the trade deficit with China has threatened the U.S. economy and stolen U.S. job opportunities; they also attributed the trade deficit to unfair trade practices by China, such as its exchange rate policy and market access obstacles, etc.

From the perspective of international trade, three reasons might explain why trade deficit has attracted so much attention in the U.S.A.

First, the total U.S. trade deficit has witnessed increasing growth in recent years. The total U.S. trade deficit first broke the benchmark of $100 billion in 1993. In only five years the deficit passed $200 billion in 1998. Then the trade

Table 7.3 U.S. trade deficit with China ($ billion)

	U.S. total trade deficit	Trade deficit with China (the U.S. statistics)	Trade surplus with the U.S.A. (China statistics)
1996	168.5	39.5	10.5
1997	182.6	49.7	16.4
1998	233.4	56.9	21.0
1999	331.9	68.7	22.5
2000	436.5	83.8	29.7
2001	410.9	83.0	28.1
2002	470.3	103.1	42.7
2003	535.7	124.0	58.6
2004	653.1	162.0	80.3
2005	766.6	201.6	114.2
2006	818.0	232.5	144.3

Source: U.S. Department of Commerce, China Customs.

deficit exceeded $300 billion in 1999, $400 billion in 2000, $500 billion in 2003, $600 billion in 2004, $700 billion in 2005, and $800 billion in 2006. The trade deficit has almost witnessed an annual increase of $100 billion since the late 1990s, and has accounted for about 6 percent of U.S. GDP.

Second, globalization has influenced not only developing countries but also developed countries such as the U.S.A. Trade liberalization is considered to benefit the U.S.A. It is estimated that U.S. annual incomes are $1 trillion higher, or $9,000 per household, due to increased trade liberalization since 1945.[1] Though both economic theory and data suggest that trade liberalization will bring consumer surplus to the U.S.A., such gains have different influences on different industries, and some industries experience consumer loss. The overall "U.S. gains" cannot compensate the specific interest groups who have been negatively influenced or have faced challenges from liberalization. These negatively influenced interest groups have more incentives to seek for protectionism and to decry China's trade surplus.

Third, the trade deficit is closely linked to America's economic cycle and economic structure. However, the influenced industries are more inclined to attribute such reasons to other countries instead of solving internal problems. It is easier for them to link trade liberalization to the loss of American manufacturing job opportunities, especially to China who has experienced dramatic trade growth since it joined the WTO in 2001. Hence China became the attack target under such background.

Although the trade imbalance has existed for over ten years and continues to expand, the bilateral economic relationship is still mutually beneficial. The USTR confessed that

the U.S.A. has also derived certain benefits from the trade relationship. American consumers now have access to a wider variety of less costly goods, and low-cost consumer and industrial goods from China have helped spur U.S. economic growth while keeping a check on inflation.[2]

The trade deficit is only a parameter in a statistical sense, and it cannot fully reflect the actual benefits achieved through bilateral trade.

China has become the most liberalized developing country, and it is the U.S.A.'s fastest growing export market among major trading partners. Since 2001 when China joined the WTO, U.S. exports to China have grown 4.5 times faster than they have to the rest of the world, and China has changed from the ninth biggest to the fourth biggest export market of the U.S.A. U.S. exports to China increased by an impressive 32 percent in 2006, building on another robust 20 percent growth in 2005.

It's true that China replaced Japan in 2000 as the largest single source of the U.S. trade deficit, but in ratio terms the U.S. trade deficit with China has not exceeded the height of its deficit with Japan. In 1989, the U.S. trade deficit with Japan accounted for 45 percent of the U.S. total trade deficit. From the 1990s, the trade deficit has diversified from Japan to many other trading partners including China. In 2000, China accounted for 19.2 percent of the U.S. trade deficit, and Japan accounted for 18.6 percent. Since 2000, the diversified sources of the U.S. trade deficit have again witnessed a gradual concentration trend to China. However, unlike Japan in the 1980s and 1990s which had maintained a trade surplus with almost all of its major trading partners, China currently has trade deficits with many of its trading partners, such as Japan, Korea, ASEAN, etc.

Causes of the trade deficits

The difference in economic structure between China and the U.S.A.

The U.S.A. is the largest developed country, and China is the largest developing country, in the world. The two countries are complementary in their economic development and economic structure.

The U.S.A. has shifted to high tech industry and services, and most of the remaining manufacturing industry is high end. This trend had already started in the 1980s, when the U.S.A. experienced trade deficits in manufacturing sectors with NIEs (Newly Industrialized Economies) such as Hong Kong, Korea, Singapore, and Taiwan. And China, currently, by its comparative advantage, especially in cheap labor costs, has developed many low end manufacturing industries, especially taking over labor-intensive industries from other countries. This is the natural reflection of optimal resources reallocation.

In its climb to the higher ladder of industrial upgrading, China was able to develop some high tech industries when it was developing labor-intensive industries, but the U.S.A. could not go back to those labor-intensive industries. In fact, 90 percent of U.S. imported products are no longer produced at all in the U.S.A., which means that even if the U.S.A. does not import from China, it has to import from other countries. The Chinese products have price advantages and it is natural that consumers prefer Chinese products. In this sense, it is the choice of the consumers and not the fault of the producers.

Difference in trade structure between China and the U.S.A.

The overall U.S. trade deficit has resulted from three categories of goods: The first category is petroleum; the second is products complementary to its economy, mainly labor-intensive products, such as textiles, shoes, toys, etc., as well as some low end mechanical and electronic products; and the third category is capital and technology-intensive products such as automobiles and auto parts, semiconductors and computers, etc.

During the period from 1996 to 2006, mineral fuels and vehicles were the two leading sources of the U.S. trade deficits, respectively 17.2 and 9.4 percent with an average annual growth rate of 17.2 and 9.4 percent respectively. The total deficit value of these two items was $421 billion in 2006, accounting for 52 percent of the U.S. total trade deficit. China has no advantages in these two items (see Tables 7.4 and 7.5).

Table 7.4 U.S. ten chapters of products with the largest trade deficit with the world and China 2006 ($ billion)

Ranking	U.S. ten chapters of products with the largest trade deficit with the world			The U.S. ten chapters of products with the largest trade deficit with China		
	HS chapter	*Value*	*Share %*	*HS chapter*	*Value*	*Share %*
1	27	−298.6	36.51	85	−54.73	23.53
2	87	−122.7	15.00	84	−54.56	23.46
3	85	−83.3	10.19	95	−20.84	8.96
4	84	−61.9	7.57	94	−19.23	8.27
5	62	−36.1	4.42	64	−13.83	5.95
6	61	−33.0	4.04	62	−11.85	5.09
7	94	−32.2	3.94	61	−8.00	3.44
8	95	−20.4	2.49	73	−7.97	3.43
9	64	−18.3	2.24	42	−6.82	2.93
10	30	−17.1	2.09	39	−4.75	2.04

Source: U.S. Department of Commerce.

Notes
Chapter 27: Mineral fuels, mineral oils, and products of their distillation; bituminous substances; mineral waxes. Chapter 87: Vehicles others than railway or tramway rolling-stock, and parts and accessories thereof. Chapter 85: Electrical machinery and equipment and parts thereof; sound recorders and reproducers, television image and sound recorders and reproducers, and parts and accessories of such articles. Chapter 84: Nuclear reactors, boilers, machinery, and mechanical appliances; parts thereof. Chapter 62: Articles of apparel and clothing accessories, not knitted or crocheted. Chapter 61: Articles of apparel and clothing accessories, knitted or crocheted. Chapter 94: Furniture; bedding, mattresses, mattress supports, cushions, and similar stuffed furnishing; lamps and lighting fittings, NES or incl.; illuminated signs or name-plates and the like; prefabricated buildings. Chapter 95: Toys, games, and sports requisites; parts and accessories thereof. Chapter 64: Footwear, gaiters and the like; parts of such articles. Chapter 30: Pharmaceutical products

Table 7.5 The U.S. top ten chapters of products with the largest trade deficit with China 2006 ($ billion)

Ranking	China statistics			U.S. statistics		
	HS chapter	Value	Share %	HS chapter	Value	Share %
	Total value of trade surplus	144.26		Total value of trade imbalance	−232.55	
1	84	36.69	25.43	85	−54.73	23.50
2	85	34.47	23.89	84	−54.56	23.46
3	94	11.48	7.95	95	−20.84	8.96
4	95	8.60	5.96	94	−19.23	8.27
5	62	7.87	5.46	64	−13.83	5.95
6	64	7.51	5.21	62	−11.85	5.09
7	73	7.06	4.89	61	−8.00	3.44
8	61	6.30	4.37	73	−7.97	3.43
9	87	4.57	3.17	42	−6.82	2.93
10	63	3.92	2.72	39	−4.75	2.04

Source: U.S. Department of Commerce, China Customs.

Notes
Chapter Description: Chapter 84: Nuclear reactors, boilers, machinery and mechanical appliances; parts thereof. Chapter 85: Electrical machinery and equipment and parts thereof; sound recorders and reproducers, television image and sound recorders and reproducers, and parts and accessories of such articles. Chapter 95: Toys, games and sports requisites; parts and accessories thereof. Chapter 94: Furniture; bedding, mattresses, mattress supports, cushions, and similar stuffed furnishing; lamps and lighting fittings, NES or incl.; illuminated signs or name-plates and the like; prefabricated buildings. Chapter 64: Footwear, gaiters and the like; parts of such articles. Chapter 62: Articles of apparel and clothing accessories, not knitted or crocheted. Chapter 61: Articles of apparel and clothing accessories, knitted or crocheted. Chapter 42: Articles of leather; saddlers and harness; travel goods, handbags and similar containers; articles of animal gut (other than silk-worn gut). Chapter 73: Articles of iron or steel. Chapter 39: Plastics and articles thereof. Chapter 87: Vehicles others than railway or tramway rolling-stock, and parts and accessories thereof. Chapter 63: Made-up textile articles; needlecraft sets; worn clothing and worn textile articles; rags.

The exported products which make up China's trade surplus were the latter two categories. In category two, the U.S. trade deficit with China in toys, furniture, lamps, footwear, apparel and clothing, articles of leather and plastics was $85 billion in 2006, accounting for 36.69 percent of the U.S. total trade deficit with China. In category three, the U.S. trade deficit with China in machinery and mechanical appliances, and electrical machinery and equipment was $109 billion in 2006, accounting for 47.00 percent of the U.S. total trade deficit with China. Simply judging from comparative advantage, category two consists of acceptable complementary deficits. Category three seems to pose some challenges to U.S. industries, but it has to be understood that most of these products are only produced in China at the final assembly stage, and the key technologies are controlled by overseas companies, including U.S. companies.

Transfer of deficits to China due to China's FDI utilization

China has become a country with one of the largest FDI inflows. By the end of 2006, China had utilized FDI amounting to $685 billion. Many overseas companies transferred their production bases to China, and the origin of production was transferred to China too, hence the trade deficits. In 2006, foreign-funded enterprises accounted for 58 percent of China's total exports.

Consequently, the U.S. trade deficit issue should be considered from a regional perspective instead of with China alone. While the U.S. trade deficit has widened with China, it has narrowed with other Asian trading partners. China's share of U.S. imports has grown from 5.8 percent to 14.6 percent over the past 11 years, while the share of the U.S. global trade deficit represented by the Asia Pacific Rim as a whole (including China) has actually fallen from 57 percent in 1999 to 43 percent in 2005.[3] Also, when the share of the U.S. trade deficit with Japan, Korea, ASEAN and China's Taiwan Province dropped from 63.46 percent in 1990 to 20.89 percent in 2006, China's share has increased from 10.11 percent to 28.43 percent, and China's trade deficit with these economies reached $153.92 billion in 2006. The trend of deficit transfer is quite obvious (see Tables 7.6 and 7.7).

In the meantime, the U.S.A. is one of the major sources of China's FDI inflows. By the end of 2006, 52,211 U.S. enterprises had invested in China with an FDI value of $53.96 billion. The previous export-to-China pattern has been replaced by more and more U.S. companies' investment, sales, and distribution in the Chinese domestic market. It was calculated that the sales to Chinese local customers of the U.S.A. MNC affiliate in China accounted for 71 percent, and 11 percent was sold back to U.S. customers.[4] This is one reason why the U.S.A.

Table 7.6 Share changes of U.S. trade deficit sources in East Asia (%)

	ASEAN* + Korea + China's Taiwan Province	Japan	China	Subtotal
1990	22.86	40.60	10.11	73.57
1995	19.29	36.94	21.07	77.30
1996	18.04	28.30	23.45	69.79
1997	18.04	30.49	27.24	75.77
1998	24.17	27.46	24.38	76.01
1999	18.74	22.27	20.69	61.70
2000	15.84	18.63	19.20	53.67
2001	14.78	16.78	20.21	51.77
2002	13.43	14.90	21.93	50.26
2003	11.87	12.31	23.14	47.32
2004	11.18	11.51	24.80	47.49
2005	10.21	10.79	26.30	47.30
2006	10.08	10.81	28.43	49.32

Source: U.S. Department of Commerce.

Note
ASEAN here refers to all the current ten members.

Table 7.7 China's trade deficits with East Asian economies ($ billion)

Year	ASEAN*	Japan	Korea	China's Taiwan Province	Subtotal
1990	0.91	1.41	n.a.	−1.94	n.a.
1995	0.58	−0.54	−3.60	−11.69	−15.25
1996	−0.54	1.69	−4.97	−13.38	−17.20
1997	0.24	2.83	−5.81	−13.05	−15.79
1998	−1.57	1.49	−8.73	−12.76	−21.58
1999	−2.65	−1.37	−9.42	−15.58	−29.02
2000	−4.84	0.14	−11.92	−20.45	−37.07
2001	−4.84	2.16	−10.87	−22.34	−35.89
2002	−7.63	−5.03	−13.08	−31.48	−57.21
2003	−16.40	−14.73	−23.04	−40.36	−94.53
2004	−20.08	−20.86	−34.43	−51.23	−126.60
2005	−19.63	−16.46	−41.71	−58.14	−135.94
2006	−18.21	−24.08	−45.25	−66.37	−153.92

Source: China Customs.

Note
ASEAN here refers to all the current ten members.

imported more from China than it exported. However, the pattern change was not reflected in the bilateral trade statistics. According to a Chinese study, it was reported that the U.S.-funded enterprises in China sold a total volume of $75 billion on the Chinese market in 2004. China's trade surplus with the U.S.A. that year was $80.2 billion according to Chinese statistics. If calculated this way, the U.S. trade deficit with China is only several billion dollars. On the other hand, the U.S.-funded enterprises in China exported over $70 billion in 2004 to foreign markets including the U.S.A. itself, and these figures were calculated in China's favor. If the trade surplus from the foreign-funded enterprises is not included, China's trade surplus with the U.S.A. would decrease by 73.4 percent.[5]

China's special feature in processing trade

With China's continual opening up and stable social environment, more enterprises have recognised China's competitiveness, especially in labor costs. These enterprises came from both developed economies such as the U.S.A. and Japan, and NIEs such as Hong Kong, Korea, and Taiwan. These economies moraly utilized China's cheap labor for assembly and then exported to the world. China has undertaken assembly tasks of products ranging from shoes and apparel to office equipment.

This makes China's foreign trade have two distinctive features: one is the rapid growth in processing trade; the other is the rapid export growth of foreign-funded enterprises. Processing trade accounted for 53 percent of China's total exports, and foreign-funded enterprises accounted for 84 percent of the total processing trade export. In fact, China's seemingly high export growth rate is driven by such FDI in assembly plants. China is only used as an assembly platform and only a tiny part of the processing fee is gained; the overseas investors or contractors get the bulk of the money. In addition, when these assembled products are exported, they are calculated in their final value, which overinflates China's trade surplus. If the trade surplus in processing trade is excluded, China's trade surplus with the U.S.A. will decrease by 91 percent.[6]

The Logitech story might provide a vivid example of this situation. A "made-in-China" Logitech's wireless mouse Wanda costs American consumers around $40. Of this, Logitech takes about $8, while distributors and retailers take $15. A further $14 goes to suppliers that provide Wanda's parts, Motorola and Agilent. China's take from each mouse comes to a meager $3, which covers wages, power, transport, and other overhead costs.[7]

Some U.S. officials have realized this. As Greenspan noticed,

> Because exports by countries are recorded on a gross basis rather than as value added, the widening of the U.S.A.' bilateral trade deficit with China, measured gross, has largely been in lieu of wider deficits with other Asian economies, including Japan. Measured by value added, the U.S. bilateral deficits with China would have been far less, and its bilateral deficits with other Asian exporters would have been far more.[8]

So, although China has a large scale of electronic production and export, China is neither a R&D center nor a profit center. Most electronic products sold worldwide should more appropriately be labeled as "assembled in China" instead of "made in China."

The U.S. statistical approach has overestimated the U.S. trade deficits

Three factors in the U.S. statistical approach overestimate China's exports to the U.S.A. First, U.S. exports are based on FAS value and China's exports are based on FOB value. FAS is smaller than FOB. The second factor is Hong Kong's role in enter-port trade. The U.S.A., based on rules of origin, treats China's exports via Hong Kong to the U.S.A. as China's exports, but it does not include its exports to China via Hong Kong as exports to China. Third, Hong Kong has also played a role in the value added to China's exported products via Hong Kong, yet in the U.S. statistics, the value-added are all calculated in China's account.

The U.S. exports restriction

Another important reason for the U.S. trade deficit with China must be pointed out. Many U.S. technologies are needed by China in its economic development, but China has to import from other countries because of the U.S. restrictions. For example, in 2004, China imported technology from the EU with a total value of $5.5 billion, a 63 percent growth over the previous year. However, China only imported a mere $2.9 billion from the U.S.A., and this is an

11 percent decrease over the previous year. In 2005, of all China's imported high tech products, the U.S. accounted for a mere 8 percent and over 90 percent are imported from other countries. It is estimated that the U.S. export restriction has made itself lose $25 billion in export opportunity to China.

RMB exchange rate and the U.S. job losses

Some Americans think the exchange rate adjustment might be a quick solution to the trade imbalances. This might sound reasonable, but it is not entirely true. First, exchange rate changes do not correspond with trade deficit changes. The U.S. dollar has depreciated from 2002, but the U.S. trade deficit still increased from $470 billion in 2002 to $818 billion in 2006. This fact showed that the dollar depreciation did not overturn the U.S. trade deficit. The other example is the yen. After the Plaza Agreement, the Japanese yen has appreciated from 238 per dollar in 1985 to 128 per dollar in 1988, but the U.S. trade deficit with Japan did not decrease but increased from $46 billion to $52 billion, reaching $88 billion in 2006. The third example is RMB. China itself has made an exchange rate adjustment in 1994, and the RMB depreciated from the 5.76 per dollar in 1993 to 8.6 in 1994, but the 1994 surplus with the U.S.A. increased by only $1.2 billion, far less than the increase of $6.6 billion in 1993 before the RMB depreciation. In this sense, there is no proof that using the exchange rate will change the trade imbalance.

Second, the exchange rate has very limited impact on trade. U.S. labor costs are about ten times, or even higher, than that in China, so it is of no use to let the RMB appreciate by 20 percent or even more. In addition, the Chinese products with a trade surplus generally have quite low price elasticity. According to Stephen S. Roach, "If the RMB peg to the dollar were adjusted upward by 20% the price of Chinese exports to the U.S. would go up by only 4% – hardly enough to trigger a major demand shift back into American-made products."[9]

On the other hand, China has its own way of solving the RMB exchange rate problem, and has already been taking measures since July 2005. But if the RMB were to revalue in a single step, for instance by 20 percent or 30 percent as some U.S. politicians suggest, it might not be a good method. If the U.S.-prescribed approach were to push China into the same position faced by the Japanese following the 1985 Plaza Agreement or like the East Asian Financial Crisis situation in 1997, it would not only be disastrous for China itself but also for regional or even world economic development.

Regarding the job losses in the manufacturing sector, it is easy to attribute this to the trade deficits with China, but such reasoning is not correct either. One explanation for U.S. manufacturing job losses is the effects of the U.S. economic cycle. Second, in the wake of economic globalization, it is natural that labor-intensive industries in the U.S.A. do not maintain their competitiveness because of the high labor costs. Even if jobs are not transferred to China, they will go to other countries with such competitiveness. Domestic enterprises tend to attribute the decrease to foreign competition instead of to domestic industrial upgrading.

Third, the decrease in job opportunities in the U.S. manufacturing sector is also closely related to its domestic industrial upgrading. Over the past 15 years, the productivity of the manufacturing sector increased at an annual rate of 3 percent, higher than the service industries; hence more labor shifted to services. According to the U.S. Bureau of Labor Statistics, from 1996 to 2005 the number of employees in manufacturing decreased by 3 million but that in services increased by 15 million, half of these in trade-related retail, transportation, etc.

Conclusion

In pure economic terms, trade deficits might not be too big a problem. The current uproar on this issue in the U.S.A. is based to a great extent on political considerations. It should be admitted that politics and economics are closely linked. It is understood that any country will not be indifferent to a huge trade deficit, because a trade deficit might result in some political pressure, and any country has a political bottom line. However, it might not be wise for two countries to have their economic relations blocked by this issue.

For China and the U.S.A. who have such a large trade volume, it is natural to encounter some problems or even trade frictions, but such problems should be resolved through constructive approaches instead of trade wars, sanctions, restrictions, or any other extreme measures. A trade war seems unlikely because both sides have already recognized the benefits derived from continuing economic linkages and cooperation, and "trade wars arise when you don't have dispute settlement mechanisms."[10]

Although a trade war is unlikely, the two countries should still actively try to resolve their trade disputes, including the trade imbalance issue. Those issues that cannot be solved immediately, can be put aside; while those issues that are mutually beneficial and have common grounds, can be solved first.

Actually, China's leaders have repeatedly emphasized that the Chinese attach importance to the China–U.S. trade imbalance issue. They hope to gradually reduce China's trade surplus with the U.S.A. and have already taken some measures to do so. On the other hand, it must be noted that the trade imbalance is also an issue of concern for China. A trade surplus is only a favorable factor in maintaining China's macroeconomic stability but it cannot determine China's national competitiveness. China tried to implement a "market diversification strategy" over 10 years ago, but its export dependence on the U.S. market has become increasingly higher, from 10.1 percent in 1992 to 21.0 percent in 2006. There is an asymmetrical interdependence between China and the U.S.A. in export terms, because China depends on the U.S. market more than the U.S. depends on the Chinese market. For example, China's exports to the U.S.A. accounted for 21.0 percent of China's total exports, but the U.S. exports to China accounted for only 5.3 percent of its total exports. In this sense, it is not the U.S.A. but China who needs to worry about the current condition.

While it is wrong to assume an exchange rate adjustment would provide a quick solution to the trade imbalance and there are few immediate solutions to the current trade imbalance, both countries could make efforts to improve it. For China's part, China will gradually shift to consumption-driven economic growth instead of the current export-driven type. The Chinese government "will adhere to the strategy of expanding domestic consumption and focus on increasing consumption demand and strengthening the role of consumption in fueling economic development."[11] China's Premier Wen Jiabao urged nationwide efforts to raise urban and rural incomes, encourage immediate consumption, encourage consumption in rural areas, and improve the consumption environment and consumption-related policies. China could also make other efforts to narrow the trade imbalance, such as upgrading its industry structure, encouraging its enterprises to invest in the U.S.A., and lessening certain export incentives. China should still stick to its market diversification policies, and might consider loosening some controls in market access beyond its WTO commitments.

China is not solely responsible for the trade imbalance and the U.S.A. should also do something to alter the situation, such as relaxing some export restrictions and adjusting certain macroeconomic policies. As the USTR noted in one report,

> the relative growth of imports and exports – and thus the trade imbalance – are [sic] affected by macroeconomic factors outside of trade. In particular, economists note that differences between the U.S. and our trading partners in national economic growth rates and patterns of saving, investment and consumption are primary reasons U.S. imports exceed exports.[12]

Yet it should be noted that the trade imbalance will not be resolved in the short term. Japan is the second largest developed country and has enjoyed a trade surplus with the U.S.A. for over 40 years, although it also has huge investment in the U.S.A. In addition, Japan has witnessed the products of their trade surplus with the U.S.A. A move from labor-intensive products to capital and technology-intensive ones, i.e. from textiles in the 1950s and iron and steel in the 1960s to automobiles in the 1980s and semiconductors in the 1990s. China is still in a preliminary development stage compared with Japan. It is possible that one day the trade disputes between China and the U.S.A. might also shift from the current textiles, footwear, and toys to automobiles, etc. The two countries still have a long way to go.

It should be understood that China–U.S. economic relations are constrained by two aspects: one is the absolute benefits from the increasing trade; the second are the costs in harming the bilateral economic relations. China's economy has witnessed several consecutive years of around a 10 percent growth rate. In 2006, China's domestic market scale was equivalent to $2.7 trillion and its imports were over $792 billion, becoming the world's third largest importer.[13] It is estimated that by 2010, China's domestic market scale will be over $4 trillion, with annual imports of over $1 trillion. In promoting the bilateral economic relations, the two countries should aim high and focus on the long-term benefits and not tangle with short-term interests.

Notes

1 The U.S. Trade Representative. *Trade Promotion Authority Delivers Jobs, Growth Prosperity and Security at Home*, January 31, 2007.
2 USTR, *U.S.–China Trade Relations: Entering a New Phase of Greater Accountability and Enforcement*, February 2006.
3 *Ibid*, p. 4.
4 J. Steven Landefeld and Raymond Mataloni, "Offshore Outsourcing and Multinational Companies," BEA working paper WP2004–06, July 16, 2004.
5 The Ministry of Commerce of China, *New Perspectives on the US Trade Deficit with China*, September 30, 2005.
6 *Ibid*.
7 Andrew Higgins, "As China Surges, It Also Proves A Buttress to American Strength," *Wall Street Journal*, January 30, 2004.
8 Statement of Alan Greenspan before the Senate Committee on Finance on June 23, 2005.
9 Stephen S. Roach, "Getting China Right," statement before the Commission on U.S.–China Economic and Security Review Hearing on China's Industrial, Investment and Exchange Rate Policies: Impact on the U.S., September 25, 2003.
10 Author's note of remarks by Karan K. Bhatia at the Shanghai Institute of Foreign Trade, March 21, 2006.
11 Wen Jiabao, "Report of the Work of the Government," delivered at the Fourth Session of the Tenth National People's Congress on March 5, 2006.
12 USTR, "U.S.–China Trade Relations: Entering a New Phase of Greater Accountability and Enforcement," February 2006, p. 11.
13 This is not the officially released GDP figure in U.S. dollars. It is a simple calculation of China's officially released GDP figure of RMB 20940.7 billion at the rate of 7.9 *yuan* = 1 dollar.

Part III

Perspectives of U.S. based scholars

8 Managing a multifaceted relationship between the U.S.A. and China

Phillip C. Saunders[1]

Of all the major powers, China arguably poses the most difficult strategic challenges for the U.S.A. The two countries have a multifaceted relationship with a complex mix of cooperative and competitive elements. Concerns about potential future conflicts have not stopped economic, political, and military interactions from deepening over the last two decades. China has become important to a wide range of U.S. interests, from managing the North Korean nuclear crisis to supplying inexpensive goods to U.S. consumers. For its part, the U.S.A. is a key market and is uniquely positioned to facilitate or obstruct Chinese goals such as Taiwan unification and China's emergence as a great power.

Despite the growing importance of relations, there have been major ups and downs over the last 15 years. The Communist Party's use of force to suppress student demonstrations in 1989 stained China's image and highlighted ongoing human rights abuses. Since then, the government has continued to pursue market reforms that have produced rapid economic growth and helped the Communist Party maintain its rule. A successful export-led growth development strategy has integrated China into the world economy, improved living standards, and widened choices for Chinese citizens, but despite limited experiments with democratic elections in the countryside, political reforms have lagged behind economic and social changes.

Chinese growth has been accompanied by a rapid expansion of Sino-U.S. economic ties. China's large bilateral trade surplus with the U.S.A. ($202 billion in 2005) has become an increasing source of friction. China's increasing global economic role has created concerns that economic growth is underwriting an ambitious military modernization program that threatens Taiwan and that may alter the balance of power in the Asia-Pacific region. These concerns are reinforced by China's growing influence in Asia and increasing economic and diplomatic involvement in regions such as Latin America and Africa. Some Americans worry about the ability of U.S. firms and workers to compete with goods produced by inexpensive Chinese labor and with state-owned firms that have access to capital at below-market rates.

The view from Beijing is equally ambivalent. Leaders and scholars recognize the importance of the U.S.A. for China's economic development, and Beijing seeks stable, cooperative relations with Washington. Yet many Chinese elites believe that the U.S.A. seeks to subvert the Chinese political system and to contain China's economic and military potential. Some believe U.S. talk about a "China threat" has been matched with policies intended to limit Chinese power. Evidence cited includes U.S. economic sanctions, efforts to limit Chinese acquisitions of military and dual-use technology, alleged tacit support for Taiwan independence, and even the accidental bombing of the Chinese embassy in Yugoslavia in 1999.

China policy in the George W. Bush administration

Given these concerns, most observers have been surprised by the newfound stability in Sino-U.S. relations and give the Bush administration relatively high marks for its handling of China. During the 2000 presidential campaign, candidate George W. Bush and prominent campaign advisers called for treating China as a "strategic competitor" rather than a "strategic partner." Many expected a tougher U.S. policy toward China that would increase tensions and reduce bilateral cooperation. Indeed, the administration's regional approach made a conscious effort to deemphasize China's importance relative to U.S. allies in Asia and to improve ties with democratic India as a potential counter-weight. The collision between a U.S. EP-3 reconnaissance plane and a Chinese fighter in April 2001 might easily have sent relations into a tailspin (especially if the EP-3 crew had been killed), but the incident was resolved diplomatically with the return of the aircrew 11 days later. China's behavior left bad feelings among Pentagon officials, but it did not have a broader negative impact on relations. By the time Secretary of State Powell visited China in July 2001, the administration had discarded "strategic competitor" rhetoric in favor of calls for "constructive, forward-looking relations" with China.

The Bush administration's shift from confrontational campaign rhetoric toward a more cooperative approach was underway prior to the September 11 terrorist attacks on the U.S.A. The reordering of U.S. security priorities following 9/11 reinforced this trend as more immediate security threats displaced China on the U.S. security agenda. Chinese leaders adroitly exploited the opportunity to improve relations by declaring vocal support for the war on terrorism. Bush administration officials praised China for choosing the right side and pursued a series of summit meetings with Chinese leaders, including Jiang Zemin's October 2002 visit to President Bush's ranch in Crawford. The shift in the U.S. agenda made it easier for China to cooperate with the U.S.A. and has shielded China from demands that are harder to satisfy. China has not emerged as a target of calls for regime change in authoritarian governments. Indeed, in 2003 the Bush administration declined to support a United Nations Human Rights Commission resolution calling for investigation of human rights conditions in China.

The Bush administration's overall approach to China actually demonstrates considerable continuity with the policies in place by the second term of the Clinton administration. Most of the language about China in the 2002 National

Security Strategy could easily have been lifted from Clinton-era strategic documents. Rather than defining China as an ally or an adversary, the U.S.A. has tried to reap the economic and security benefits of cooperation while hedging against the potential emergence of China as a future threat.[2] This approach reflects uncertainty about China's future political and military evolution. The U.S. strategy has two elements. The first emphasizes the role of cooperation and integration into global institutions (including the global economy) as a means of influencing Chinese behavior and shaping China's future evolution in positive directions. The second emphasizes maintenance of U.S. military capabilities and alliances as a hedge against the possibility of a future China that becomes aggressive or threatening. The challenge in implementing this strategy is to keep the two elements in balance, so that overemphasis on cooperation does not leave the U.S.A. in an unfavorable strategic position and overemphasis on the military dimension does not stimulate nationalism and push China in the direction of confrontation. One concern is that treating China as an inevitable threat could become a self-fulfilling prophecy.

The chief differences between the Bush and Clinton approaches lie in the realm of tactics. The Clinton administration tended to downplay the military dimension of U.S. strategy in order to limit the negative impact on China's domestic political evolution. This reflected a belief that confrontational U.S. policies might increase the influence of the military and nationalist political actors and impede Chinese political reforms. The administration undertook significant efforts to rebuild the political foundations of the U.S. alliance with Japan, to strengthen security ties with Taiwan, and to increase military planning aimed at China contingencies, but used ambiguity to try to limit the impact in China. (For example, the revision of the U.S.–Japan guidelines for defense cooperation referred to "areas surrounding Japan" but remained vague about whether this included Taiwan.) The administration often preferred to address conflicts over issues such as Chinese proliferation activities via quiet diplomacy rather than sanctions. This approach, coupled with efforts to work toward a "constructive, strategic partnership," rendered the Clinton administration vulnerable to charges that it was too soft on China.

Conversely, the Bush administration's approach reflects the view that differences should be expressed frankly and that clear statements of U.S. commitments and capabilities reinforce deterrence and reduce the likelihood of challenges to U.S. interests. The Bush administration has made frequent use of sanctions against Chinese firms for violations of U.S. nonproliferation laws and has been vocal about disagreements on issues such as missile defense and space weapons. It has also been more open about efforts to improve U.S. military capabilities in Asia and to increase security cooperation with Japan, India, and Taiwan. In addition to authorizing the sale to Taiwan of advanced weapons (including diesel submarines that had been denied by previous administrations), President Bush clarified the U.S. security commitment by declaring that the U.S.A. would do "whatever it takes" to help Taiwan defend itself.

Within the context of this hedge strategy, the Bush administration has gradually sought to increase cooperation with China on a range of important economic and security issues including energy security, nonproliferation, and counter-terrorism. It has also sought to shape Chinese thinking about its own long-term interests by proposing the vision of China as a "responsible stakeholder" that helps maintain the current international system. This concept, elaborated in a 2005 speech by then Deputy Secretary of State Robert Zoellick, recognizes China's increasing impact on the international system and seeks to obtain Chinese support in sustaining the global institutions and norms that have contributed to its remarkable economic success. It represents an effort to expand the scope of U.S. and Chinese common interests and to place potential conflicts of interests within a larger framework of cooperation.

The Bush administration has sought to engage Chinese leaders and senior officials in discussions about China's global responsibilities through a variety of mechanisms. In addition to formal summits, President Bush and President Hu see each other regularly at international meetings. The "senior dialogue" between Deputy Secretary Zoellick and Vice Foreign Minister Dai Bingguo has been the principal vehicle for explaining and elaborating on the responsible stakeholder concept. These discussions, which have continued with Undersecretary of State Nicholas Burns and Vice Foreign Minister Yang Jiechi following Zoellick's departure from the government, explicitly address a range of global issues of common concern. This political dialogue has been joined by a cabinet-level U.S–China "strategic economic dialogue" led by Treasury Secretary Henry Paulson and Vice Premier Wu Yi. High-level military-to-military talks have also resumed, with then Defense Secretary Rumsfeld visiting China in October 2005 and Central Military Commission Vice-Chairman Guo Boxiong visiting the U.S.A. in July 2006.

A variety of bilateral cooperative mechanisms have been established to follow up on the issues raised in these dialogues and pursue practical cooperation on areas on common interest. These include the Defense Consultative Talks, an ongoing dialogue on nonproliferation, and the shuttle diplomacy associated with the Six Party talks on the North Korean nuclear issue. Economic issues have been addressed through a range of bilateral channels, including the Joint Commission on Commerce and Trade. These executive branch mechanisms play a vital role in engaging various branches of the Chinese government and connecting a potentially abstract debate about "responsible behavior" to concrete policy issues and policy implementation.

While providing a useful framework, the responsible stakeholder concept contains a number of ambiguities that deserve attention. First, there is no clear definition of what constitutes "responsible behavior" in specific issue areas. China is unlikely to accept a definition of responsibility based on what behavior is most helpful for American interests or most congruent with American policy. The U.S.A. will also have difficulty holding China accountable to international rules and norms that it does not always respect. Second, Zoellick's speech recognizes the reality of the increasing Chinese influence in Asia but avoids taking a position on Chinese long-term regional intentions or specifying which

Chinese interests are legitimate and must be respected by the U.S.A. Third, while Zoellick highlighted U.S. willingness to work with China in shaping new international rules, it is unclear whether the U.S.A. is willing to consider changes in existing rules and institutions to accommodate Chinese concerns and interests. Finally, the responsible stakeholder concept implicitly assumes that China will have influence within an international system where the U.S.A. plays the leading role. If China's power increases significantly, or if U.S. power wanes, the U.S. ability to continue to shape the international system may eventually come into question.

China's "Washington problem"

Chinese leaders have ample reasons to want good Sino-U.S. relations, or at least to avoid a major military confrontation, but China's options in dealing with the U.S.A. are limited. The traditional strategy for middle powers to constrain a dominant power is to seek formal or informal allies to create a balance of power. However, the current U.S. position is so powerful that other countries are reluctant to align themselves overtly against the U.S.A. The failure of China's 1999–2001 campaign to mobilize international opposition to U.S. ballistic missile defense (BMD) plans shows the limits of such a strategy. China viewed its "strategic partnership" with Russia as a crucial means of dissuading the U.S.A. from moving ahead with BMD deployment. Yet Russia ultimately made its own arrangements with the U.S.A. by signing the Strategic Offensive Reductions Treaty in May 2002 without taking China's strategic interests into account. Although other countries share some of China's concerns about U.S. dominance, their unwillingness to actively oppose the U.S.A. limits China's diplomatic options. Chinese leaders also recognize that provocative behavior is likely to strengthen the hand of those within the Bush administration who support a more confrontational China policy.

As a result, China appears to have decided to accommodate the U.S.A. and acquiesce to U.S. policies that run counter to the Chinese leadership's preferences and sense of Chinese interests. China has accepted a number of U.S. actions with minimal or *pro forma* complaint, including U.S. withdrawal from the ABM treaty, U.S. pursuit of missile defenses and missile defense cooperation with allies in Asia, sales of advanced weapons to Taiwan, deployment of U.S. military forces to Central Asian bases along China's borders, diplomatic pressure on North Korea and Iran, and the U.S. invasions of Afghanistan and Iraq. China opposes all these actions to varying degrees, but Chinese leaders have not made cooperation in other areas or the overall relationship conditional on changes in U.S. policy.

The decision to accommodate Washington has had a positive impact on the tone of bilateral relations. Chinese official media have moderated criticism of the U.S.A.; Chinese officials have participated in official dialogues with their U.S. counterparts on a range of economic and security issues; and China has increased security cooperation in areas where U.S. and Chinese strategic interests coincide (such as counter-terrorism and joint efforts to respond to the North Korean nuclear weapons crisis). Statements about the need to take advantage of a period of strategic opportunity "to speed up economic construction and reform and build a well-off society" in the first two decades of the twenty-first century provide a domestic political justification for compromises necessary to maintain stable relations with the U.S.A.

While avoiding direct confrontation with Washington, China has sometimes quietly pursued policies such as economic assistance to North Korea and efforts to limit U.S. influence and military presence in Central Asia that complicate U.S. diplomatic strategies and make it harder for the U.S.A. to achieve its policy objectives. China has also accelerated efforts to improve Chinese military capabilities. China's military budget rose by approximately 17 percent in 2001 and 2002, with double-digit real increases continuing in 2003, 2004, and 2005. The official 2006 military budget was approximately $35 billion, but DIA estimated China's total defense spending would be between $70 billion and $135 billion in 2006.[3] China's 2007 defense budget was announced as $44.9 billion, which was cited as a 17.8 percent increase over the 2006 figure.[4]

The leadership transition from Jiang Zemin to Hu Jintao has resulted in some changes in Chinese domestic priorities but has not reduced the importance of getting along with Washington or had a major impact on Chinese foreign policy. President Hu has advocated the goal of building a "harmonious society" and made greater efforts to ameliorate the negative side-effects of rapid economic growth. Economic inequality has grown rapidly in China in recent years as some individuals and regions have benefited more from reforms than others. Hu has sought to reduce the tax burden on China's farmers and raise rural incomes to reduce the potential for unrest in the countryside. He has also emphasized the goal of balanced development that gives greater weight to environmental considerations and seeks to make domestic demand an engine of growth for the Chinese economy.

Zoellick's speech sparked widespread debate in China about how to translate the concept of "responsible stakeholder" and whether it was in China's interests to accept the current rules and norms of the international system. Chinese experts noted that the U.S.A. also needed to behave responsibly and should not be the sole judge of whether international behavior was responsible. After much debate, Chinese President Hu Jintao endorsed the concept during his April 2006 summit with President Bush, agreeing that "China and the U.S.A. are not only stakeholders, but they should also be constructive partners."[5] Hu's phrasing highlighted the point that both countries have global responsibilities and placed China's acceptance of the stakeholder concept within the context of an ongoing, positive U.S.–China relationship.

Managing a multifaceted relationship

The relative stability and cooperation in U.S.–China relations during the Bush administration's tenure in office conceals a range of underlying tensions and potential conflicts. The wide range of U.S. interests affected by China requires an approach that can deal with both the cooperative and competitive dimensions of Sino-U.S. relations. In some areas, common interests make *cooperation* the dominant element of the relationship. Examples include a shared interest in maintaining stability in the Asia-Pacific region, fostering a global system that supports trade and economic development, pursuing a denuclearized Korean peninsula, and counter-terrorism. In these areas and others, common and over-lapping interests provide a basis for cooperation and joint action on both a bilat-eral and a multilateral basis. The task is defining and aligning U.S. and Chinese interests and finding ways to cooperate effectively. The existence of common interests does not guarantee that cooperation will actually take place. States can agree on the importance of a common objective but disagree about the most effective means of pursuing it. (U.S. and Chinese disagreements about how to deal with North Korea's nuclear weapons programs provide an obvious example.)

In other areas *engagement* is an important way to push China to redefine its interests and change its behavior. Examples of areas and issues where engage-ment is appropriate include nonproliferation, human rights, constructive Chinese participation in multilateral institutions, economic policy, protection of intellec-tual property rights, and environmental protection. In these cases, common inter-ests may exist (but not be recognized) or the two countries may have differing priorities. Engagement seeks to alter Chinese thinking about interests and prior-ities to produce changes in Chinese behavior and to create a basis for longer-term cooperation. Sanctions and incentives may sometimes play a useful role in sensitizing China to U.S. concerns and stimulating policy change. However, the core mechanisms are education and inclusion in international institutions and organizations in order to change Chinese thinking and definitions of interests. This process seeks to build and strengthen groups within the Chinese bureau-cracy who believe that the changes the U.S.A. seeks are also in China's interest.

Engagement has had a significant positive impact on Chinese economic policy and nonproliferation behavior. In both areas, Chinese leaders and officials have been exposed to Western views and learned how international mechanisms work, built a core of technical expertise within China, and eventually redefined China's national interests and policies. The result has been significant changes in Chinese behavior, usually in directions compatible with U.S. interests. In eco-nomic policy, fellowships in Western universities, technical advice by the World Bank and Western experts, and participation in international organizations have dramatically increased the sophistication of Chinese economic policy-makers and supported reforms that have moved China toward a more market-oriented economy. A similar process has occurred in nonproliferation, where China has gradually shifted from a stance of regarding nonproliferation as inherently dis-criminatory against developing countries to a position where China now accepts nonproliferation norms, participates in key organizations (including export control regimes that had previously been anathema), and has passed domestic export control laws that meet international standards. Although the U.S.A. still has concerns about Chinese proliferation behavior, China has made remarkable progress considering where it started.

Cooperation and engagement are important means of pursuing U.S. interests, but conflicts between China's preferred policies and U.S. interests sometimes require more assertive policies. The U.S.A. seeks to *deter* China from undertaking certain actions such as invading or attacking Taiwan or using force to pursue Chinese claims in territorial and resource disputes. Deterrence requires clear communication about which specific actions are prohibited and the consequences if they are attempted. Deterrence in the Taiwan Strait is complicated by the fact that the U.S.A. is trying to deter or discourage efforts to challenge the status quo by either China or Taiwan. Washington has therefore maintained a degree of ambiguity about the circumstances under which the U.S.A. would intervene in a conflict.

The credibility of deterrent threats rests upon the capability and willingness to impose the threatened costs if deterrence fails. U.S. alliances and the ability of U.S. military forces to project power in the Asia-Pacific region underpin deterrence. China's ongoing military modernization program, which is focused on acquiring capabilities that would complicate or delay U.S. military intervention in the event of a Taiwan crisis, therefore represents a potential challenge to the U.S. ability to deter China. But deterrence does not rest solely on the military balance. A conflict with the U.S.A. would set back China's economic modernization efforts substantially, a factor that enhances deterrence by making the use of force to settle the Taiwan issue costly and unattractive to PRC decision-makers. Using force would also undercut China's considerable investment in reassuring Asian countries of China's benign intentions.

While deterrence attempts to deal with immediate challenges, *dissuasion* attempts to deal with future conflicts of interest by shaping a potential adversary's strategic choices. One definition of dissuasion involves discouraging current or potential adversaries from developing, deploying, augmenting (quantitatively) or enhancing (qualitatively) military capabilities or pursuing objectives that would threaten the U.S.A., its forces, or its interests. Potential means include altering a potential adversary's calculus by imposing costs, denying gains, increasing risks, maintaining advantages, exploiting weaknesses, raising the barriers to entry or competition, and/or providing more acceptable alternatives. Dissuasion can be thought of in a narrow technical sense (efforts to discourage China from developing anti-satellite weapons) or a broader strategic sense (efforts to discourage China from challenging the U.S. global position). Some conceptions of dissuasion are compatible with the U.S. hedging strategy discussed above, especially those that work indirectly by influencing the costs and benefits of Chinese strategic choices. However given that economic growth is vital to the leadership's efforts to maintain social stability and Communist Party rule, dissuasion efforts are unlikely to prevent Chinese leaders from pursuing economic modernization that will eventually provide the resource and technology base for improved military capabilities. Efforts to dissuade Chinese leaders from converting power potential into actual capabilities in specific areas are more promising but will still be difficult.

Deterrence and dissuasion are most effective when employed for specific, limited objectives. However, U.S. and Chinese interests may conflict in areas such as human rights, intervention, and currency policy where these tools are inappropriate. The U.S.A. must therefore be prepared for *competition* with China. Competition is a normal part of how states pursue their interests, and does not necessarily imply a hostile relationship. Competition can consist of efforts to win political support for specific regional and global initiatives or more abstract efforts to encourage countries to emulate broad political and cultural values. In recent years, China has started or supported a variety of initiatives for regional cooperation in Asia that do not include the U.S.A. Some see these initiatives as evidence of increasing Sino-U.S. competition for influence in Asia, with both countries trying to strengthen ties with key countries. The U.S.A. has considerable hard and soft power resources and is well positioned to compete effectively with China. However, the U.S.A. must use its resources as part of integrated strategy that responds to the concerns of other countries while advancing U.S. interests.

The U.S.A. and China have a complex, multifaceted relationship that cannot be reduced to a simple slogan or described in a single phrase. Depending on the issue and the time period under consideration, the U.S.A. may need to rely on cooperation, engagement, deterrence, dissuasion, or competition to pursue its interests in China (or interests affected by China). This complexity does not mean that the two countries are fated to be enemies, but it does mean that a degree of ambivalence and tension is unavoidable.

Key strategic challenges for the U.S.A.

China's domestic developments

Despite the many cooperative elements in U.S.–China relations, China is likely to pose strategic challenges for the U.S.A. in a number of areas. Chinese leaders are focused on the domestic tasks of maintaining social stability and preventing challenges to Communist Party rule. Economic growth is viewed as a critical means of building legitimacy and maintaining stability. But the economic reforms that have promoted growth and raised living standards have also created serious social problems such as unemployment, an inadequate social safety net, and a collapsing rural health care system. One measure of these problems is the increasing number of protests in China. A senior public security official recently revealed that there were more than 74,000 large-scale public protests involving 3.7 million people in 2004.[6]

Protests generally have local causes, but they also reflect underlying systemic problems. One major issue for Chinese leaders is the declining legitimacy of the Chinese Communist Party. Party leaders have attempted to compensate for declining belief in communism by building legitimacy through economic performance and appeals to nationalism. Economic reforms have been remarkably successful but have generated significant negative side-effects. Economic inequality has increased rapidly as some individuals and regions have benefited more from reforms than others. China's southeastern coastal provinces are big winners, while the northeastern rust belt and interior provinces face serious economic difficulties. Another dimension of inequality lies in the large gap between urban and rural incomes and standards of living. Corruption is also a serious problem. There is increasing resentment of cases where politically connected individuals have profited from enterprise closures or privatizations, violated labor and environmental laws for private gain, or used official positions to extort money.

Protests to date have remained isolated and have not presented a major threat to the regime, but Chinese leaders are worried about the "colored revolutions" that toppled authoritarian governments in Georgia, Ukraine, and Kyrgyzstan. The immediate response has been a crackdown on press freedom and intensified controls on nongovernmental organizations and the Internet.[7] The longer-term response appears to be efforts to address underlying causes by reducing the tax burden on rural residents and seeking economic policies that will produce more balanced growth with fewer negative environmental and social side-effects. Reports from the Communist Party's fifth plenum in October 2005 suggest that the next five-year program will stress common prosperity and sustainable development. This may represent a significant shift from recent policies focused on maximizing growth rates, which have averaged 8 to 9 percent over the last decade. Chinese leaders will still emphasize the importance of economic growth in maintaining domestic stability, because a slower growth or a prolonged economic downturn would aggravate social problems and stimulate increased protests.

The broader question is whether China can continue rapid economic growth without undertaking significant political reforms. Party goals of building a "harmonious society" cannot compensate for the lack of effective political institutions to represent diverse social interests and reconcile competing political demands. But Chinese leaders appear determined to prevent the emergence of any organized political groups and to resist independent monitoring of government officials by the press or the public. The Party seeks to rely on intra-party supervision and anti-corruption campaigns that are unlikely to be effective. Technocratic approaches and buzzwords like "scientific management" are unlikely to solve China's serious social problems. The party maintains considerable coercive tools, but an economic slowdown would greatly increase the challenge of maintaining social stability.

Instability in China would pose a variety of challenges for the U.S.A. Chinese leaders would likely respond to widespread instability with a political crackdown to maintain order, possibly involving the use of force. This would raise the profile of human rights issues in U.S.–China policy and heighten concerns that China was moving toward greater authoritarianism rather than democracy. Chinese leaders would likely also seek to accelerate economic growth via increased exports to ameliorate underlying social problems. This might lead to increased government subsidies or incentives for exporters, further aggravating U.S. concerns about China's trade practices and undervalued currency. The Chinese leadership might also be tempted to blame domestic problems on outside influences in an effort to justify a political crackdown and harness nationalist sentiment behind government policy. Despite concerns that authoritarian regimes sometimes seek foreign conflicts to unify the population and divert attention from domestic problems, Chinese leaders are unlikely to engage in foreign adventures that would further aggravate their troubles.

Taiwan

Another strategic challenge involves Taiwan. The "one China" framework whereby the U.S.A. recognizes the People's Republic of China as the sole official government of China while maintaining unofficial economic and cultural relations with Taiwan has allowed the U.S.A. to enjoy the economic and security benefits of cooperation with China without paying the domestic and international political costs of abandoning Taiwan. This approach has been remarkably successful in pursuing U.S. interests while facilitating economic, social, and political development on both sides of the Taiwan Strait. The U.S. long-term objective is a peaceful resolution of the dispute over Taiwan's status that is acceptable to the Taiwan people. U.S. short-term policy seeks to maintain stability and prevent unilateral challenges to the status quo (as defined by the U.S.A.) by either side.[8] The U.S.A. also encourages dialogue and cooperation between China and Taiwan.

However, a number of trends are gradually eroding the stability of the status quo and challenging the viability of the "one China" framework.[9] In Taiwan, a growing sense of separate identity and efforts by leaders to highlight Taiwan's separate status have raised concerns in Beijing about "creeping independence." Chinese leaders regard Taiwan independence as a threat to China's territorial integrity and to the continued rule of the current Chinese leadership. Beijing has had difficulty formulating an effective response to gradual moves toward independence, with leaders seeking to reinforce the credibility of threats to use force (most recently via the anti-succession law) while simultaneously pressing the U.S.A. to rein in Taiwan. China has also accelerated its military modernization efforts, with a focus on weapons that can be used to delay or deter U.S. military intervention in the event of a conflict. These trends are occurring against a backdrop of increasing economic integration and interdependence across the Taiwan Strait and the increasing influence of domestic politics in Washington, Taipei, and Beijing on cross-Strait relations.

The U.S.A. has been forced to become more deeply involved simply to maintain the status quo. Both China and Taiwan regularly push the U.S.A. to back their position in the dispute. For Taiwan, this involves attempts to obtain symbolic gestures of U.S. support, such as congressional resolutions, diplomatic support for Taiwan's participation in the World Health Organization, or permission for Taiwan leaders to make transit visits through the U.S.A.

Democratization has given Taiwan's appeals for support more legitimacy, allowing a push for greater U.S. recognition of Taiwan's elected leaders. Taiwan's successes include President Clinton's February 2000 statement that any resolution of Taiwan's status must be "peaceful and acceptable to the Taiwan people" and President Bush's April 2001 statement that the U.S.A. would do "whatever it takes to help Taiwan defend itself."[10] However, Taiwan leaders have been unable to win U.S. endorsement of their claim that Taiwan is already an independent sovereign state. At the same time, China regularly pushes the U.S.A. to reaffirm its "one China" policy and to make statements opposing Taiwan independence. China also tries to use previous U.S. commitments and cooperation in other areas to limit U.S. political and security ties with Taiwan (with arms sales being a particular sore point). An important success was President Bush's statement in a meeting with Chinese Premier Wen Jiabao in December 2003 that the U.S.A. opposes "comments and actions made by the leader of Taiwan" that "indicate that he may be willing to unilaterally change the status quo."[11]

Changes in the military balance are also increasing U.S. involvement. Taiwan's technological edge is eroding as China's military modernization efforts begin to pay dividends. Over the past decade China has acquired advanced Russian weapons systems such as Su-27 and Su-30 fighters, S-300 surface-to-air missiles, Kilo class submarines, and Sovremenny destroyers equipped with advanced anti-ship missiles. China's own defense industries are now producing higher-quality weapons that incorporate advanced technologies. China's expanding deployments of short-range ballistic missiles (now estimated at 700–800 missiles) are increasing the PLA's military reach.[12] In contrast, Taiwan's defense spending has declined in real terms over the last decade, and the opposition-controlled legislature has been unwilling to authorize the purchase of advanced U.S. weapons systems such as the Patriot PAC-3 and conventional submarines. As the military balance has shifted, U.S. officials and military planners have focused on the practical issues involved if a military conflict broke out. One response has been increased U.S.–Taiwan security cooperation that includes strategic defense dialogues, visits by military officers and senior civilian officials, educational exchanges, observation of exercises, and assessment team visits.[13] The U.S.A. has long used ambiguity about the circumstances under which it would intervene to discourage destabilizing actions by both China and Taiwan. If deterring a possible Chinese attack requires a clearer U.S. commitment and increased cooperation with the Taiwan military, however, this ambiguity will be eroded. Greater confidence in U.S. intervention increases the chances that Taiwan will either shirk responsibility for its own defense or engage in risky behavior in the belief that China will not risk a military conflict with the U.S.A.

The "one China" framework has served U.S. interests effectively for three decades, but the U.S.A. is being drawn more deeply into the dispute to preserve the status quo in the face of potentially destabilizing trends. Can the status quo be sustained indefinitely? Stability requires China, Taiwan, and the U.S.A. to make pragmatic compromises and to tolerate continued ambiguity about Taiwan's status. Chinese leaders are currently focused on stopping Taiwan independence, but unification remains China's long-term objective. Despite strong support on Taiwan for the status quo, democratization and the development of a separate Taiwan identity have encouraged political leaders to assert Taiwan's status as an independent state. A key question is whether increasing economic integration and the changing military balance will lead Taiwan to seek an accommodation with Beijing or whether Taiwan leaders will see a window of opportunity to achieve independence that is closing. Some signs, such as public approval for Nationalist Party chairman Lien Chan's visit to mainland China, suggest that popular support for Taiwan independence may be declining. However, the U.S.A. will have to reckon with the possibility that developments in either China or Taiwan could cause a major crisis.

The U.S.A. could respond to these challenges by increasing diplomatic efforts to promote dialogue across the Taiwan Strait and by supporting efforts to establish political and military confidence-building measures to increase stability. One interesting suggestion is to explore an "interim agreement" for 20–50 years whereby China would agree not to use force and Taiwan would agree not to declare independence.[14] Yet in the absense of major domestic political changes, both China and Taiwan are likely to use negotiations as means of pursuing their long-term political objectives. The possibility of a conflict (and the growing U.S. role) may make it increasingly difficult to manage the Taiwan issue within the broader U.S.–China relationship.

Nuclear modernization and ballistic missile defense

The potential for a military confrontation over Taiwan complicates a third strategic challenge: the interaction between Chinese strategic force modernization and U.S. ballistic missile defenses. After more than two decades of development, China will soon begin deploying a new generation of mobile land-based intercontinental ballistic missiles (ICBMs) and sea-launched ballistic missiles (SLBMs) on nuclear submarines.[15] These new missiles will improve the survivability of China's nuclear deterrent and double or triple the number of Chinese nuclear warheads that can reach the continental U.S.A. Interactions between China's strategic modernization and U.S. ballistic missile defense (BMD) deployments could generate an action-reaction spiral that leads to a strategic arms race. Even if this outcome is avoided, increased strategic mistrust and suspicion could spill over into bilateral relations in negative and potentially destabilizing ways.

China's nuclear deterrent relies primarily on cave- and silo-based DF-4 and DF-5A ICBMs. These missiles must be fueled and have warheads attached before launch, resulting in a force with low readiness and high vulnerability to attack. China's modernization program will deploy new solid-fueled, road-mobile ICBMs and SLBMs, resulting in significant improvements in launch preparation time, survivability, and accuracy. The DF-31, a road-mobile ICBM with an 7,250 km range that can reach parts of the western U.S.A., will likely begin deployment in 2006. The DF-31 will probably be a single-warhead missile, although it may employ decoys or other counter-measures to penetrate U.S. missile defenses. China is also developing the DF-31A, a 12,000 km range missile expected to enter service in 2007.[16] China has replaced older DF-5 ICBMs with new DF-5A variants that could potentially be fitted with multiple warheads or missile defense countermeasures. These land-based ICBMs will be supplemented by the Julang-2 (JL-2), a SLBM that will be deployed on the new JIN Class (Type 094) SSBN (which should be operational by the end of the decade).[17] As a result, the number of Chinese missiles capable of reaching the U.S.A. is likely to increase from the current 18–26 to at least 50–60. Some of this expansion is dictated by the fact that the addition of just two Type 094 SSBNs would add 32 additional warheads to China's arsenal.[18]

Deployment of even a thin U.S. BMD system would threaten China's goal of a credible strategic nuclear deterrent. Chinese leaders are determined not to accept permanent vulnerability to perceived U.S. nuclear blackmail. The size, perceived effectiveness, and potential expandability of U.S. missile defenses are likely to have a direct impact on the pace and scope of China's strategic modernization. China will most likely respond by increasing force levels and deploying new technologies as necessary to maintain a credible nuclear deterrent.[19] This could involve a significant increase in the number of Chinese ICBMs aimed at U.S. targets, retention of older strategic missile systems, deployment of countermeasures to penetrate or defeat U.S. missile defenses, and the possible deployment of multiple warheads on China's DF-5A ICBMs.

Although the initial U.S. BMD system has very limited operational capabilities against Chinese ICBMs, the U.S.A. is currently pursuing a wide range of systems and technologies, including boost-phase, mid-course, and terminal defense systems. The Missile Defense Agency is also considering future concepts that might include space-based weapons.[20] Chinese planners therefore confront considerable uncertainty about the ultimate size and effectiveness of future U.S. missile defenses. More advanced U.S. BMD architectures would likely result in correspondingly larger increases in China's ICBM force. This situation is further complicated by changes in U.S. nuclear doctrine. The "new strategic triad" introduced in the 2002 Nuclear Posture Review highlighted the role of conventional strike capabilities in targeting an adversary's weapons of mass destruction.[21] Moreover, once the Chinese Type 094 submarine is operational, U.S. Navy efforts to shadow it on patrol increase the possibility of an incident at sea.

From a political standpoint, the key question is whether China's strategic modernization and U.S. missile defense deployments are viewed as rational responses to real strategic vulnerabilities or as indicators of hostile political intentions. This issue will receive increasing attention as Chinese deployments of new strategic missiles are reported, especially given ongoing debates about the possible need for new nuclear weapons designs to improve the capability and reliability of the U.S. arsenal. The fact that China will be expanding its nuclear forces at a time when the U.S.A. is reducing its arsenal will highlight the question of Chinese strategic intentions. Uncertainty about the ultimate size and effectiveness of U.S. missile defenses and China's reluctance to discuss its force structure plans creates a high potential for misperception on both sides. Most Chinese officials and analysts dismiss U.S. fears of rogue state missile threats and view China as the real target of U.S. missile defenses. U.S. interest in space-based weapons and the range of BMD technologies being explored raise the possibility of a surprise technological breakthrough. These factors are likely to cause China to overestimate the effectiveness of U.S. missile defenses and plan for a nuclear force structure that U.S. officials view as excessive.

There is considerable U.S. ambivalence about a strategic deterrence relationship with China. Some former officials have argued that the U.S.A. must maintain overwhelming strategic superiority so that China's limited nuclear retaliatory capability is neutralized.[22] However, it is unclear that U.S. missile defenses will ever have the technical capability to negate China's current nuclear forces reliably, much less defend against the larger forces China would likely deploy in response. An explicit U.S. effort to nullify China's nuclear deterrent would have an extremely damaging effect on bilateral relations, and likely limit future security cooperation. These issues are further complicated by Chinese concerns about potential U.S. development of space weapons and by the U.S. belief that China is developing anti-satellite weapons that might target U.S. space assets.[23]

The potential negative political effects of such strategic interactions might be limited through mutual strategic reassurance. The U.S.A. could clarify the technical parameters of its planned BMD architecture and discuss China's potential responses. At some point, the U.S.A. might be able to offer assurances about the ultimate scope of its BMD system, while China might offer greater transparency about its modernization plans, possibly including force structure levels keyed to specific missile defense architectures. The Bush administration has expanded consultations with Chinese officials on a range of political, economic, and security issues, including some discussion of strategic nuclear issues. Addressing Chinese concerns without allowing Beijing to dictate U.S. policy could help avert misperceptions and potentially moderate the size of China's nuclear build-up. However, this approach would require accepting the inevitability of a nuclear deterrent relationship with China, a controversial position in the U.S.A. Moreover, any serious strategic dialogue requires reciprocity in the form of greater transparency about China's nuclear doctrine and planned force structure.

While a franker dialogue on strategic issues would be useful, the potential for a U.S.–China conflict over Taiwan to escalate to the nuclear level raises the stakes and will make it hard for either side to react passively to improvements in the other's strategic capabilities. The U.S. reaction to the recent remarks of a Chinese general that China was prepared to use nuclear weapons if attacked by Washington during a confrontation over Taiwan highlights the potential for strategic issues to affect broader relations, as does the U.S. outcry over China's successful test of a ground-based anti-satellite (ASAT) weapon in January 2007.[24]

Chinese influence in Asia

China's expanding influence in Asia poses a fourth strategic challenge. Many expected that China's military actions to defend its territorial claims in the South China Sea and use of "missile diplomacy" against Taiwan in 1995–96 signaled a more aggressive regional stance that would eventually cause Asian countries to balance against China. But as Beijing became aware of regional concerns, it moderated its behavior and sought to reassure its neighbors that China's rising power would not threaten them. One initial means was the articulation of a "New Security Concept" which emphasized the importance of dialogue and negotiations as means of resolving disputes. China's settlement of numerous land border disputes, signature of the Declaration on Conduct of Parties in the South China Sea, and accession to ASEAN's Treaty of Amity and Cooperation have all helped reassure China's neighbors.

Chinese diplomacy has become more sophisticated, embracing multilateralism and launching new initiatives aimed at spurring regional cooperation. China initially resisted participation in multilateral security forums due to fears that countries would gang up against it. But as China gained experience in the U.N. Security Council and the Conference on Disarmament, Chinese diplomats learned how to operate effectively in a multilateral context. China has taken the initiative in establishing new organizations such as the Shanghai Cooperation Organization (SCO) and the ASEAN + China grouping. China has supported the ASEAN initiative for an East Asian Summit, which will include the major Northeast and Southeast Asian countries as well as Australia, India, and New Zealand. China has also proposed cooperation on nontraditional security issues within the ASEAN + 3 (China, Japan, South Korea) framework. These initiatives have created new venues for regional cooperation that do not include the U.S.A. The July 2005 SCO declaration calling for the U.S.A. to set a deadline for withdrawing from bases in Central Asia is one indicator of China's ability to wield influence within regional organizations.

China's efforts to reassure its neighbors have calmed regional fears about China's rising power. Asian countries increasingly view China as a partner and market opportunity rather than a potential threat. Beijing's embrace of multilateralism and cooperation on issues of concern to Asian governments contrasts positively with a perceived U.S. unilateralism and narrow focus on fighting terrorism. The result has been a substantial increase in Chinese influence, including with traditional U.S. allies such as Australia and South Korea. The desire to benefit from China's future economic growth further increases Beijing's leverage. China has signed a China–ASEAN free trade agreement that includes "early harvest" provisions benefiting ASEAN's poorer members. Arguments that neighboring countries will benefit economically from China's rise figure prominently in speeches by Chinese leaders. China is now the number one trading partner for Japan, South Korea, and Taiwan. Asia has been the primary focus of China's diplomacy, but the need for energy, natural resources, and markets has prompted an expansion of Chinese activities in Latin America, Africa, and the Middle East.

Beijing's use of economic and political tools to pursue its regional goals is certainly preferable to the use of military instruments, but China's increasing influence complicates U.S. efforts to pursue its own regional interests. Influence is not necessarily a zero-sum game, but China's growing ties with U.S. friends and allies in Asia could limit U.S. ability to respond to Chinese actions that threaten U.S. interests. This is already evident in the U.S. alliance with South Korea, where Seoul has pointedly rebuffed suggestions that the U.S.–ROK alliance might be used to deal with a Taiwan contingency. China's preference for regional institutions that do not include the U.S.A. and U.S. ambivalence about supporting multilateral organizations in Asia raise the possibility that the U.S.A. could be excluded from key decisions about Asia's future. China's increasing influence could eventually affect the viability of the U.S. alliances in Asia that have helped underpin regional stability and prosperity.

A U.S. policy response must recognize that Asian countries do not want to be forced to choose between China and the U.S.A., especially in the event of a military crisis over Taiwan. However, most Asian governments welcome a continuing U.S. presence, which they expect will help preserve a balance of power and reduce their vulnerability to Chinese demands. The U.S.A. should broaden its regional agenda to place greater emphasis on economic development and on non-traditional security issues of interest to Asian governments. Greater responsiveness to Asian concerns might also increase the willingness of countries to cooperate on counterterrorism. One important role for the U.S.A. is to provide alternative modes of security cooperation within Asia, including options that fall short of formal alliances or security partnerships. As the U.S. response to the South Asian tsunami indicated, the U.S.A. has resources and unique capabilities that make it the preferred partner for cooperation in many areas, but these resources must be applied more actively and within the context of a broader regional strategy.

China as a potential strategic rival

A final strategic challenge involves China's long-term power potential. China has enjoyed the most rapid economic growth in the world over the last 25 years and is the only potential peer competitor for the U.S.A. on the horizon. Although the Chinese economy faces a number of difficult challenges, most economists expect that economic growth will continue, albeit at a somewhat slower pace. Aided by foreign investment, China has begun to move up the technology ladder from labor-intensive goods to exports that incorporate advanced technology. As China moves up the technology curve, many Americans view it as a looming economic and a strategic challenge. This anxiety is reinforced by the realpolitik worldview of Chinese leaders, who are committed to realizing the goal of a "rich country, strong army." U.S. policy-makers, including former Secretary of Defense Donald Rumsfeld, expressed concerns about the purposes behind China's increasing military spending and military modernization efforts.[25] These factors led many U.S. analysts to worry that China might eventually challenge the U.S. global position.

These concerns are reinforced by China's role as a successful "communist development state" where the Communist Party plays a leading role in fostering economic development. Some argue that the Chinese approach of reforming the economy while limiting political reforms represents a new model with considerable appeal to leaders in developing countries.[26] Chinese leaders remain committed to Communist Party rule and have explicitly rejected multi-party democracy. The human rights Americans care about most – political rights, freedom of speech, and freedom of religion – are the areas where China has made the least progress. Moreover, recent crackdowns on press freedom and nongovernmental organizations have eroded some of the limited progress that had been made.

The prospect that the Chinese government may continue to be authoritarian (and increasingly nationalist) highlights questions about how a stronger China might behave in the future. Besides Taiwan, China has a host of unresolved maritime and territorial disputes, including claims to the Spratly Islands, disputes with Japan over the Senkaku/Diaoyu Islands and the East China Sea, and disputes with Vietnam over the Paracel Islands. These issues are complicated by the existence of considerable natural gas and possible oil resources in the disputed territories. China's increasing demand for energy to fuel its economic growth has prompted concerns that Beijing might defend its maritime claims more aggressively and seek to develop a blue water navy to protect its sea lines of communications to the Middle East.

These concerns have been part of the China debate since the mid-1990s, but several recent developments are giving them increased salience. The first is a sense that China is improving its military capabilities more rapidly than expected. This reflects the cumulative impact of a double-digit real increase in Chinese military spending since 1999, "software" reforms in training, education, doctrine, and logistics that are improving PLA operational capabilities, and increased Chinese deployments of both Russian and domestically produced weapons systems. Analysts disagree about the significance of some of these developments, but most agree that Chinese military modernization is moving faster than anticipated in the late 1990s.

A second factor is the realization that integration in the world economy and membership in international and regional organizations has given China new opportunities to influence how these institutions operate. While membership shapes China's foreign-policy choices (through socialization and by raising the costs of aggressive policies), it also enables Chinese foreign policy as China learns how to operate in a multilateral setting and how to employ political and economic levers to exercise influence. This is a logical consequence of China's increasing integration into international organizations, but it has caught many observers by surprise. China's increasing ability to influence the rules and operations of international institutions may limit the degree to which these institutions can shape China's international behavior and political evolution.

A third factor is impatience that economic growth and integration in the world community have not produced dramatic changes in the Chinese political system. There has been significant progress in building the legal institutions that are a precondition for establishing the rule of law, but key political decisions remain firmly in control of the Communist Party. Although Chinese citizens enjoy greater freedom in their daily lives, they do not enjoy freedom of speech or full political rights. It is logical to expect the military and the core institutions of the Communist Party control to be the last to liberalize, but the slow pace of political change in China has led some to question the assumptions underpinning engagement.

Despite these concerns, the hedge strategy the U.S.A. has pursued since the mid-1990s remains the most appropriate way of responding to the potential long-term challenges posed by China. Alternative strategies such as containment have high costs and limited benefits. A containment strategy would require the U.S.A. to significantly increase military spending and to develop expensive new capabilities such as space weapons to negate Chinese asymmetrical warfare options. Containment would not only require the U.S.A. to forego the benefits of cooperation with China, but also have a destabilizing impact in Asia as the U.S.A. tried to force unwilling countries to act against their perceived interests by lining up against China. Containment would also impose high economic costs on American businesses and consumers, including significant damage to the global competitive position of U.S. companies.

A better approach is to continue engaging China while simultaneously working to improve the U.S. strategic position. This requires enhanced efforts to engage Chinese leaders and to enhance bilateral cooperation. The Bush administration has launched a number of initiatives such as the "senior dialogue" and the "strategic economic dialogue" that could play a useful role in this respect. The "responsible stakeholder" concept outlines a useful framework for long-term U.S.–China cooperation. Nevertheless, there are significant operational challenges to using this framework as a basis for bilateral relations. A sustainable China policy will also need to pay greater attention to Congressional concerns about the U.S. bilateral trade deficit and the value of the Chinese currency. Maintaining the balance between aggressively pursuing short-term U.S. economic and security interests and longer-term efforts to shape Chinese thinking about its global interests will be difficult. With Deputy Secretary Zoellick's departure, it will also be important to identify a senior member of the administration who can continue the high-level dialogue and help coordinate relations with China across the economic, security, and diplomatic domains.

Conclusion

Although Sino-U.S. relations have been undergoing a period of relative stability, bilateral tensions are likely to increase significantly over the next few years. Congress has been reluctant to challenge the Bush administration on China policy, but this may be changing. Increased Congressional activism is currently focused on economic issues such as surges in Chinese textile imports, the ballooning U.S. trade deficit with China, and concerns about the impact of an undervalued Chinese currency on U.S. manufacturers. But issues such as

Taiwan, China's relations with North Korea, human rights, and the ongoing Chinese government crackdown on the press, Internet, and nongovernmental organizations are also matters of concern. Increased Congressional activism may challenge the administration's efforts to set clear priorities and to implement a balanced China policy. Renewed Chinese efforts to link cooperation with U.S. concessions on issues such as Taiwan would make China policy-making much more difficult.

The U.S.–China relationship will continue to be characterized by ambiguity and ambivalence. The complex mix of cooperative and competitive elements in the relationship will require patience and persistence in pursuing U.S. objectives. The multifaceted nature of U.S.–China relations requires the U.S.A. simultaneously to cooperate with China in the pursuit of common interests, to engage China to alter its behavior, and to deter China from unwanted military actions. All these activities take place within a broader context where the U.S.A. is attempting to influence China's political evolution and long-term strategic choices in positive directions through initiatives such as dialogue with China about the "responsible stakeholder" concept. Given the range of U.S. interests and the difficult trade-offs between short-term policy goals and long-term strategy, it is not surprising that the U.S.A. has sometimes experienced difficulty in prioritizing its interests and pursuing them effectively. Different parts of the U.S. government have different priorities in dealing with China, making policy coordination inherently difficult. Leadership, vision, and patience will be necessary for the U.S.A. to take full advantage of the benefits that cooperation with China offers while successfully meeting the strategic challenges China poses to U.S. interests.

Notes

1 The views expressed are those of the author and do not reflect the official policy or position of the National Defense University, the Department of Defense, or the U.S. government.
2 Jonathan Pollack was one of the first to articulate the logic of a hedge strategy in a 1995 working paper for the Council on Foreign Relations. A revised version, "Designing a New American Security Strategy for Asia," was published in James J. Shinn, ed., *Weaving the Net: Conditional Engagement with China*, New York: Council on Foreign Relations, 1996, pp. 99–132.
3 Keith Crane, Roger Cliff, Evan Medeiros, James Mulvenon, and William Overholt, *Modernizing China's Military: Opportunities and Constraints*, Santa Monica, Cal: RAND, 2005, pp. 91–134; and Department of Defense, *Military Power of the People's Republic of China 2006*, May 2006, pp. 18–21, available at <http://www.defenselink.mil/pubs/pdfs/China Report 2006.pdf>
4 China's 2007 military budget announcement revealed that official defense spending for 2006 was actually 297.93 billion RMB, or about $36.3 billion U.S. dollars at the current exchange rate of 8.2 RMB per dollar. "China's defense budget to rise 17.8 percent in 2007," *People's Daily*, March 4, 2007.
5 "Remarks by President Hu Jintao of The People's Republic of China at Welcoming Luncheon at the White House Hosted by President George W. Bush of the U.S.A. of America," April 20, 2006, available at <http://www.fmprc.gov.cn/eng/zxxx/t259220.htm>
6 "The cauldron boils," *The Economist*, 29 September 2005. Also see Murray Scot

Tanner, "China Rethinks Unrest," *Washington Quarterly*, 27 Vol. 1, No. 3 2004, pp. 137–156, available at http://www.twq.com/04summer/docs/04summer_tanner.pdf Comparable figures for 2005 are not yet available.

7 Yongding, "China's Color-Coded Crackdown," www.foreignpolicy.com, October 2005, available at http://www.foreignpolicy.com/story/cms.php?story_id=3251

8 James A. Kelly, "Overview of U.S. Policy Toward Taiwan," testimony at a hearing on Taiwan, House International Relations Committee, Washington, D.C., April 21, 2004, available at http://www.state.gov/p/eap/rls/rm/2004/31649.htm

9 This section draws upon Phillip C. Saunders, "Long-Term Trends in China-Taiwan Relations: Implications for U.S. Taiwan Policy," *Asian Survey*, Vol. 45, No. 6, 2005, pp. 970–991.

10 William J. Clinton, "Remarks by the President to the Business Council," February 24 2000, available at http://hongkong.usconsulate.gov/uscn/wh/2000/022401.htm; "Bush vows 'whatever it takes' to defend Taiwan," cnn.com, (25 April, 2001) available at http://archives.cnn.com/2001/ALLPOLITICS/04/25/bush.taiwan.03/

11 "Bush Reaffirms U.S. Commitment to One-China Policy," usinfo.state.gov, 9 December, 2003, available at http://usinfo.state.gov/xarchives/display.html?p=washfile-english&y=2003&m=December&x=20031209173641esuarKS0.2866632&t=xarchives/xarchitem.html

12 David Shambaugh, "A Matter of Time: Taiwan's Eroding Military Advantage," *The Washington Quarterly*, Vol. 23, No. 2, 2000, pp. 119–133 and Department of Defense, *The Military Power of the People's Republic of China 2006*, p. 50.

13 Michael S. Chase, "U.S.–Taiwan Security Cooperation: Enhancing an Unofficial Relationship," in Nancy Bernkopf Tucker, ed., *Dangerous Strait: The U.S.–Taiwan–China Crisis*, New York: Columbia University Press, 2005, pp. 162–185.

14 David M. Lampton and Kenneth Lieberthal, "Heading off the Next War," *Washington Post*, 13 April, 2004.

15 This section draws upon arguments in Phillip C. Saunders and Jing-dong Yuan, "China's Strategic Force Modernization," in Albert Willner and Paul Bolt, eds, *China's Nuclear Future*, Boulder, CO.: Lynn Rienner, 2006, pp. 79–118.

16 U.S. Department of Defense, *Military Power of the People's Republic of China 2006*, May 2006, p. 27; also see remarks of an anonymous U.S. official in Howard Diamond, "Chinese Strategic Plans Move Forward with Missile Test," *Arms Control Today*, Vol. 29, No. 5, 1999, p. 27, available at http://www.armscontrol.org/act/1999_07–08/chija99.asp

17 John Wilson Lewis and Hua Di, "China's Ballistic Missile Programs: Technologies, Strategies, Goals," *International Security*, Vol. 27, No. 2, 1992, p. 28; and U.S. Department of Defense, *Annual Report on the Military Power of the People's Republic of China* (2003) (Department of Defense: Washington, D.C.: 2003), p. 31, available at http://www.defenselink.mil/pubs/20030730chinaex.pdf

18 A minimum of two submarines is necessary to keep one on operational patrol at all times; the U.S. Navy typically requires three submarines in order to have one operationally deployed at all times.

19 Alan D. Romberg and Michael McDevitt, eds, *China and Missile Defense: Managing U.S.–PRC Strategic Relations*, Washington, D.C.: The Henry L. Stimson Center, February 2003; Paul H.B. Godwin and Evan S. Medeiros, "China, America, and Missile Defense: Conflicting National Interests," *Current History*, Vol. 99, No. 638, 2000, pp. 285–289; Charles Ferguson, "Sparking a Buildup: U.S. Missile Defense and China's Nuclear Arsenal," *Arms Control Today*, Vol .30, No. 2, 2000, pp. 13–18.

20 Missile Defense Agency, "A Day in the Life of the BMDS, Third Edition," circa 2005, p. 23, available at http://www.mda.mil/mdalink/pdf/bmdsbook.pdf

21 U.S. Department of Defense, "Findings of the Nuclear Posture Review," 9 January, 2002, available at http://www.defenselink.mil/news/Jan2002/020109-D-6570C-001.pdf

22 Peter Brookes, "The Case for Missile Defense," *Far Eastern Economic Review*, 7 September, 2000, p. 33.
23 U.S. Department of Defense 2005, p. 36; and Phillip C. Saunders, "China's Future in Space: Implications for U.S. Security," Space.com, May 2005, available at http://www.space.com/adastra/china_implications_0505.html
24 Alexandra Harney, Demetri Sevastopulo, and Edward Alden, "Top Chinese general warns US over attack," *Financial Times*, (14 July, 2005).
25 "Secretary Rumsfeld's Remarks to the International Institute for Strategic Studies," Singapore, June 4, 2005, available at http://www.defenselink.mil/transcripts/2005/tr20050604-secdef3002.html
26 Joshua Cooper Ramos, *The Beijing Consensus*, London: Foreign Policy Centre, 2004, available at http://fpc.org.uk/fsblob/244.pdf; and Joshua Kurlantzick, "Cultural Revolution: How China Is Changing Global Diplomacy," *New Republic*, June 27, 200), pp. 16–21.

9 The domestic political game behind the engagement strategy

Jean A. Garrison

Despite 35 years of engagement with the People's Republic of China (PRC) and a continued deepening of the relationship, a dichotomous dialogue on China policy within the U.S. government persists, reflecting competing assessments as to China's role in the world. Consistently, one assessment emphasizing common interests is optimistic about China's future cooperation with the U.S.A., while a second focuses on its hostility or threat to U.S. interests. This shifting rhetoric has been visible within the George W. Bush administraton in the highs represented by Colin Powell's claim while secretary of state that the relationship was the "best it has been in thirty years" to lows characterized by the Department of Defense's yearly reports focusing on China's growing military threat.

This debate has become deeply imbedded in the U.S. domestic policy context. Recurring controversies with China have become the norm and each situation (whether a discussion of trade policy, human rights, or security issues) reinvigorates the controversy over China policy. Especially since the events of June 3–4, 1989 in Tiananmen Square, domestic critics of China have aggressively attacked America's bipartisan engagement policy. During each new election cycle American presidents become particularly vulnerable to this. In 2004 Democratic nominee Senator John Kerry's get-tough message claimed that President George W. Bush's policies had led to the loss of tens of thousands of American manufacturing jobs. Previously Republicans accused Bill Clinton of appeasing China and abandoning Taiwan. The Democrats, in turn, had accused George H.W. Bush of being soft on the "butchers of Beijing" after Tiananmen Square. These examples highlight how popular it has become for some on both sides of the political aisle to attack portions of the U.S.A.'s long-standing engagement policy.

Why and how does such a schitzophrenic domestic political pattern regarding China occur? Part of the reason is that the concept of "engagement" represents a convergence around a broad range of discrete policy choices including tough discussions on problematic security, and commercial and social issues rather than a coherent policy consensus. Today's engagement policy is fought over by diverse domestic interests within Congress *and* presidential administrations. This breadth of bureaucratic and policy differences creates competing policy agendas (with competing strategic assessments) and provides a daunting picture for effective policy-making vis-à-vis America's China policy. One important reason this pattern has emerged is that Tiananmen Square as a symbolic event has permanently affected the American psyche regarding China – i.e., one that resonates with deeply held American beliefs about democracy and possibilities for political reform.

The discussion in this chapter will illustrate how U.S. bureaucratic decision-making practices have affected policy-making and policy choices regarding China since Tiananmen Square. It covers policy-making processes and patterns within the George H.W. Bush, Bill Clinton, and George W. Bush administrations.[1] The chapter concludes with a discussion of some implications this policy-making process has for U.S. policy and the U.S. relationship with China.

Who gets what, when, how in China policy?

Just as Harold Lasswell in *Politics: Who Gets What, When, How* and Graham Allison in *Essence of Decision* argue in discussing general policy-making patterns, China policy results from a political struggle (or "pulling and hauling") among various stakeholders – a process in which the president is only one among many players. Within the president's inner circle executive branch policy-makers come to the table with particular preferences based on their view of how to balance strategic and domestic imperatives with their own policy preferences. In complex foreign-policy problems like American policy toward the PRC involving uncertainty, political controversy, and conflicting values, these decision-makers struggle to define the nature of the problem and build consensus behind particular policy choices.

Competing strategic assessments

With China, many pundits focus first and foremost on strategic assessments – looking at the systemic level – making different assessments of China's future role in the world as a force for stability or instability. Pessimists such as Richard Bernstein, Ross Munro, Bill Gertz, and Constantine Menges, among others, emphasize the current and future threat China represents for American national security, noting that a zero-sum, self-help world requires constant vigilance for survival.[2] In contrast, more optimistic assessments come with those who argue that states operate in a web of interdependence where rules and norms of behavior constrain the actions of states. Thus conflict, to scholars who share these assumptions such as Andrew Nathan, Robert Ross, David Shambaugh, and David Lampton, is not inevitable if a rising China can be peacefully integrated into the international system.[3] These competing visions frame the domestic-policy debate over China and depending on your perspective fundamentally lead decision-makers to ask different questions and assess possibilities for conflict and cooperation differently.

This renewed debate comes at a time of great uncertainty about China's future direction and corresponds to a time when the president faces greater criticism from a Democratic Congress. The tarnished image of political progress in China since Tiananmen Square, along with recurring problems, has created a political environment where it is difficult for presidents to maintain a coherent China policy.

Competing institutional priorities

Fundamentally the struggle for control of the China policy agenda is exacerbated by a political system with different institutions sharing power. Because Congress represents narrow interests (with corresponding lobbying groups) while the administration, in general, must focus on the general health of the bilateral relationship, they begin from different reference points, which result in a series of fights that are reinvigorated each time a new controversy emerges. The controversy over the proposed purchase of Unocal by the China National Offshore Oil Company (CNOOC) in summer 2005 illustrates a fundamental concern many in Congress have about the nature of China's potential threat. This feeling is exacerbated by the fact that where once the U.S. business community was united in its efforts to promote closer trade ties, today many groups are critical of Chinese practices. A mixed assessment exists because some small companies fear Chinese competition and piracy while larger businesses are concerned about China's overall mercantilist policies. In other areas, influential interest groups representing interests ranging from human rights and religious freedom to organized labor have flourished since Tiananmen Square and placed pressure on presidents to elevate their particular issues to a prominent place in the bilateral dialogue.

Developing a coherent policy strategy

In this political environment the president and his advisors work to control the policy agenda and to build a governing coalition inside and outside the administration. Within the president's inner circle, an important part of controlling the policy is controlling how the problem is defined and alternatives are assessed (i.e., who gets what, when, how). To build support, leaders try to create common reference points to categorize information, to provide for its efficient communication, and to establish important distinctions among policy alternatives so that appropriate policy choices stand out. Political elites who want to reshape the policy debate to favor their cause emphasize the opportunities their alternatives provide in a deliberate campaign using rhetorical tools such as historical analogies, stereotypes, or images that will resonate with the targeted audience. Scholarship on American public opinion and the study of social movements suggests that leaders can use cultural themes that resonate with the public to strengthen their policy positions and to build support for their preferred options. Studies of the media illustrate that those themes that are primed and readily available will be most persuasive.

Specific focusing events such as Tiananmen Square can act as symbols that prime an audience by highlighting new positive or negative themes that create new opportunities, in this case for China's critics.[4] In this way the image of the young protestor blocking a tank in Tiananmen Square remains a powerful visual of Chinese oppression – one that still haunts those American decision-makers pushing for closer Sino-American ties. Images such as this have provided fodder for China's critics and undermined the bipartisan consensus on engagement policy. As Graham Allison anticipates in his work, a competition over the policy agenda and definition of the policy problem become a likely bureaucratic pattern. As we will see, George H.W. Bush faced the immediate task in the wake of Tiananmen Square to resist a strong political backlash, while Bill Clinton faced critics who questioned his overall stewardship of American foreign policy. These fights with Congress created a political pattern inherited by President George W. Bush as well.

George H.W. Bush and Bill Clinton – common policy strategies but mixed success

President George Bush worked to strengthen engagement with China and to usher in a new level of stability in Sino-American bilateral relations despite Beijing's Tiananmen Square crackdown. The Chinese government crackdown on protesters led to congressional condemnation and a bipartisan call for tough sanctions. Correspondingly the decline of the Cold War added new fodder because it represented the end to the strategic glue justifying close relations with the PRC. Long-ignored frictions over issues such as China's arms sales to other countries, problems in the trade relationship, and China's human rights abuses came to the fore. Maintaining the relationship with China, given this political climate, became President Bush's greatest challenge. Ironically, President Clinton who had criticized Bush for his close relationship to Beijing, faced the same pressures as president and eventually adopted a similar policy to maintain the status quo in U.S.–China relations despite an initial focus on linking progress in human rights to possible sanctions and the extension of trade rights.

Within Congress, Tiananmen Square set the stage for a long-term alliance between hardline anti-Communists and advocates for religious freedom. A lasting core of opposition was formed to the Bush and Clinton administration efforts to foster a strong Sino-American relationship. In the post-Tiananmen Square context, the challenge for each administration was to define the problem in positive terms while maintaining as much presidential autonomy as possible.

The challenges – downplaying Tiananmen Square and managing the fallout

President Bush's immediate challenge following Tiananmen Square was to make sure that congressional sanctions pressure did not threaten the stable relationship that his predecessors had forged. To do this, the administration defined the problem as the need to maintain the mutually rewarding relationship that had developed with China since the 1970s. This perspective downplayed the Tiananmen problem by putting it into its broader historic context, by emphasizing the value of the administration's long-term perspective, and specifically emphasizing the success of Deng Xiaoping's economic reforms that created greater freedoms for China's people.[5] Bush argued the U.S.A. must remain engaged if it was to have any opportunity to continue to influence China to embrace political reform. For him, the Tiananmen Square massacre called for reasoned and careful action that took into account U.S. long-term strategic and economic interests and recognized the complex internal situation in China.[6] The dilemma James Baker identified was that this task "forced a risky juggling act upon our new administration . . . encompassing geo-strategic, commercial, and human rights interests that in large measure conflicted."[7]

When Bill Clinton entered office, he initially accepted the Democratic congressional leadership's position that prioritized human rights and linked the renewal of China's most-favored nation (MFN) status to progress in human rights. The Clinton administration's approach differed from the Bush administration's in its human rights emphasis and its willingness to employ economic sanctions as a tool to encourage Chinese reform. Clinton's national security adviser, Anthony Lake, argued the U.S.A. could help to steer countries like China down a reform path by "providing penalties that raise the costs of repression and aggressive behavior."[8] This policy attempted to integrate the values and interests of the U.S.A. in a policy that would open China to free trade, human rights, and international norms regarding a host of other issues.

Although they used different tactics, underpinning both positions was the same neo-liberal assumption that trade and commercial ties promote reform. Secretary of State James Baker argued that economic and political reform was "two sides of the same coin."[9] To Clinton's Secretary of State, Warren Christopher, a peaceful evolution in China could be helped by U.S. policies that encouraged the forces of economic and political reform.[10] These beliefs rested on the assumption that more trade and investment would increase economic growth and build a middle class with both consumerism and democracy in mind. Both administrations – Bush immediately and Clinton after May 1994 when he abandoned sanctions as a tactic (i.e., linking human rights progress to MFN renewal) – argued that foreign trade and investment were essential tools to keep China open to the outside world and to encourage responsible behavior in areas important for American interests. With Congress, both argued that if China's MFN status was not renewed it could reduce U.S. leverage in market access by hurting U.S. exports and other issues as it set back meaningful reform in China.[11] This sentiment prompted Bush to resist sanctions pressure and by May 1994 Bill Clinton to abandon his linkage policy.

Clinton's MFN reversal in 1994 was a painful change and hard policy lesson to learn. It marked the end of the early administration view that had elevated human rights over other issues and led to a new commercial rationale emphasizing mutual dependence and overall stability in the U.S.–China relationship. Mickey Kantor, Clinton's first trade representative, characterized the elevation of commercial interests over human rights as recognition that the U.S.A. had strategic, economic, and regional concerns beyond human rights.[12] A new economic equation emerged in which Chinese trade benefits without condition were argued to be a matter of economic security and vital to American national security.[13]

In addition, China was seen by both administrations as an important strategic actor beyond the economic equation. For Bush the Cold War strategic equation was still relevant. Maintaining a strong Sino-American relationship was important to discourage any deepening of ties between the Chinese and the Soviets.[14] While Clinton did not have the Soviet context as an element of his strategic thinking, China's growing regional and international influence became an important consideration. Both presidents recognized that China was destined to become a powerful influence in the Asian region and China's restraint should be sought on issues of interest to the U.S.A. such as arms proliferation.

Bureaucratic challenges to the developing policy agenda

Why did Bush weather domestic pressures to change his policy agenda more successfully than Bill Clinton? The answer can be found, in part, in the different organization and practices of their advisory systems. Following Tiananmen, the Bush administration succeeded in maintaining White House control of China policy and in maintaining one voice in policy-making in response to the tough domestic environment. According to National Security Adviser Brent Scowcroft the worst bureaucratic politics were avoided because "everyone knew where the president stood."[15] Bush argued for presidential prerogative and by emphasizing his experience in foreign affairs he countered a lot of the congressional sanctions pressure. The administration's unity and the president's active involvement helped the administration forge a measured response after Tiananmen despite congressional sanctions pressure.[16] In doing so he kept the harshest sanctions from passing, and specifically kept Congress from rescinding China's MFN status.

To maintain his authority Bush did compromise with Congress and signed some revised sanctions legislation, but only when the White House retained policy flexibility. For example, once MFN was off the table, Bush signed a watered-downed sanctions package when he gained the authority to designate important exceptions – which he did immediately by waiving the prohibitions on the Export-Import Bank's financing of trade with the PRC.[17] When Bush faced legislation introduced by Congresswoman Nancy Pelosi (D-California) in November 1989 that would extend protection to Chinese students studying in the U.S.A., he pocket-vetoed the Pelosi legislation, arguing that it unnecessarily tied the hands of the president in the conduct of foreign policy.[18] After 1989 congressional opposition galvanized by Tiananmen Square settled into a familiar yearly pattern each spring when MFN came up for renewal (until the U.S.A. granted China permanent normal trade relations – PNTR – during the Clinton administration).

In contrast in the Clinton administration, the president was relatively uninterested in China policy (and traditional foreign policy generally) and organizationally proved to be a hands-off administrator. Without the central involvement of the president, bureaucratic politics flourished with multiple advisers, each with different strategies of engagement, sending mixed signals domestically and to the Chinese. For example, human rights advocates in the State Department who favored sanctions linked to MFN renewal if China did not reform its human rights record were challenged by commercial officials who feared that linkage would undercut U.S. commercial interests and long-term trade prospects. Particularly Secretary of the Treasury Lloyd Bentsen and Robert Rubin, assistant to the president for economic policy and director of the National Economic Council, pushed for U.S. accommodation on the MFN issue to preserve the overall trade relationship.

Secretary of State Warren Christopher's failure to gain significant human rights concessions in meetings with Chinese officials by March 1994 led Clinton to retreat to the commercial policy position favored by the Treasury and the previous administration. Christopher's efforts to get broader concessions on human rights had been undermined by a commercial agenda which publicly emphasized the immediate need to maintain the commercial relationship for the sake of national security and indirectly to work for evolutionary progress in human rights. For example, a January 1994 trip by Rubin and Bentson to China focused on the conditions under which the administration would end its linkage as part of their agenda to promote trade and investment in China.[19] These efforts sent mixed messages to the Chinese and seemed to convince them to hold out for a change in administration policy.

When the administration failed to get Chinese concessions, even former supporters of linkage such as National Security Advisor Lake, Deputy National Security Advisor Sandy Berger, and Christopher became convinced that a change in tactics was needed.[20] The challenge was how to placate congressional human rights advocates. In crafting the president's May 26, 1994 announcement of de-linkage of human rights from MFN renewal, the administration argued it had not abandoned its human rights goals but would pursue them through new steps with the business community and multilaterally through the U.N. Commission on Human Rights.

Pentagon officials joined commercial interests in pushing for the broader focus because trade relations and MFN renewal were seen as important first steps to make its proposed military dialogue with China possible – a move that improved the U.S. security posture.[21] Officials such as Assistant Defense Secretary Joseph Nye emphasized the need to jointly manage new security threats because of the interrelated nature of the system that meant that crises in different parts of the world could cause markets to crash in others.[22] Like George Bush, this position also recognized that China was a player with which the U.S.A. had to deal because of its economic power, its U.N. PermFive status, its nuclear weapons, its modernizing military, etc.[23]

The MFN linkage policy reversal set a pattern of bureaucratic politics and congressional opposition from which Clinton never completely recovered. Events such as Taiwan's democratization, Chinese missile firings across the Taiwan Straits, and recurring domestic scandals repeatedly made Clinton vulnerable to congressional pressures. These situations sparked a new domestic debate, precipitated by critics who feared that China's reemergence as an Asian power was a threat to U.S. interests in East Asia. Conservative voices in the Republican Party, in particular, called for an aggressive foreign-policy campaign targeting China as a threat that needed to be contained. Evidence of China's threat was gathered in the Congress through a series of investigations by congressional committees. The most prominent of these investigations, chaired by Representative Christopher Cox, released an unclassified report in May 1999 focusing on Chinese espionage activities, including information obtained on the American neutron bomb and the W-88 thermonuclear warhead in the 1980s. A pattern of domestic pressure focusing consistently on MFN, and sporadically on other issues, pitted each president against his China policy critics.

Mixed messages and confusion over a China policy flourished more in Clinton's than in Bush's administration, in part, because he and his White House never maintained a consistent focus on China policy. Only when the president and the White House became directly involved in policy-making did Clinton respond to his critics effectively. Gradually, under Sandy Berger's leadership within the NSC in the second term, policy-making became more centralized to the White House with greater presidential involvement. This change helped the administration weather the worst from its critics and set the stage for Clinton's success in securing passage of PNTR and China's entry into the World Trade Organization (WTO) in 2000. Passage of PNTR was a moment when the president and the White House worked together to build policy consensus. In familiar terms the White House insisted PNTR was a step in the right direction that enhanced chances for reform and rule of law in China while it brought tangible economic benefits to the U.S.A. (including access to China's market and lowered tariffs on U.S. exports).[24] Further, Clinton emphasized strategic and security dimensions of the overall relationship with the PRC that made it more than just trade benefits at stake. Arguing that China's entry into the WTO was about U.S. "national interest," it was an opportunity to influence China's future choices in the "right" direction.[25]

Despite opposition from various unions, human rights organizations, key Democrats, and conservatives in both houses, the PNTR legislation passed in the House and Senate with more Republicans than Democrats voting in favor. The administration's compromise behind the scenes to put in congressional oversight provisions and additional reporting requirements involving areas such as human rights paid off. It gave comfort to those members of the Congress that otherwise might not have voted for PNTR.[26]

One lesson to be drawn by comparing Bush's and Clinton's policy efforts is that the president needed to remain involved and be willing to engage the prestige of his office to shape the policy agenda during tough times. The compromises each made with the Congress also established a new pattern in which the

Congress had a more formal oversight role in the making of America's China policy. Today the Congress has gained leverage through annual reporting requirements on China's human rights record as well as the Defense Department's annual report on China's military. For George W. Bush the Congress has remained a voice challenging the status quo in the U.S.–China relationship.

G.W. Bush and mixed policy priorities

China policy-making in the G.W. Bush administration shows a bureaucratic pattern more similar to Clinton's administration than to that of his father. A fundamental disagreement in the administration emerged over the degree to which China could be trusted and how to balance the need for China's cooperation in areas of strategic common interest such as North Korea without undermining the long-term U.S. commitment to Taiwan. Two distinct positions – pragmatic engagers like Colin Powell and the State Department and hardliners such as Vice President Dick Cheney, Secretary of Defense Donald Rumsfeld, and the Department of Defense – vied for bureaucratic dominance of the East Asian policy agenda. The collision of an EP-3 surveillance plane with a Chinese F-8 fighter on April 1, 2001 brought pragmatists to the forefront, diffusing the crisis and shifting the administration away from the confrontational tone in U.S. China policy. Despite President Bush's new pragmatic focus, however, he remained caught between the two groups vying for power and control over the framing of China policy, and simultaneously the proper approach to the North Korean problem.

The challenge – defining the China problem

The overall challenge that Secretary of State Colin Powell, and ironically Condoleezza Rice after him, faced was how to gain and maintain the authority to coordinate policy toward China in the State Department and to contain hardline elements in the White House and Defense Department who were more hostile toward China. As the State Department fostered a productive dialogue on a range of issues with China to set the groundwork for a more stable and enduring relationship, others in the administration pursued an East Asian policy emphasizing the need to consolidate relations with key allies such as Japan and Taiwan and to promote national and theatre missile defense systems in order to address China's rising challenge.

Following the events of September 11, 2001, however, the administration more commonly argued that a China positively engaged in the world was conducive to both the stability and security of East Asia and U.S. security interests. More and more Bush's statements showed that the White House now felt it was not smart to let symbolic issues such as Taiwan's status interfere with the more general foreign-policy agenda which sought to rally China's support for the war on terror among other issues.[27]

For policy advisers such as Colin Powell, and the State Department more generally, the important point was to maintain the cross-strait status quo to prevent confrontation and to emphasize how dealing constructively with China promoted American interests for regional security and stability. Given the broad ties that existed with China, Powell's emphasis included an agenda focusing on cooperation in counter-terrorism, promotion of mutual economic prosperity through economic/financial reform while managing the trade relationship, promoting democracy and human rights, and urging adherence to international and bilateral nonproliferation and arms control arrangements. The breadth of this list included areas of agreement and disagreement but also demonstrated a shared commitment for pragmatic discussions to address differences as well as common interests.

Despite a fragile convergence around the pragmatic position noted above, hardliners continued to emphasize China's growing military threat to U.S. interests in separate policy channels. The September 30, 2001 *Quadrennial Defense Review Report* (QDR), for example, emphasized the potential for regional powers (namely China) to develop capabilities to threaten stability in regions critical to U.S. interests and for a military competitor with a formidable resource base to emerge.[28] Various other Pentagon reports, such as its annual report to Congress on China's military, concluded that Chinese political leaders and commanders in the People's Liberation Army (PLA) had developed credible military options to prevent Taiwan from achieving independence; thus fueling the Pentagon's call for a consistent strategic harmonization between the U.S.A. and Taiwan which would make Taiwan part of the U.S. force structure and create a de facto military alliance.[29] The Pentagon's 2005 report to Congress noted China's heavy investment in its military although it faced no direct threat from any state. It warned "current trends in China's military modernization could provide China with a force capable of prosecuting a range of military operations in Asia – well beyond Taiwan – potentially posing a credible threat to modern militaries operating in the region." It went on to state that China's leaders might be tempted to resort to force or coercion more quickly to press diplomatic advantage, advance security interests, or resolve disputes as its power grew.[30] In 2006, the Pentagon noted that China's fast economic growth, foreign diplomatic leverage and improvements in the PLA's military capabilities in contrast with Taiwan's modest defense efforts had "the effect of shifting the cross-Strait balance in Beijing's favor," making it "critical that Taiwan strengthen its defenses with a sense of urgency."[31]

The most recent QDR, published on February 6, 2006, also expressed concern about China's expanding military development. It now identified China as a country that could "compete militarily" with the U.S.A., noting specifically that China fields "disruptive military technologies" that might "offset traditional U.S. military advantages."[32] Robert Sutter has argued that the QDR reflects "continued strong US government (not just DoD) concern about China's military build-up and other policies [that are] seen as disruptive or potentially disruptive to international norms supported by the US government."[33] In its discussion the QDR labels China a great-power competitor, making the management of China's disruptive capabilities the logical policy prescription. In June 2006 Rumsfeld argued that the pace and scope of Beijing's strategic forces' modernization was a cause for concern and that its lack of transparency justified international reaction to hedge against the unknown and the development of a broad network of security relationships in Asia to hedge against the Chinese. Similarly for some, China's successful test of its anti-satellite technology on January 11, 2007 demonstrated a victory for Beijing's military strategy over the U.S.A. that aims to bridge the technology gap between the two countries.[34]

Pragmatists in the State Department have faced a consistent challenge to put these concerns in perspective. Regarding Taiwan, they fear that expanded military ties advocated by hardline elements risk triggering a sharp response from China that would threaten many areas of cooperative relations. Although Taiwan has needed to be assisted, relations with Taiwan should be kept low key so that the U.S.A. avoids any unnecessary and potentially destabilizing political confrontations with the PRC. Regarding broader military issues, the need has been to avoid a crisis and to emphasize a broad range of common interests.

Former Deputy Secretary of State Robert Zoelleck's speech before the National Committee on U.S.–China Relations in September 2005 articulated a new engagement policy that seemed meant to counter the hardline position. Noting China's embrace of globalization and market reform, Zoellick called on China to become a "responsible stakeholder" in the international system. He made it clear that neither the Cold War analogy nor balance-of-power politics of nineteenth-century Europe applied to China. "The U.S.A. welcomes a confident, peaceful, and prosperous China, one that appreciates that its growth and development depends on constructive connections with the rest of the world. Indeed, we hope to intensify work with a China that not only adjusts to the international rules developed over the last century, but also joins us and others to address the challenges of the new century."[35] Cooperation with China would promote U.S. interests in areas such as counter-terrorism, the proliferation of WMD, poverty, and disease. In an interview on April 18, 2006 Zoellick emphasized long-term and shared interests and focused on laying a strong foundation for the future. Like George H.W. Bush's logic, the responsible stakeholder concept acknowledged China's success over three decades in integrating itself into the international system and its subsequent interest in sustaining and strengthening that system in areas such as trade, currency markets, or nuclear proliferation. This concept was meant to set the long-term policy agenda, focusing on building a constructive relationship that would shape China's role in the global system.[36]

The impact of bureaucratic politics and an isolated president

Underlying the pragmatic and hardline positions noted above were different assumptions about the geopolitical landscape in East Asia. As the QDR and annual Pentagon reports illustrate, this pattern of mixed signals has continued despite Condoleezza Rice's close relationship to the president or Zoelleck's restatement of the administration's policy. With Zoelleck's resignation in

summer 2006 the new treasury secretary, Henry Paulson, became the administration's central player in China policy. Although the December 2006 Strategic
Economic Dialogue with China was a historic meeting in which Zoelleck's
responsible stakeholder language was reiterated, the vagueness of the language
creates a broad umbrella under which engagement and hedging strategies continue to coexist.

The negative impact of a policy with competing strains of emphases can be
seen more clearly in the administration's approach to North Korea. Not unlike
the split in views over China, irreconcilable agendas regarding North Korea
have persisted in both Bush terms. In 2001, Powell's first instinct to continue
Clinton's efforts to solve the North Korean nuclear issue through bilateral negotiations was blocked by hardliners who felt negotiation was not an option. Only
reluctantly did the White House enter multiparty talks at Powell's urging even
after North Korea announced that it had nuclear weapons and admitted it might
be willing to sell them in 2003. Through several rounds of six-party talks the
State Department promoted a more accommodating stance (i.e., greater willingness to manage the crisis through negotiation) while hardliners led by Vice
President Cheney, Rumsfeld, and Undersecretary of State for Arms Control and
International Security John Bolton (in Bush's first term) were lukewarm and
insisted on regime change. Although hardliners tentatively endorsed the six-
party process, their accusations that the State Department was "soft" on North
Korea consistently undermined the legitimacy of the talks. While the president
said he wanted a negotiated solution, his negotiators were never allowed the
flexibility to carry out such a mandate.[37]

In September 2005, a breakthrough seemed imminent. Secretary of State Condoleezza Rice provided broad guidelines to U.S. negotiators which gave them
more flexibility to seek a deal and to meet directly with their North Korean counterparts. This change produced a tentative agreement that gave some hope that
North Korea's search for nuclear weapons would end in return for economic and
energy assistance from U.S allies. However, because the agreement was vague and
left contentious issues to be solved in future discussions its hope for real success
was tenuous at best. By arguing that the wording of the agreement called on North
Korea to disarm first before discussing the idea of a nuclear reactor, the agreement
was doomed.[38] Although Rice's close relationship with the president had made the
return to diplomacy possible, as Ivo Daalder argued at the time, the failure to
move forward seemed to demonstrate the administration's inflexibility and lack of
agreement to pursue a compromise diplomatic solution to the problem. Daalder
concluded that the public disavowal of the September 2005 compromise with
North Korea demonstrated the power of the administration's naysayers, who mis-
trusted North Korea and China's intentions.[39]

The real test for the administration's flexibility seemed to come with the February 2007 round of six-party talks. In January 2007, Assistant Secretary of
State Christopher Hill met one-on-one with his North Korean counterpart to
move forward again with six-party talks. There was cautious optimism and after
two days of talks he noted that the U.S.A. was "willing to engage in 'a bilateral

process' to establish 'a normal relationship.'" Asked about Hill's progress Rice endorsed the assistant secretary's work while reiterating the September 2005 joint declaration's need for "complete, verifiable denuclearization" and "irreversible denuclearization." She called for North Korea to move first before assurances of aid were given.[40]

Rice's endorsement of Hill's "progress" with a continued emphasis on timing and sequencing issues seemed to demonstrate that the administration's "flexibility" still had limits. The continued insistence that no talks could go forward without North Korea first giving up its nuclear capability reflected the earlier nonnegotiating position of administration hardliners. Although the renewed six-party talks in February 2007 hit some of the same snags over North Korea's demand for fuel oil shipments and electricity before agreeing to start to disable its nuclear facilities, a broad general agreement was made. Although this agreement left the hard negotiation for later, it was a start toward a negotiated solution to the North Korean problem.[41] The agreement on the U.S. side seems linked to the continued crisis in Iraq and the administration's need for a policy win. Ironically, the outline of the deal the administration was ready to sign onto in February 2007 was very nearly Clinton's "freeze" in the 1994 agreement which Bush had repudiated when he came into office.

These circumstances illustrate that the domestic context and internal policy climate can and do shape an administration's foreign-policy choices. It also shows that policy dynamics can shift across administrations so that policy change under certain circumstances is possible.

Conclusion

These three administrations have shared elements in their China policy and faced their share of domestic controversy. Each eventually advocated similar broad engagement policies, if with different degrees of agreement within their administrations. Clinton was initially much more confrontational toward China tactically in comparison to George H.W. Bush, but once he recognized the costs of his approach his policy soon shifted to reflect the viewpoint that China's cooperation was critical in multiple areas of shared interests. Both advocated policies that pushed to involve China in a web of interdependence that would shape its behavior. For his part, George W. Bush came to office more hostile to China rhetorically, but September 11th became an opportunity for pragmatists in the administration to endorse a position closer to both previous presidents.

These similarities in approach, however, should not lead us into a false sense of consensus and stability in America's China policy. As a closer look at the bureaucratic political patterns illustrates, engagement, and its latest incarnation in the responsible stakeholder concept, remains an umbrella concept under which many specific policies can flourish. If engagement represents a convenient convergence around a policy concept rather than a consensus then its stability and the stability of "responsible stakeholder" must also be called into question. The consistent contrast between the language of the State Department and the Defense Department and the overall hedging strategy throughout the G.W. Bush administration demonstrates how different interpretations of China continue to flourish.

From a policy-making perspective it is important to note that these conflicts flourish most when the president has been uninterested, uninvolved, or undecided on the proper approach to China, and when no one plays a brokering role among competing agendas. The presence of entrenched factions that compete for dominance within an administration makes the president's noninvolvement even more serious. As the first Bush administration shows, an active president and national security adviser can mitigate these conflicts. The complexity of the Sino-American relationship today makes it more important to generate an agreed upon policy frame so that the administration can speak with a unified policy voice regarding China. Even in a White House such as G.W. Bush's that talked about its centralization, bureaucratic wars have raged so that mixed messages flourished in China policy. Some would argue that the stalemate in Korean policy caused by conflicting viewpoints allowed North Korea's nuclear program to continue, which increased rather than decreased instability in the region.

In policy terms the lesson each president has learned is that in managing the relationship with the PRC we need to focus on long-term opportunities rather than short-term problems which generate the most domestic controversy. The sooner the U.S.A. closes the gaps between its rhetoric (and expectations for China policy) to fit the pragmatic political reality, the sooner a truly "normal" relationship that openly acknowledges areas of shared interest and disagreement can flourish. Part of the problem has been the unrealistic assumptions Americans hold for U.S.–China policy.

America's engagement policy (even the concept of "responsible stakeholder") still rests on the dangerous hope for regime change in China. Rather than pressuring for immediate change through military means, America's engagement policy rests on the notion that placing China into a web of interdependence eventually will lead to political reforms. This "hope" raises expectations among certain constituencies that make presidents susceptible to political backlash when progress is not forthcoming. It simultaneously rests on the unrealistic assumption that the U.S.A. maintains the top position in the relationship and thus has the means to influence China directly. China's rise and the dependence the U.S.A. has on its economy should outline the dangers of this simplistic assumption.

The U.S. government and public must recognize that the only pragmatic orientation that remains is an engagement policy with China that openly acknowledges shared interests as well as areas of disagreement. Single interest agendas must be prevented from capturing the China policy agenda. Similarly, we need to avoid the dangers of symbolic politics and not be quick to paint China in the role of an enemy or a friend. In this context China is neither an "us" nor a "them" but embodies a complex relationship made up of daily contacts between multiple agencies and departments at various levels of importance, including the most mundane tasks to the occasional high politics.

Notes

1 A more thorough discussion of the China policy approach in these administrations as well as the Nixon, Carter, and Reagan administrations is available in Jean A. Garrison, *Making China Policy: From Nixon to G.W. Bush*, Boulder, CO: Lynne Rienner Publishers, 2005. This chapter draws material from this earlier volume but more clearly compares and contrasts George H.W. Bush with Bill Clinton in order to compare each to the policy approach of George W. Bush. The discussion of George W. Bush also includes a new analysis of his policy in his second term.
2 Richard Bernstein and Ross H. Munro, "The Coming Conflict with America." *Foreign Affairs*, vol. 76, no. 2, March/April, 1997, pp. 18–32; Richard Bernstein and Ross H. Munro, *The Coming Conflict with China*, New York, NY: Alfred A. Knopf, 1997; Bill Gertz, *China Threat: the Plan to Defeat America*, Washington, D.C.: Regnery, 2002; Constantine C. Menges, *China: The Gathering Threat*, Nashville, TN: Thomas Nelson, 2005.
3 Andrew J. Nathan and Robert S. Ross, *The Great Wall and the Empty Fortress: China's Search for Security*, Boston, MA: Norton, 1997; David Shambaugh, "Containment or Engagement of China: Calculating Beijing's Responses." *International Security*, vol. 21, no. 2, 1996, pp. 185–86; David M. Lampton, "Paradigm Lost: the Demise of the 'Weak China.'" *The National Interest*, Fall 2005, Issue 81, pp. 67–74.
4 John Kingdon, *Agendas, Alternatives, and Public Policies*, 2nd ed., Boston: Little, Brown, 1994, pp. 98–112.
5 Robert W. Barnett, Oral history interview, 3/2/90, *Foreign Affairs Oral History Collection* (CD-ROM, 2000), Association for Diplomatic Studies and Training; Thomas Friedman, "Crackdown in China; Foley says U.S. Should Consider Further Sanctions Against China," *New York Times*, June 19, 1989, pp. A1, A10; Thomas Friedman, "Congress, Angry at China, Moves to Impose Sanctions," *New York Times*, June 23, 1989, p. A5.
6 Talking Points on China and Chronology of White House Comments on the Situation in China, June 1989, Folder: China [OA/ID 06786], White House Press Office Marlin Fitzwater Files, CBS [OA6786 through Christmas Card/Part [2] [OA6786], Box 4, Bush Presidential Library; George Bush and Brent Scowcroft. *A World Transformed*, New York: Alfred A. Knopf, 1998, pp. 98–102.
7 James A. Baker, III with Thomas M. DeFrank, *The Politics of Diplomacy: Revolution, War, and Peace, 1989–1992*, New York: G.P. Putnam's Sons, 1996, p. 98; see also Raymond Garthoff. *Détente and Confrontation: American-Soviet Relations from Nixon to Reagan*, Washington, D.C.: Brookings Institution, (1994), pp. 640–643; Harry Harding. *A Fragile Relationship: The U.S.A. and China Since 1972*, Washington, D.C.: Brookings Institution, 1992, pp. 173–214; Steven Hurst, *The Foreign Policy of the Bush Administration*, London: Cassel, 1999, pp. 38–40.
8 Remarks by Anthony Lake before the Japan-America Society, Washington, D.C. on October 23, 1996, available: http://clinton3.nara.gov/WH/EOP/NSC/html/speeches/19961023.html (Last accessed 10/25/02.)
9 Baker, *Politics of Diplomacy*, pp. 99–101; Bush and Scowcroft, *World Transformed*, pp. 91–97.
10 Quote in James Mann, *About Face: A History of America's Curious Relationship with China, from Nixon to Clinton*, New York: Alfred A. Knopf, 1999, p. 276.
11 Letter with attachments to Senator Max Baucus from the White House, July 17, 1991, Folder: TPRG: China [OA/ID F01855], Box 1 of 5, Council of Economic Advisers Paul Wonnacott TPRG Files, A-M, Bush Presidential Library; Statement of Administration Policy, July 15, 1991, Folder: MFN for China O/A/ID 07687, Box 1 of 5, Paul Korfonta Files, White House Office of Cabinet Affairs Collection, Bush Presidential Library, p. 1; Fact Sheet on Continuation of MFN For China, June 18, 1991, Folder: MFN Status for China [OA/ID 08202], Box 1 of 5, White House Office of Correspondence, Beverly Ward Files, Bush Presidential Library, pp. 1–3.

12 Mickey Kantor interview with author, Washington, D.C., June 13, 2002.
13 Secretary of Commerce Ron Brown's Remarks to the American Chamber of Commerce Breakfast in Beijing, 8/28/94 (Doc.#01763); Department of State Briefing Memorandum from EAP Peter Tomsen to the Acting Secretary, 8/24/94 (Doc.#01762); Department of State Information memorandum from EAP Thomas Hubbard to the Secretary, 9/2/94 (Doc.#01772) National Security Archives Collection: China and the U.S.A. from Hostility to Engagement, 1960–1998 (published and post-publication collections), Washington, D.C.
14 National Security Directive (NSD) 23 from September 1989 reinforced the message that the Soviet military threat had not diminished. See National Security Directive 23, "U.S.A. Relations with the Soviet Union," September 22, 1989, Bush Presidential Library online research resources, http://bushlibrary.tamu.edu (last accessed 6/3/03), p. 2.
15 Brent Scowcroft telephone interview with author, 9/16/02.
16 George H.W. Bush, "The President's News Conference," June 5, 1989. Bush Presidential Library online research resources, available: http://bushlibrary.tamu.edu (last accessed 12/9/04); George H.W. Bush, "The President's News Conference," June 27, 1989. Bush Presidential Library online research resources, available: http://bushlibrary.tamu.edu (last accessed 12/9/04).
17 "Letter to the Speaker of the House of Representatives and the President of the Senate on Trade with China," December 19, 1989. Bush Presidential Library online research resources, available: http://bushlibrary.tamu.edu (last accessed 12/9/04); see also Baker, *Politics of Diplomacy*, p. 114.
18 See also Draft Presidential Statement, Folder: China–U.S. October–December 1989 [3] [OA/ID cf. 00316], NSC Douglas Paal Files, Box 3 of 5, Bush Presidential Library. Interestingly, the administration never enacted an executive order and instead relied on an administrative order issued from the Department of Justice. When this became public in several stories in the *New York Times* and *Washington Post*, beginning on April 5, 1990, it added fuel to Bush's China policy critics who saw it as further evidence of the administration's duplicity. See David Hoffman, "Bush Never Issued Executive Order Protecting Chinese Students in U.S.", *Washington Post*, April 5, 1990, p. A25.
19 Quoted in James Mann, *About Face: A History of America's Curious Relationship with China, from Nixon to Clinton*, New York: Alfred A. Knopf, 1999, p. 294; See also Clay Chandler and Daniel Williams, "Bentsen to Push China on Economic Reforms," *Washington Post*, January 6, 1994, p. D10; Thomas Friedman, "Trade vs. Human Rights," *New York Times*, February 6, 1994, p. 1.
20 Warren Christopher. *In the Stream of History: Shaping Foreign Policy for a New Era*, Stanford, Connecticut: Stanford University Press, 1998, pp. 153–156; Douglas Jehl, "Clinton Makes No Progress with Beijing," *New York Times*, May 3, 1994, p. A8.
21 Confidential Department of Defense Cable, "Press Guidance for Xu Huizi Visit," 8/3/94 (Doc.#01753); Confidential Cable from Secretary of Defense to the Beijing Embassy on Plenary Session with PLA General Xu Huizi, 8/19/94 (Doc.#01758); Cable from Office of Secretary of Defense to Beijing Embassy on Secretary Perry's discussion with Xu Huizi, 8/19/94 (Doc.#01759); Briefing Book for Secretary Perry's visit to China 16–19, 10/94 (Doc.#01778) available National Security Archives Collection: China and the United States from Hostility to Engagement, 1960–1998 (published and post-publication collections), Washington, D.C.
22 Assistant Secretary of Defense Explanation of Pentagon Regional Security Strategies After the Cold War, no date, Post-Publication File, National Security Archives Collection China and the United States.
23 One senior Defense Department official described this as William Perry's effort to "lead the relationship in a positive direction but also to hedge against the possibility of failure and trouble." While the Pentagon had a fundamental, long-term strategic

interest in decent relations with China, it still did not want to abandon important inter-ests like Taiwan. Interview by author with senior Pentagon official from the Clinton administration, June 2002; Talking Points for Meeting with LTG She-Ung To Discuss Sino-American Military Activities in 1996, 11/95, National Security Archives post-publication Collection China and the United States; Memo to Branch Secretaries from the Secretary of Defense, "U.S.–China Military Relationship," 8/94 (Doc.#01751) National Security Archives Collection China and the United States.

24 Granting PNTR involved preparing legislation declaring the Jackson–Vanik amend-ment (Title IV of the 1974 Trade Act) no longer applicable to China and to recom-mend that nondiscriminatory trade treatment be extended to all Chinese products.

25 Office of the Press Secretary, 'Remarks by the President on China,' 3/8/00; Back-ground paper on WTO and PNTR for Ambassador Holbrooke visit to PRC 3/16–20/2000, no date, Post-Publication File, National Security Archives Collection China and the United States; William J. Clinton, *My Life*, New York: Alfred A. Knopf, 2004, p. 768.

26 Author's telephone interview with member of the Clinton administration's NSC staff, 7/9/02; State Department PNTR Background Paper, no date and Background Paper on WTO and PNTR for Ambassador Holbrooke visit, no date, Post-Publication File, National Security Archives Collection China and the United States.

27 Bruce J. Dickson, 'New President adjusts old policies: U.S.–Taiwan relations under Chen and Bush,' *Journal of Contemporary China*, vol. 11, no. 33, November 2002, pp. 653–654.

28 Department of Defense, *Quadrennial Defense Review Report*, Washington, D.C.: Department of Defense, 2001, p. 4.

29 Maxim Kniazkov, "China Developing 'Credible Military Options' to Confront Taiwan, US Warns," Agence France-Presse, 5/30/04, available: http//web.lexis-nexis.com (last accessed 10/1/04); Bill Gertz, "Taiwan Shoring up Defenses with U.S. Assistance," *Washington Times*, February 29, 2004, p. A3.

30 Office of the Secretary of Defense, Annual Report to Congress, *The Military Power of the People's Republic of China 2005*, Washington, D.C.: Department of Defense, (2005) pp. 13–14.

31 Office of the Secretary of Defense, Annual report to Congress, *Military Power of the People's Republic of China 2006*, p. 1.

32 Department of Defense, *Quadrennial Defense Review Report*, February 6, 2006, available online http://www.qr.hq.af.mil/pdf/2006%20QDR%20Report.pdf (last accessed 3/16/06); Thomas Donnelly, "The 2006 Quadrennial Defense Review," Tes-timony before the Armed Services Committee, March 14, 2006, available http://www.aei.org/publications/filter.all,pubID.24047/pub_detail.asp (last accessed 3/16/06).

33 John Hill, "U.S. Quadrennial Defense Review sparks anger in China," *Janes Defense Review online*, March 7, 2006, available from http://www.janes.com/defence/news/jir/jir060307_2_n.shtml (last accessed 3/16/06).

34 Geoffrey York, "China's Anti-Satellite Weapon Fuels Anxiety," *Globe and Mail* online (posted January 22, 2007), http://www.theglobeandmail.com/servlet/story/LAC.20070122.CHINA22/TPStory/TPInternational/America (last accessed 1/22/07).

35 Robert Zoellick, "Whither China: From Membership to Responsibility," Remarks to the National Committee on U.S.–China Relations, 9/21/05, U.S. Department of State, www.state.gov/s/d/rem/53682.htm (last accessed 6/21/06).

36 Robert Zoellick, Interview with Phoenix TV, April 18, 2006, U.S. Department of State, available www.hongkong.usconsulate.gov/uscn/state/2006/041801.htm (last accessed 6/21/06).

37 Joshua Kurlantzick, "Look Away, a Do-Nothing Korea Policy," *New Republic*, December 15, 2003, pp. 14–16.

38 David Sanger, "Yes, parallel tracks to North, but parallel tracks don't meet," *New*

York Times, September 20, 2005, p. 6; Joseph Kahn and David Sanger, "U.S.–Korean Deal on Arms Leaves Key Points Open," *New York Times*, September 20, 2005, p. 1.

39 Ivo Daalder, "The Limits of Rice's Diplomacy," *NRC Handelsblad*, January 17, 2006, available online from http://www.tpmcafe.com/story/2006/1/18/12256/8615 (last accessed 3/16/06).

40 Glenn Kessler, "U.S. Open to Bilateral Talks on Ties with North Korea," *Washington Post*, January 18, 2007, p. A18.

41 Jim Yardley and David E. Sanger, "In Shift, Accord on North Korea Seems to Be Set," *New York Times*, February 13, 2007, pp. A1, A11.

10 Chinese military modernization and energy security

Conflict or cooperation?

Bernard D. Cole

This chapter addresses China's energy security concerns as a rising power in the first half of the twenty-first century. The discussion will consider the geographical, economic, and political contexts of the issues, including interaction with the U.S.A.

Energy security describes the measures necessary to "assure adequate, reliable supplies of energy at reasonable prices and in ways that do not jeopardize major national values and objectives."[1] This includes, first, energy availability: the confirmed location and accessibility of the energy reserves – especially the fossil fuels – including petroleum, natural gas, and coal – required by an early twenty-first-century nation to satisfy its economic demands. Second is affordability: the fuel so delineated must be available at a cost aceptable to the consuming nation. Third is the military aspect, the focus of this essay: a nation must be able safely and confidently to obtain and import the required energy supplies. These three elements of energy security are not completely discrete, but are linked by common geographical, geological, economic, political, and military factors.

Two major developments have been part of China's emergence as a global power: dramatically increasing energy demand and naval modernization. Its economy is in the midst of history's longest period of double-digit annual economic growth, which in turn is raising its demand for energy. At the same time, Beijing is modernizing its military to carry out specific national security missions. These economic and military developments will to a large extent determine the current and future degree of security China expects and will demand for energy supplies. These developments are affected by the U.S.A.'s ubiquitous maritime presence in Asia and dominance as a consumer in global energy markets; Beijing is also very much aware of the American role in the energy calculus.

Geography and energy security

China has been a continental power throughout its history, but the country's 11,000 miles of coastline and more than 5,000 islands make it a maritime nation as well. First, China relies on its extensive river network for communication, commerce, and energy production. The Yangtze River is particularly important, bisecting the country with its 6,300 kilometer (km) length, more than 700 tributaries, and draining a basin of 1.8 million km that contains one-third of China's population. Harnessing the hydroelectric power potential of this vast river network is an important part of China's energy plan. Best known is the Three Gorges Dam project, the most extensive hydroelectric project in history, in terms of both geographical reach and production potential. China also is building other large dams to take advantage of its riverine resources, estimating its hydroelectric reserves at 40 percent of the country's total conventional energy sources.[2]

Second, coastal waters provide China with critical maritime highways, as do the regional waters of East Asia, the third maritime category. These seas are important sources of food, minerals, transportation, and defense. They are international bodies of water, linking China to friends and opponents. Hence, any evaluation of East Asian military balances must include the linkages between China and Russia, Korea, Japan, and the nations of Southeast Asia. And the U.S.A., by virtue of its omnipresent naval and air forces throughout the Pacific Ocean and adjacent seas, is linked directly to maritime China.

Finally, the oceans of the world are increasingly vital to China's continued economic growth and national well-being, especially under the aegis of "comprehensive national power" and "peaceful rise" so frequently trumpeted by Beijing. All these maritime areas are connected, of course, but they are characterized by different conditions and pose different problems for China's civilian and military leaders. Riverine issues are in the main domestic, although international complications arise from rivers with international borders or whose management affects other nations. The Amur, bordered by China and Russia, is an example of the first; the Mekong (called the Lancang by China) marks the second case. This river's headwaters are in southwestern China, but its course through Southeast Asia gives most of the nations of that region – Myanmar, Vietnam, Laos, Thailand, Cambodia – an intense interest in Beijing's attempts to harness the upper reaches of the Mekong for generating hydroelectric power. These are already reducing the river's flow downstream where it is a vital resource.[3] The Southeast Asian nations' concerns could provide a point of leverage for the U.S.A. to counter China's increasing influence in the region.

Coastal waters, those lying within 100 nautical miles (nm) of China's shore, are in part sovereign, in part international, and marked by the thousands of islands belonging to or claimed by China.[4] Of particular note are the islands disputed with Japan, Taiwan, and Vietnam. These waters are trafficked by ocean-going vessels making or leaving port, of course, but also serve hundreds of thousands of fishing boats, ferries, and coastal commercial craft, including energy carriers. Coastal waters are also the most sensitive from a naval viewpoint, since their control is absolutely necessary for China to maintain national sovereignty, economic autonomy, and security. China's vital maritime arena includes the Yellow, East, and South China Seas, which define the region from Japan and the Korean Peninsula in the north to the Strait of Malacca in the south. Beijing's interests in these waters by definition pose international issues: including shared maritime boundaries and disputes with North Korea, South Korea, Japan, Vietnam, the Philippines, Brunei, Indonesia, and Malaysia.

The U.S. position on these sovereignty disputes has three tenets. First, the U.S.A. will take no position on ownership of disputed islands or land features, but second, urges all disputants to resolve the issue peacefully. Third, if, however, any claimant attempts in the course of enforcing sovereignty to restrict freedom of navigation, the U.S.A. will intervene to ensure the sanctity of that principle. The obvious exception to this three-step policy is the status of Taiwan, which the U.S.A. insists be resolved peacefully.

Beijing is increasingly concerned about the global oceans, since they are necessary for continued economic growth, consolidation of its status as a world power, and the continued legitimacy of the Chinese Communist Party (CCP) regime. China already deploys the world's second largest merchant marine, trailing only Panama's "flag of convenience" fleet.[5] China's shipbuilding industry is also among the world's most robust, with the largest shipyard in history under construction in the Shanghai estuary. This city is also the principal container port for Northeast Asia, and the third largest in the world. Its maritime importance to China is matched by Hong Kong, which is the maritime doorway to the southern half of China, and the world's busiest container port. In fact, seven of the world's largest container ports are in China.

Beijing's White Paper, "China's National Defense in 2006," focuses on basic changes to the PLA that follow trend lines adumbrated in the 2004 Defense White Paper. Navy organization remains based on three fleets – North, East, and South Sea fleets – but reports continuation of the significant changes begun following the 2003 loss of the *Ming* submarine. These focus on streamlining and clarifying the organization and chain of command for maintenance and logistics responsibilities; the 2006 White Paper reemphasizes these processes and further highlights the reduction in headquarters personnel. While the PLAN has reportedly "cut some ship groups ... the naval aviation department and converted naval bases into support ones," this process does not reflect a lessening of the PLAN's importance to China's leadership. Rather it results from Beijing's determination to increase the power and usefulness of the navy as an instrument of national statecraft. This is strongly reflected in the paper's noting that the navy remains unaffected by reductions in PLA manpower.

Taiwan continues to head the list of China's security concerns, and hence the PLAN's primary concern. China's *2006 White Paper on National Defense* directly addresses the importance of national security interests in the coastal and regional maritime areas, emphasizing the strategy of "active defense."[6] The defense of national sovereignty, territorial integrity, and "maritime rights and interest" were all named in this White Paper as "national security goals." These maritime interests include energy resources, both proven and estimated, that are of vital importance to China. The White Paper notes the "priority [of] the building of the Navy, Air Force and Second Artillery force," while PLAN strategists view the American presence in Japan, Taiwan, and the Philippines as forming a "blockade" of China's legitimate maritime security interests. "Active Defense" remains the strategic coda, supported by the need to improve capabilities in "joint operations and integrated maritime support," particularly in coastal waters. The White Paper repeatedly emphasizes the importance of "science and technology" and "informationization" as the key guide posts for naval modernization. A naval role in nuclear deterrence is noted, probably reflecting the national investment in the new *Jin*-class ballistic missile submarines currently under construction.

The 2006 White Paper repeats earlier statements about improvements to China's naval reserve and militia forces, as it does to the continuing codification of military laws. The paper also emphasizes the maritime laws that follow the U.N. Convention on the Law of the Sea (UNCLOS), reflecting Beijing's continuing concerns with maritime sovereignty disputes in the East and South China Seas. In the near term, Beijing's efforts to build a navy able to satisfy maritime security concerns focus on Taiwan; in the mid-term, they include the disputes with Japan over natural gas deposits in the East China Seabed and with the claimants to South China Sea territories. Beijing and Tokyo concluded their fourth round of talks about the East China sea dispute in late 2006, still without reaching a settlement. Both sides remain intransigent, insisting on a broad interpretation of sovereignty in the area.[7]

China has signed two significant diplomatic instruments with respect to disputes in the South China Sea. In 2002, Beijing and the other claimants to South China Sea land features agreed in a written concordat to resolve their claims peacefully; in March 2005, China, the Philippines, and Vietnam signed an agreement to conduct joint seismic petroleum surveys in disputed areas of the South China Sea. The effort is estimated to last three years and cost $15 million.[8]

Energy sector vulnerabilities

Longer-term maritime security interests are particularly important to China's energy future, reaching beyond Taiwan and East Asian sovereignty issues. Future concerns focus on the long sea lines of communications (SLOCs) on which China depends for petroleum imports from Southwest Asia. The U.S. Navy currently guarantees the security of these long SLOCs, but their future remains central to Chinese strategic thought.

Beijing faces two major problems in securing the energy supplies it needs to sustain economic growth and societal tranquility: locating and procuring those supplies, and then distributing them throughout the enormous Chinese hinterland. Distribution issues are particularly critical for the coal on which China is dependent as a source for approximately 65–70 percent of its energy production.[9] Regional imbalances within China between coal supply and demand require transporting large quantities of the mineral, generally from northern areas to the south and east by rail, augmented by riverine and coastal carriers. In fact, coal accounts for a larger percentage of freight than any other commodity in China. More than 50 percent of the coal is shipped by rail, and 60 percent of rail transport is tied up in transporting coal. The inadequacy of the rail system was underlined by an April 2006 complaint by the vice-president of China's Coal Industry Association that "the biggest hurdle" in developing huge reserves in Xinjiang Province was "transportation – we just cannot get the coal out of there cheaply."[10] China is also an important participant in the international coal exporting market, providing 24 percent of all Asian coal imports in 2003. These exports of course go by sea, primarily to Japan and South Korea. Japan also has become a partner in the industry, providing loans for improved mining technology, and for improved rail transport.[11]

China's economy is growing faster than its available energy supply, a phenomenon exacerbated by declining domestic petroleum production. In 2003, the nation surpassed Japan to become the world's second largest oil consumer, behind the U.S.A.

Indeed, *per capita* oil use in China currently is nearly 30 times less than that in the U.S.A., which indicates the range of possible growth.[12] The Chinese Academy of Geological Sciences has estimated the national demand for oil in 2020 as 700 million tons, while domestic production will not exceed 200 million tons.[13] The nation still has unexploited reserves, both proven and estimated, but these amount to just 2.3 percent of the world's total, and will be inadequate for China's energy needs. Approximately 90 percent of China's oil production capacity is located onshore. One complex alone, the Daqing fields in Heilongjiang Province, accounts for a third of that production, 1 million barrels (bbl) per day of China's total crude production of 3.2 million bbl per day. Daqing is a mature field, however, and is expected to show a declining output in future years.[14]

China's oil consumption grew by 42 percent between 2001 and 2005, while production went up 25 percent.[15] This disparity between domestic production and consumption indicates how fast China's energy demands will almost certainly continue to grow, as disposable income increases and WTO membership results in lower automobile prices for the huge population. China's energy production-consumption equation is further unbalanced by the inefficiency that is endemic in the petroleum industry; most Chinese refineries operate at financial losses usually hidden by state ownership. For instance, the estimated cost per barrel of Chinese refining is $1.50; the cost for Western refineries is $1.20. Similarly, natural gas exploration costs for Chinese firms are $3.90; that for Western firms is $3.00.[16] Additionally, since the U.S.A. has not adopted meaningful energy consumption reduction measures since the 1970s (indeed, the restrictions instituted following the 1973 oil shock have been relaxed), American petroleum consumption will continue to rise and continue as a direct competitor to Chinese requirements.

Natural gas has not been a major fuel in China, but offers a cleaner alternative to coal and could relieve reliance on imported oil. Gas currently accounts for less than 3 percent of total energy usage in China, however, compared to a world average of 24 percent and an Asia-wide average of 8.8 percent. Beijing is trying to boost its production and consumption, but with little success to date.

Beijing wants gas to provide 8 to 10 percent of the nation's total energy consumption by 2020.[17] This will increase the reliance on imports, either by pipeline or in the form of liquefied natural gas (LNG). The import issue is complicated by the fact that in its natural form, gas can be piped only a limited distance without being liquefied. Furthermore, for liquefaction to be economical, the gas deposit must be 3 to 5 trillion cubic meters (tcm) in size. This has possible surprising international political implications, since liquefication plants need to be located near the source of the natural gas. Hence, cooperative relations will be needed between China and the nations of Southeast Asia, the location of extensive natural gas resources.

Natural gas demands also exceed domestic supplies, and this is another energy resource China has to import to benefit fully from its advantages.[18] Natural gas is being sought in the form of liquefied natural gas from overseas sources. Beijing's plans for domestic pipeline construction are very ambitious, and are necessary to increase the efficient energy distribution. More than a half-dozen major pipeline projects have been built, are under construction, or are in the planning stage, all involving foreign investment and/or technical assistance.[19] These are intended both to facilitate the distribution of oil and natural gas within China, primarily bringing oil and natural gas from western and northern sources across the country to Shanghai and the rest of economically expanding eastern China, and to increase the availability of foreign sources.

Three major issues hinder domestic and international pipeline projects, exemplified by Moscow's plans to construct a pipeline from Siberia to China and or the Sea of Okhotsk coast. First is to fund and to actually build it. Both Tokyo and Beijing have made multi-billion dollar offers to Moscow for the Siberian project, but solving the technical complexity of the proposed pipeline project remains a work in progress; hence, cost estimates are not precise. Nonetheless, China is looking to Russia as a major source of future energy resources.

Second is the recoverability of sufficient petroleum for the Siberian project to make the pipeline profitable. This factor is related directly to the distance and the complexity of the geographical environment through which pipeline routing options pass. The potential market is another factor affecting pipeline routing. In the case of Siberian reserves, China's huge population and continuing, unprecedented economic growth offer far more potential than Japan's graying population and inconsistent economic performance since the early 1990s. But routing Siberian resources to the Sea of Japan would make them more readily available for export to the entire Pacific basin, including the apparently insatiable U.S. energy market. Washington presumably would prefer that Beijing not have direct access to the "on-off" switch for Siberian resources.

A third concern about pipeline viability is the apparent lack of planning at the national level to de-conflict natural gas piped from the far west with that being imported from Indonesia, Papua New Guinea, and Australia. In other words, the key to maximizing efficient energy utilization in China may be as much a problem of prioritization and distribution of known resources as much as it is one of locating new supplies.

There is no doubt about Beijing's deliberate, well-funded global effort to locate and secure energy supplies, an effort dependent on being able to use long SLOCs. Furthermore, China is already concerned about its reliance on Middle Eastern sources, which provide at least 60 percent of China's imported oil. This heightens Beijing's strategic interest in an area of key concern to Washington, posing a competitive situation with naval as well as economic aspects. Barring a currently unforeseen domestic bonanza, foreign sources will likely remain China's only option for increasing petroleum supplies. To this end, Beijing has made recent investments in exploration and production in Southeast, Southwest, and Central Asia (including the Caspian Basin); North and South America; the Middle East; and Africa.

China is making an extensive effort to include the energy sector in its "strategic partnership" with Moscow, as well as with Russia's former republics in Central Asia. Extensive programs have been launched in Kazakhstan, for instance, with whom Beijing has signed agreements and contracts and from whom it has purchased a small amount of oil. Significant shipments of oil to China from the central Asian nation remain, and may soon start flowing, but past reports of progress have been problematical. With respect to Siberian reserves, China wants Russia to build the pipeline either directly across their common border to Daqing, rather than to the coastal port of Nakodka. Despite the economic and technical factors affecting the selection of a route for a Siberian pipeline, Moscow's final decision will most likely reflect political rather than economic factors. The current state of good relations between Russia and China is unprecedented in length, and historical factors of mistrust and fears may reasonably be expected to cool the relationship to the point where Moscow would simply be too uncomfortable with a routing that placed control of the pipeline terminus in Chinese hands.

Indeed, in early March 2006, Beijing expressed its dissatisfaction "with the development of energy cooperation with Russia," based largely on the lack of progress in selecting a route for the Siberian pipeline. Zhang Guobao, deputy director of the Chinese National Development and Reform Commission, stated that while "Russia has undertaken various oral obligations," there "has been no practical progress."[20] Russia, however, has pointed out that while the Resolution of the Russian Government #1737 of 31 December, 2004, demonstrates "the political will of the Russian Government to take specific steps in the development of the Eastern direction of the Russian oil exports," the decision about the "Far East Pipeline ... still remains tentative and leaves far too many uncertainties," some of which are credited to "the Chinese factor still remain[ing] a mystery."[21] The most likely outcome is for the pipeline to be built to Nakhodka, with a spur constructed to Daqing or some other Chinese terminal. U.S. strategists should take satisfaction in the lack of agreement between Moscow and Beijing.

China is pursuing oil and natural gas reserves wherever located, around the world. This has led to many investments considered inefficient by global energy companies, but the relatively closed nature of the economy, especially the state controlled energy sector, is allowing Beijing to pursue a very active acquisition policy.

Defense of the energy sector

China also is seeking to emulate the U.S.A. by establishing a strategic reserve of petroleum supplies (90 days' worth, in Beijing's case) to counter fluctuations in the international oil market. The first of four approved petroleum reserve installations is under construction near Shanghai, with others to be built along China's coast. Two reserves are planned for Zhejiang and Shandong Provinces, with the fourth in the northeastern province of Liaoning. Guangdong Province officials are also campaigning for such facilities, to "ensure the economic security of the [Pearl River] delta."[22] The nonmilitary character of these strategic reserves is evidenced in their planned construction as above-ground tank farms near China's vulnerable coastline, and supports the conclusion that Beijing's interest in securing energy supplies springs primarily from an economic rather than military rationale.

People's Liberation Army (PLA)

Although China has been a net energy importer for more than a decade, the country retains more than adequate supplies to meet all conceivable PLA missions to defend Chinese vital national security interests. The PLA thus can count on China's indigenous petroleum supplies to fuel its platforms; another resource for the PLA is nuclear power, already used in six operating and three under-construction submarines.

But the military is deeply involved in the nation's hunger for nondomestic energy resources, specifically assigned a role in modernizing and expanding China's energy infrastructure. Beijing's 2002 Defense White Paper notes PLA participation in "the construction of nine energy facilities such as pipelines, natural gas fields and oil-and-gas fields; the construction of seven hydropower stations and nineteen trunk diversion channels [and for] the protection and construction of the ecological environment." The PLA is also tasked with countering possible threats to domestic sources. The White Paper notes that the military is responsible for "maintaining and promoting social stability and harmony," to include "cracking down on all criminal activities that threaten public order."[23] Beijing typically classifies as "threats to public order" incidents of labor unrest and other similar activities, which means that the People's Armed Police (PAP) and the PLA are primary instruments of government control as the energy infrastructure undergoes the sometimes traumatic effects of privatization and modernization.

The military is especially concerned, of course, about possibly violent threats to power sources and pipelines. Some steps have been taken to protect domestic energy facilities against organized attack, although defensive measures appear limited to those by local police and PAP units and those attendant to routine defense plans of Military Region staffs. For instance, in mid-2001, the State Council promulgated revised Regulations for Protecting Oil and Natural Gas Pipelines, a measure intended to defend against "seizing, sabotaging, stealing, and looting pipelines and facilities."[24] The PLA will continue to serve as the "police force" of last resort, should civilian and PAP authorities require assistance. The Central Asian member-states of the Shanghai Cooperative Organization represent one of Beijing's most significant efforts at multilateralism and delineate the theater most likely to demand PLA missions in the realm of protecting continental energy resources. Xinjiang's energy resource infrastructure, including the Tarim Basin fields, conceivably is a target of Uighur separtists.

Beijing has built more than a half-dozen major pipeline projects; others are under construction or being planned. As demonstrated by T.E. Lawrence in the Middle East during World War I and currently by the Ejército de Liberación Nacional (ELN) in Colombia, pipelines can be difficult to protect. The PLA is directly involved in China's search for energy security through its mission of securing SLOCs and ocean bed energy fields, with the U.S.A. viewed as the most likely threat. However, even the U.S. military would find it difficult to interrupt China's SLOCs over which international energy flows, but they appear vulnerable to PLAN eyes. Should the U.S.A. attempt physically to interrupt either SLOCs or overland pipelines, it would almost certainly mean directly attacking China, directly attacking other nations' hosting pipelines and their pumping stations, interfering with the peacetime passage of third-country tankers at sea, or all of the above.

Petroleum imports from Southeast Asia and the Middle East, including the Persian Gulf, do face a long seaborne transit. And the Gulf is the source of 60 percent of China's imported oil, while most of its imported natural gas comes from Southeast Asia.[25] The SLOCs are most vulnerable not on the high seas, but at narrow straits, including Hormuz, the 9-Degree Channel, Malacca, Luzon, and Taiwan. The most likely tactic for the U.S.A. to employ would be a blockade of Chinese oil port terminals, or of these chokepoints. Even these steps would not significantly reduce China's overall energy supply.

Beijing's decision-making process about using the PLAN to ensure energy security includes several factors. First, how secure does the CCP leadership feel about their place in power in Beijing? Second, how willing is the Chinese leadership to rely on the world energy market to ensure the affordability, availability, and safe passage of imported supplies? Third, how confident is the leadership about U.S. peaceful intentions, possibly in the face of contentious Chinese actions, such as increasing military pressure against Taiwan? Finally, how much confidence does the leadership have in PLAN capabilities?

The U.S. Navy will protect these SLOCs for the foreseeable future, but a Sino-American crisis (over Taiwan for instance) might lead Beijing to decide that the PLAN has to be able to defend these SLOCs. This would require Beijing to make a major change in national budgeting priorities to build a navy and air force capable of protecting the extended SLOCs to the Middle East. This decision would have to override other serious concerns. First, Beijing's national priorities continue to fall under the rubric of "rich country, strong army": Developing China's economy and ensuring the welfare of its people remains the government's and the CCP's top priority. Second, while Taiwan remains the most sensitive issue between Beijing and Washington, the present economic and political situation on the island, U.S. and Chinese interest in keeping the issue within peaceful bounds, and common interest in the campaign against terrorism, all mitigate against the reunification issue deteriorating to the point of hostilities. Third, there is little indication that the Chinese military's strategic paradigm is going to change significantly in the near future. The PLA remains dominated by the army, with the navy only as strong as specific maritime-associated national interests justify. Current PLAN modernization seems fueled by increased national revenues rather than by a reordering of budgeting priorities within the PLA.

People's Liberation Army – Navy (PLAN) modernization

China's navy has been modernizing since its inception in 1950, but this process intensified during the 1980s and especially after the 1996 Taiwan Strait crisis. However, naval modernization has not been balanced. Despite observing the effective use of American naval airpower in 1996, the PLAN's aviation force remains restricted to shore-based fixed wing aircraft, with only limited numbers of helicopters operating from shipboard. The former assets consist mostly of fighter and bomber aircraft, although some longer-range aircraft capable of launching anti-ship cruise missiles are maintained. Chinese naval aviation is notably deficient in anti-submarine warfare (ASW) and long-range search aircraft; its airborne electronic warfare (EW) capability is also weak.

The PLAN's helicopter force is small but growing in capability and numbers. Especially significant has been recent at-sea exercises demonstrating the navy's emphasis on operations between ships and aircraft, both fixed- and rotary-wing. PLAN combatants also have finally achieved the capability of data-linking with embarked helos.[26] The Chinese navy currently includes fewer than 20 warships capable of operating in the twenty-first-century naval environment. And these ships – 4 *Sovremenny*-class, 1 *Luhai*-class, 2 *Luhu*-class guided-missile destroyers (DDGs), and approximately 12 *Jiangwei*-class guided-missile frigates – are equipped with very limited anti-air warfare (AAW) systems. The U.S. Navy, by contrast, deploys more than 50 ships equipped with the Aegis AAW system, the most advanced in the world. Another 40 or so Chinese surface combatants are armed with anti-surface ship cruise missiles and, in a nonair threat environment, could perform SLOC defense duties in Chinese littoral waters. The PLAN ability to deploy at extended ranges is also limited by an inventory of only five replenishment-at-sea ships. Again, by contrast the U.S. Navy operates more than 30 such ships.

PLAN surface forces are improving at a steady pace, however, both in terms of capabilities and numbers. Older destroyers and frigates are being replaced at a measured pace by newer, near state-of-the-art combatants. The most recent classes appear to include ships equipped with an area-capable AAW system, which would be a very significant advance for the PLAN, hitherto incapable of operating safely in a hostile air threat environment. The navy's most potent strength lies in its numerous, modernizing submarine force. The five nuclear-powered *Han*-class attack submarines (SSN) are capable of extended deployments but are noisy and difficult to maintain. The nuclear-powered submarine force will soon improve as the new Type 093-class SSN becomes operational. With the advent late in this decade of the Type 094-class fleet ballistic missile submarines (FBM), China will for the first time deploy a dependable maritime nuclear deterrent force.

The PLAN already deploys the world's most impressive, improving force of conventionally powered submarines. The 12 *Kilo*-class and 12–15 *Song*-class conventionally powered attack boats are not well suited for long-range deployments (to the Indian Ocean, for example) but are formidable weapons systems within approximately 1,000 miles of China's coast. The new *Yuan*-class boat unveiled in the summer of 2004 appears to incorporate Russian *Amur*-class characteristics and may become a platform for installation of air-independent-propulsion (AIP). As Beijing continues to build *Songs* and buy *Kilos* from Russia, the 30 or 40 older *Ming*- and *Romeo*-class boats will probably be decommissioned. By contrast, the U.S.A. deploys only nuclear-powered submarines, including approximately 50 attack boats and 18 subs equipped with either ICBMs or land attack cruise missiles. This decision reflects superior U.S. nuclear propulsion technology and the great distances over which the U.S. submarine force has to operate. China is following another U.S. example by employing its navy as a diplomatic instrument. Since 1983, the PLAN has periodically deployed two- or three-ship task forces on diplomatic missions to Southeast, South, and Southwest Asia and to the Western Hemisphere. In 2002, a *Luhu*-class DDG and an oiler completed a circumnavigation of the globe, a significant accomplishment. Another task force visited the U.S.A. in 2006.

Defense of China's economic offshore infrastructure is a prominent PLAN concern; the South China Sea would become an area of primary operations should significant energy resources be discovered in waters claimed by Beijing in that sea. PLAN forces have regularly been deployed to the South China Sea's Paracel Islands since the early 1970s and to the Spratly Islands since the early 1980s, with a military presence on more than a half-dozen of the islands. The PLAN presently is capable only of defending littoral SLOCs (those lying no more than 200 nm from China's coast), however, and even that capability is limited by the proven difficulty of defending surface ships against submarine attack.

China describes its maritime strategy as "offshore defense," requiring the PLAN to "maintain control over the maritime traffic in the coastal waters of the mainland" and the resources in those waters.[27] This area is not well defined, and a more useful approach is to look at specific missions and sea lines. This still delineates formidable ocean areas for the PLAN to defend: all of the South China Sea, the western half of the East China Sea, the waters extending from the

Chinese coast to at least 100 nm east of Taiwan along a line from the Philippines to Japan, and all of the Yellow Sea. Continued constructive relations with the nations of Southeast Asia should relieve Beijing of concern for commanding the narrow Malacca Strait. Defense of more distant SLOCs, from that strait between the South China Sea and the Indian Ocean, to the Hormuz Strait between that ocean and the Persian Gulf, would require a quantum leap in PLAN capabilities. Conceivably, however, China could choose to deploy PLAN units as part of a multinational force in those distant waters.

SLOC defense

The dramatic rise in pirate attacks in Southeast Asian waters concerns all Asian nations; these attacks caused an estimated annual loss of $25 billion in 2004. While a multinational effort is under way to combat these attacks, China verbally supports this campaign but is not participating directly in the anti-piracy center established in Kuala Lumpur by ASEAN.[28]

West of Malacca, across the vast Indian Ocean distances, China faces a wary India with its own formidable navy. Beijing maintains a close relationship with India's long-time enemy, Pakistan, whose navy receives strong support from China. Islamabad's force of seven modern conventionally powered submarines is augmented by eight frigates – none of them new, but most armed with guided missiles – and two replenishment-at-sea oilers. China is also helping Pakistan build a deepwater port at Gwadar, nominally for commercial traffic. This port, however is located in Balochistan, perhaps Pakistan's least stable province. And its usefulness as a terminus for pipelines from Iran or the Caspian Basin may be constrained by the extremely difficult terrain through which a pipeline would have to pass. Furthermore, Islamabad has consistently come out second best in wars with New Delhi, and the advent of the two nations as nuclear powers casts future contests in a different light, especially as India's nuclear arsenal forms its only way of effectively threatening China.

Beijing has established a maritime presence in the Indian Ocean and no doubt hopes it will be able to count on the Pakistani navy in a regional contest. China also has established a strategic economic and military relationship with Myanmar by providing advisers and material assistance. The Chinese military and contractor personnel in that country – involved in projects ranging from road-building in the far north to manning listening stations in the Andaman Sea – represent the first Chinese military presence on foreign soil since the Vietnam War, other than PLA participation in U.N. peacekeeping missions.

Beijing's policy in Myanmar is motivated by several factors. First is concern for their common border, rife with drug traffickers and other smugglers, and at one time a refuge for former Nationalist soldiers. Second are the economic advantages China is gaining from near-domination of Myanmar's international commerce. Energy is a potentially important element in this commerce, evidenced in the modernization of the old Myanmar Road into a modern eight-lane highway, and the recent announcement of construction of a petroleum pipeline from the Burmese coast all the way to China's Yunnan Province. When completed, this pipeline will relieve dependence on the Malacca Strait transit. Third is the desire to counter Indian influence in the region – important because of its location between the subcontinent and Southeast Asia, an area to which Beijing is devoting increasing political and economic resources. Fourth is concern for the Indian Ocean SLOCs on which China depends for so much of its energy imports. India is trying to establish a stronger political and naval presence east of Malacca, evidenced in New Delhi's increased attention to ASEAN and the 2001 deployments by the Indian Navy to East Asia, from Singapore to Japan. This development, combined with improving Indian naval strength in the Indian Ocean, poses a classic problem in maritime strategy for Beijing: Its most important source of petroleum imports, the Persian Gulf area, lies at the end of very long SLOCs that are dominated by another nation's navy.

The Indian Navy continues to modernize and expand. It currently includes an aircraft carrier and at least 17 conventionally powered submarines, with several newer models under construction. The navy surface force centers around eight DDGs, perhaps 15 older destroyers and frigates, and three replenishment-at-sea ships. More importantly, India has funded an ambitious plan to modernize its navy, from new aircraft carriers to submarines. The Indian force does not outnumber China's, but PLAN presence in that distant region is limited by the distances involved and its lack of maritime airpower. How will China address the problem of Indian Ocean SLOCs? Beijing apparently has decided not to build a navy capable of patrolling these long SLOCs to the Middle East. Instead, Beijing is forming supportive relationships with the nations bordering those routes, from Vietnam and the Philippines to Saudi Arabia.

Given China's significant draw on Middle Eastern-Southwest Asian oil, a prolonged war in that region might seriously disrupt the outflow of petroleum products. To forestall that eventuality, Beijing is engaging in diplomatic activity both to signal its interest in the welfare of the Arab states and to offer mediation services in the Israeli–Palestinian conflict. This activity backs up and possibly extends Beijing's activities with petroleum companies in the region, including investments or extraction activities in Iran, Iraq, Kuwait, Saudi Arabia, Egypt, Sudan, and Somalia.

Unrest in Southeast Asia also has the potential to disrupt the maritime oil flow to China. The political situation in that region is so fractured, however, as to make effective multilateral action against freedom of navigation extremely unlikely. Even if the Malacca Strait–South China Sea route was interrupted, oil could be shipped via alternate routes at an acceptable increase in cost. These options include rerouting tankers through other straits in the Indonesian archipelago or completely around Australia. Other alternatives – in addition to the Myanmar–Yunnan pipeline – currently being discussed include building a canal or pipeline across the Kra Isthmus, a pipeline north through Thailand to China.

Conclusion

China's leaders view energy issues and maritime interests as vital elements in their nation's economic health and their own political legitimacy. The PLAN is tasked with energy security as a mission, but China's concern for the security of its overseas energy supplies does not dominate its national security policy process. The most important aspects of energy security for Beijing are economic and political, not military. In his March 2006 report to the People's Congress, for instance, Vice-Premier Zeng Peiyan listed five "problems in the energy sector," but included neither military threats nor security concerns.[29]

While China currently imports approximately 45 percent of its oil, this is only slightly more than 6 percent of its national energy needs.[30] The chairman of the China National Offshore Oil Corporation (CNOOC) has stated flatly that "China's oil demand will remain fairly stable" and will not expand as some analysts have predicted.[31] Furthermore, China has codified the world's most stringent automobile efficiency standards and announced "a sharp tax increase on big cars and a matching reduction for smaller models"; additionally, Beijing's State Council Energy Leading group has delineated an "oil alternative strategy," which prioritizes gas over oil, coal over either, and renewable energy (hydro, wind, solar, biomass, nuclear) over fossil fuels.[32]

Beijing is also concerned about growing reliance on foreign ships for petroleum carriage. Speaking at a January 2004 energy industry conference, Zhang Guofa, deputy director of China's Water Transport Department, of the Ministry of Communications, noted that while 90 percent of China's crude oil imports came by sea, only 10 percent is transported by Chinese flagged carriers. Other conference speakers noted that the present 50 million tons of oil imported by sea in 2003 was estimated to grow to 75 million tons by 2010 and to 130 million tons by 2020. Current Chinese tanker capacity of 5.2 million tons was targeted to grow to 10 million tons in the near term, but that would still be far too inadequate to reduce the risk of China getting "in trouble once emergencies such as wars occur."[33]

Perhaps most significantly, coal will almost certainly remain the source of at least 65–70 percent of China's total energy requirements for the foreseeable future. That dependence poses problems of inefficiencies and environmental deficiencies, but these are amenable to technical solutions and do not detract from the very considerable "comfort blanket" provided to China by its huge coal reserves, third largest in the world.

The maritime dispute with Japan may pose the most serious risk of possible armed conflict between the two nations' navies, despite the relatively modest amounts of energy resources contained in the disputed Chunxiao natural gas field. But almost certainly, any clash would be brief and quickly resolved by Tokyo and Beijing. The South China Sea is potentially contentious because of the number of claimants to the bits and pieces of land that dot that body of water. Little chance of armed conflict presently exists, however, since no significant energy reserves have been found in the disputed central areas of the

Sea. In fact, China, the Philippines, and Vietnam have signed an agreement to jointly explore the area.

There are two certainties in assessing the military element in energy security for China. First, Beijing is building and deploying a new navy; second, China is dependent on imported energy supplies to maintain its growing economy, which in turn is necessary to maintain societal cohesion and the CCP in power. These two facts and Beijing's concerns about potential U.S. interference do not, however, necessarily mean that future energy security concerns will lead to armed conflict with the U.S.A.

Notes

1 Daniel Yergin, "Energy Security in the 1990s," *Foreign Affairs*, vol. 67, no. 1, Fall 1988, p. 11.
2 Zhang Guobao [vice-minister, State Development and Reform Commission], quoted in "Hydroelectric Power Accounts for 40% of Conventional Energy," *Xinhua*, October 27, 2004, at: http:www.chinadaily.com.cn/English/doc/2004–10/27/content_386292.htm
3 Chen Liang, "For China, Xiaowang Dam a Reservoir for Progress," at http://www.ipsnews.net/mekong/stories/xiaowan.html
4 One nautical mile equals approximately 1.2 statute miles. Maritime sovereignty is defined by the 1982 United Nations Convention on the Law of the Sea (UNCLOS), which has been accepted – if not formally signed and ratified – by almost all the world's nations with coastlines. Briefly, it delineates four primary areas of national maritime control: (a) the Territorial Sea extends from a nation's coastline 12 nm seaward and gives sovereign rights over the sea, airspace above it, seabed, and subsoil; (b) the Contiguous Zone (CZ) extends from a nation's coastline 24 nm seaward and gives the control to prevent and punish infringement of its customs, fiscal, immigration or sanitary laws, and regulations within its territory or territorial sea; (c) the Exclusive Economic Zone (EEZ) extends to a maximum of 200 nm from a nation's coastline and gives sovereign rights with respect to natural resources and certain economic activities, and exercise jurisdiction over marine science research and environmental protection; d) the Continental Shelf (the national area of the seabed) may be claimed out to a maximum distance of 350 nm from a nation's coastline and gives sovereign rights for exploring and exploiting the seabed.
5 *CIA World Factbook*, at http://www.cia.gov/cia/publications/factbook/rankorder/2108rank.html
6 China's previous defense White Papers may be found at http://www.china.org.cn/e-white/index.htm; the 2006 iteration is at "Full Text: China's National Defense in 2006," *Xinhua* (Beijing), December 29, 2006, in FBIS-CPP2006122968070.
7 Rich Chapman, "Japan–China: Disputed Gas Talks Have Familiar Ending – A Special Press Summary," U.S. Pacific Command's Virtual Intelligence Center (referred hereafter as "*VIC Site*"): at www.vic-info.org/RegionsTop.nsf/ce7a71ce 2912c7330a25707c0065b5f9/2d5cf58d253ee2bfoa257131000177a3?, March 13 2006.
8 The 2002 "Declaration on the Conduct of Parties in the South China Sea" falls short of the legally binding "code of conduct" desired by the other signatories. The 2004 Tripartite Agreement is described at: http://www.china.org.cn/english/2005/Mar/122853.htm
9 The U.S. Department of Energy cited the 65 percent figure in August 2005, but also noted the uncertainty of the data: http://www.eia.doe.gov/emeu/cabs/china.html

10 Zhu Deren, quoted in "Shuenhua to Develop Xinjiang Coal Mines," *China Daily*, Beijing, April 12, 2006, p. 10.

11 See "Japan to Help China Liquefy Coal as Oil Alternative," *AFP*, April 14, 2006, in *Alexander's Gas & Oil Connections*, vol. 11, no. 9, May 4, 2006, at: www.gasandoil.com.

12 Robert A. Manning, *The Asian Energy Factor: Myths and Dilemmas of Energy, Security, and the Pacific Future*, New York: Palgrave, 2000, p. 104.

13 Cited in Takio Murkami, "China Becomes World-Class Oil Buyer," *Asahi Shimbun* (Tokyo), July 23, 2003, in *Alexander's*, vol. 8, no. 16, August 21 2003.

14 Mai Tian, "Daqing to Cut Oil Production," *China Daily*, "Business" page (September 16, 2003), in FBIS-CPP20030922000015, September 22, 2003, reports that Daqing's production "will be cut by 2 million tons next year, after its output went below 50 million tons this year for the first time in two decades," and "may further drop by 40 percent to 30 million tons by 2010."

15 DOE, EIA: Tables 2.4 and E.1, at http://www.eia.doe.gov/emeu/cabs/china.html

16 Cited in Felix Chang, "Chinese Energy and Asian Security," *Orbis*, vol. 45, no. 2, Spring 2001, p. 226.

17 The 8 percent figure is cited in "China's Modernization May Be Slowed Down by Oil Shortage," *People's Daily*, in *Alexander's*, vol. 6, no. 15, August 14, 2001; Mai Tian, "Sinopec, PetroChina Reach Agreement on Pipeline Project," *China Daily*, October 6, 2001, in FBIS-CPP20011006000032, reports the goal as 10 percent.

18 "China to Require Natural Gas Imports From 2005," *Interfax Information Services, B.V.*, January 29, 2003 in *Alexander's*, vol. 8, no. 4, February 20, 2003.

19 Philip Andrews-Speed, et al., *The Strategic Implications of China's Energy Needs*, Adelphi Paper 346, London: International Institute of Strategic Studies, 2002, pp. 35 ff.

20 Quoted in "Beijing Says Not Fully Satisfied with Oil, Gas Cooperation With Russia," *Moscow Interfax*, March 3, 2006, in FBIS-CEP20060303027121.

21 Vladimir Milov (President, Institute of Energy Policy, Moscow), quoted in "The Russian Pacific Oil Pipeline: More Questions Than Answers," *The Northeast Energy Focus*, vol. 2, no. 3, August 2005, p. 1, available online at: www.energypolicy.ru/eanalit.php?printversion=yes&id=1001959.

22 "Guangdong to House Oil Reserve Bases," *People's Daily*, February 28, 2006, at: http://english.people.com.cn/200602/28/eng20060228_246572.html

23 "China's National Defense in 2002 'White Paper,'" December 9, 2002, 34, at http://www.china-embassy.org/eng/38991.html

24 Yang Ron, "Perspective on Hot Spots," *Zhongguo Kongjun*, February 1, 1998, pp. 4–6, in FBIS-FTS20000113001050.

25 Philip Bowring, "Oil-Thirsty Asia Looks to Calm Gulf Waters," *International Herald Tribune*, February 9, 2006, at http://www.iht.com/bin/print_ipub.php?file=/articles/2006/02/08/opinion/edbowring.php

26 Author's discussion with *Jiangwei III*-class frigate Commanding Officer (CO) in May 2006.

27 PLAN Commander (Admiral Shi Yunsheng) quoted in "Jiang Made the Final Decision on Adopting Offshore Defense Strategy," *Tung Fang Jih Pao* (Hong Kong), August 24, 2001, in FBIS-CPP20010824000062.

28 Anthony Davis, "Piracy in Southeast Asia Shows Signs of Increased Organization," *Jane's Intelligence Review*, June 1, 2004.

29 Wenran Jiang, "Beijing's 'New Thinking' on Energy Security," *China Brief: A Journal of Analysis and Information*, vol. VI, no. 8, The Jamestown Foundation: April 12, 2006, p. 2, at: www.jamestown.org

30 Margaret Kriz, "Fueling the Dragon," *National Journal*, August 6, 2005, p. 2512.

31 Fu Chengyu, quoted in Paula Dittrick, "CNOOC Chairman Sees Steady Chinese Oil

Demand," at: http://ogj.pennet.com/articles/article_display.cfm?Section=ONART& C=Genln&ARTICLE_ID=247605&p=7
32 Xiao Fuyu, "Dependence on Oil Needs to be Cut, Says Panel," *China Daily*, February 13, 2006, at http://www.chinadaily.com.cn
33 "China to Increase Oil-Supply Security," *People's Daily* (Beijing). January 1, 2004, at: english.people.com.cn/200401/09print20040109_132208.html

11 The rise of China and Sino-American energy cooperation

June Teufel Dreyer

As oil prices spiked toward US$75 a barrel in the summer of 2005, energy competition seemed poised to replace the war on terrorism as the focus of world attention. The *New York Times* deemed it appropriate to headline its lead story on Chinese president Hu Jintao's April 2006 visit to the U.S.A., "China's Big Need for Oil Is High On U.S. Agenda,"[1] and two Chinese researchers entitled their article, published in *Far Eastern Economic Review* at the same time, "Will China Go To War Over Oil?"[2] A cartoonist portrayed Uncle Sam and a generic Chinese leader of 2020 circling each other menacingly as each prepared to grab the last gallon of oil on Earth. While a Council on Foreign Relations/Baker Institute report observes that in fact the global hydrocarbon resource base remains enormous, it notes the potential for sudden, severe strains at critical links in the energy supply chain.[3]

The impressive growth of the Chinese economy over the past three decades has literally been fueled by energy, and more growth means greater energy demands. In 1985, the People's Republic of China (PRC) was self-sufficient in energy and a net exporter of crude oil. In 1993, with demand growing and domestic production virtually flat, it became a net importer. Ten years later, the PRC became the world's second-largest consumer of petroleum. The same is true for other sources of energy. In 1985, China's share of world energy consumption was relatively modest: 20.2 percent for coal, 3.3 percent for oil, 0.8 percent for natural gas, and 4.2 percent for hydroelectricity. By 2003, the figures had risen to 29.2 percent of world coal consumption, 7.0 percent of oil consumption, 1.4 percent of gas consumption, and 10.5 percent of hydroelectricity consumption.[4] Current estimates are that the PRC's demand for oil will double in the next twenty years and, given a continuation of stagnant domestic production, two-thirds of this will have to be obtained from abroad.

This rapid increase, as well as predictions that the PRC's economy will continue its rapid growth, has caused concerns among other countries about whether energy supplies will be available to them, and at an affordable price, in the future. China's purchases were not solely responsible for the spike in oil prices: Disruptions in oil supply due to instability in producer states and rising demand in other large countries, including India, Brazil, and the U.S.A., were also factors. But it is China's purchases that have attracted the most attention.

In part, this concern exists because Chinese companies have sought to secure oil supplies through buying equity oil, which Chinese firms have a right to take or market as a result of equity ownership in development projects rather than purchasing it on the international market. Potential competitors fear that the PRC intends to sequester supplies through this technique. In an exceptionally blunt speech in September 2005, U.S. Deputy Secretary of State Robert Zoellick accused the PRC of exhibiting increasing signs of mercantilism in seeking to lock up energy supplies and advised its government to take concrete steps to address what he called a cauldron of anxiety in the U.S.A. and other parts of the world about Chinese intentions. The path to energy security, said Zoellick, was not through arousing anxieties.[5]

Unsurprisingly, Zoellick's speech was controversial. It confirmed the suspicions of a number of Chinese analysts that the world's sole superpower was trying to contain the rising power of the PRC in order to maintain its own privileged position, and to prevent their country from becoming the comfortably well-off society [*xiaokang shehui*] envisioned in former president Jiang Zemin's valedictory speech. Some Americans pointed out that the U.S.A. must look like a mercantilist state to the Chinese, given its war against Iraq and close ties with the Saudi monarchy.

In an insecure world, it is understandable that nations are concerned with ensuring energy independence. Simultaneously, however, the world is becoming more energy interdependent. For most countries, energy independence is unrealistic unless new, as yet undiscovered, technologies are developed. This would indicate the wisdom of a policy of energy cooperation rather than energy competition. Yet mutual suspicions make this hard to achieve. In February 2006, an American air force general opined that "confrontation is not inevitable, but it might be possible if China sees it as a pragmatic way of achieving their [sic] ends. Competition over resources, and particularly energy resources, would likely be the number one driver of future conflict in Sino-American relations."[6] And an influential U.S. senator described energy dependence as "the albatross of U.S. national security."[7]

There are also concerns related to human rights: A number of the countries that the PRC has signed energy contracts with have poor to reprehensible records of respecting the dignity and well-being of their citizens. Most prominent among these are the Sudan, Zimbabwe, Venezuela, and Iran. In the case of Iran, there are concerns about nuclear proliferation as well, and even hints that Beijing may have aided Iran's weapons development programs in exchange for oil. The rapidly expanding capabilities of the PRC's armed forces have caused worries that Beijing may resort to aggressive tactics in order to achieve its energy goals.

China's leaders, though less inclined to voice their insecurities publicly, seem to have the same concerns. The country's energy industry is dominated by three state-owned oil companies, all established within the last quarter century. The China National Offshore Oil Corporation, better known as CNOOC, was established in February 1982, followed by the China Petrochemical Corporation, or

Sinopec, in July 1983. These two were joined by the China National Petroleum Corporation, CNPC, in August 1988. Also in that year, as part of a government initiative to separate policy making and supervision from business operations, CNPC was given control over most of the upstream oil producing fields previously managed by the Ministry of Petroleum Industry. The three corporations have become active players, often competing successfully with more established multinational firms in identifying new resources, acquiring drilling rights, and contracting for pipeline construction.

Chinese leaders, however, argue that one reason they must exploit the morality gap by dealing with pariah countries is precisely because the major energy multinationals have eschewed dealings with them: Here, unlike elsewhere, Chinese firms do not have to compete with far more experienced conglomerates. They state that their help to Iran is solely for the purpose of peaceful uses of nuclear energy.[8] As for military expansion, more than half of the PRC's current oil imports travel through the Straits of Malacca, one of the least secure shipping lanes in the world. Should there be a war, those straits could be blockaded. The People's Liberation Army Navy (PLAN) is currently unable to defend against the blockade, but must be able to do so to protect the nation's economic lifeline.

Cooperation

While concern with energy independence and sovereign rights are understandable, they also enhance the possibilities of conflict. In a major address to the Council on Foreign Relations in November 2005, Senator Joseph Lieberman posed the issue as a stark choice between cooperation and collision. He likened Sino-American energy engagement to a twenty-first-century version of what arms control negotiations with the Soviet Union were in the last century, but cautioned that it would be necessary to start discussions with China before the race for oil became as hot and dangerous as the nuclear arms race between the U.S.A. and the Soviet Union did in the twentieth century.[9]

In fact, cooperation has existed for a quarter century. Each side recognizes that the U.S.A. and China face common challenges to provide adequate and reliable energy services in both the near and long terms while minimizing the adverse health, economic, and environmental issues that are associated with energy production and use. These may be briefly summarized as

- coping with problems associated with increasing dependence on petroleum imports;
- addressing the harmful economic, health, and environmental impacts of energy-related emissions;
- dealing with safety and waste disposal concerns associated with nuclear power generation.

As a developing country, and because of its particular resource endowment, China has specific issues concerning limited per capita energy resources due to its large population; difficulties in accessing existing energy resources, since most of the PRC's coal, oil, and hydropower resources are located far from population centers; limited access to electricity, which is unavailable to an estimated 40 million people; an underdeveloped energy infrastructure, particularly for electricity and natural gas; inefficient use of existing energy supplies.

The U.S.A. also faces issues specific to it, including: organized interest groups who oppose commercial nuclear power; and disagreement on the need and the means to deal with global climate change, particularly given the imminent retirement of several nuclear power plants.

Cooperation, which is understood to mean governmental, non-governmental, academic, scientific, commercial and financial, provides opportunities to address these challenges through better use of currently available energy-efficient technologies; moving to cleaner, more efficient varieties of fossil fuels; expanded research and development of technologies; mutually beneficial transfers of human and financial capital and technologies; and collaborative economic and environmental initiatives that benefit both the two nations and the international community at large.

The first efforts at energy cooperation date from 1979, with an accord on high energy physics signed between the U.S. Department of Energy (DOE) and China's State Development Commission (CSCC). Major conduits through which cooperation currently occurs include the U.S.–China Energy Policy Dialogue, the U.S.–China Oil and Gas Industry Forum, the U.S.–China Economic Development and Reform Dialogue, and the U.S.–China Defense Consultative Talks.

U.S.–China energy policy dialogue

Formed in May 2004 through a Memorandum of Understanding signed by then Secretary of Energy Spencer Abraham, the U.S.–China Energy Policy Dialogue (EPD) established a partnership between the DOE and China's National Development Reform Commission (NDRC). Topics have included energy policy making, supply security, power sector reform, regulatory issues, energy efficiency, and the development of energy technology.[10] China has been encouraged to establish a strategic petroleum reserve as a hedge against supply disruptions and other emergencies. Experts agree that the use of strategic petroleum reserves must be coordinated internationally to maximize the efficiency of energy markets. Ideally the Bush administration would also like the PRC leadership to provide a clear statement on how and under what circumstances China would use its strategic reserves.[11] In summer 2005, the DOE opened an office in Beijing to support the activities of the EPD.

The energy efficiency steering committee

Founded in 1995, the committee met for the first time two years later, in Beijing. Cooperating agencies include, in addition to the DOE, the American Council for an Energy-Efficient Economy, the Lawrence-Berkeley National Laboratory, and the China State Bureau of Technology Quality Supervision.

According to Chinese studies, if the PRC can raise its industrial energy efficiency levels to international standards, it has the technical potential to achieve a 40–50 percent reduction in energy use. Since the industrial sector consumes nearly two-thirds of commercial energy and is highly dependent on coal, it is particularly important in this endeavor. A DOE study notes that, because China is undergoing a critical phase of technology implementation and much of the industrial production capacity that will exist there in 15 years has yet to be built, the technologies that are chosen today will affect patterns of energy use and the efficiencies thereof for decades to come.

Cooperation in electric motor systems, which consume about half of the PRC's electricity demand, has been a major area of mutual interest. Efforts on this front aim at reducing greenhouse gases by improving motor systems in factories. They have included a forum held in conjunction with the International Institute for Energy Conservation on international motor standards and testing procedures, the formation of a working group to select a motor test procedure suitable for the PRC; three workshops on motor systems; an experts' tour of Chinese industrial sites to identify potential case studies; a study of China's motors market; and a workshop on motor testing procedures.

Pilot programs are to be implemented in Shanghai and in Jiangsu province; these will provide models for a national program tailored to the PRC's needs. Workshops have presented U.S. laws and discussed to what extent they would be applicable in the Chinese context. Training and collaboration on standards for energy-efficient air conditioners and lamp ballasts have been completed, and the Lawrence-Berkeley National Laboratory has assisted in the development of standards. A DOE program carried out with China's Brightness Program is providing training on solar energy, rural electrification, and renewable energy policy. Two hundred homes in Tibet have been supplied with solar systems. Wind energy development programs have focused on sustainable large-scale development of wind power in both off-grid and grid-connected power applications. A cooperative pilot project between DOE's National Energy Renewable Lab and China's State Power Corporation is using a wind/diesel/battery system to electrify 120 households on Xiao Qing Island in the Yellow Sea, off Shandong province.[12]

U.S.–China Oil and Gas Industry Forum

Founded in 1998 to facilitate Chinese familiarity with Western business practices as well as open the PRC market to American and Western investment, the Oil and Gas Forum has held seven formal meetings in the intervening years. Co-hosted on the U.S. side by the Departments of Energy and Commerce with China's NDRC, the organization has been described as playing an important role in bringing representatives of the two countries together for discussion on available technologies for such topics as deep water and unconventional oil and gas exploration, coal bed methane production, and risk management for large energy infrastructure projects. U.S. industry is already the largest investor in the PRC's petroleum sector.[13]

U.S.–China Economic Development and Reform Dialogue

Initiated in 2003 by the U.S. Department of State with the NDRC, its discussions have included market approaches to energy security as well as broader topics such as agriculture, investment, and telecommunications.

U.S.–China Defense Consultative Talks

Begun in December 1997, the seventh meeting of this dialogue in April 2005 featured an in-depth discussion between then Undersecretary of Defense Douglas Feith and Deputy Chief of the PLA General Staff Xiong Guangkai on global energy security issues. There has also been science and technology cooperation on issues including energy. A *Fossil Energy Protocol* was signed in April 1985 between the U.S. DOE and China's Ministry of Coal Industry. It has sponsored seminars and joint projects in such areas as distributed generation fuel cell development, the economic and ecological impacts of coal liquefaction plants, the technological feasibility of coal bed methane development, and a joint carbon capture and sequestration leadership forum (CSLF). None of these is a perfect solution. For example, the process used to release methane from subterranean coal creates huge volumes of waste water that can destroy soil for agricultural purposes.[14] And coal sequestration, which involves capturing carbon dioxide and placing it underground in tapped-out oil fields or deep saline aquifers, can cause deadly accidents if the gas escapes. It can also trigger earthquakes.

The U.S.A. has sponsored several pollution control workshops in China since 2003. The two countries are working together through the International Partnership for a Hydrogen Economy (IPHE), which hopes to bring hydrogen-based vehicles to the international market. The U.S. National Safety Council has a contract to improve mine safety inspection and mine rescue operations. The PRC's mines are currently the most dangerous in the world. Higher prices for energy have been a disincentive to close down unsafe or marginal mines, thus increasing the danger to those who work in them.

There is also cooperation in so-called smart buildings. According to American energy expert Robert Watson, the PRC's buildings use more energy than its cars or industries. Taken together, households and office buildings account for an estimated 45 percent of the country's energy consumption. The cooperation project has involved training building designers and helping to develop technology to produce green buildings that feature energy-saving air conditioning systems and reflectors to maximize natural lighting. Ultimately, argues Watson, the increased cost will pay for itself: Every dollar invested in green buildings results in savings of $12 in operating and even health care costs.[15]

In the summer of 1999, the Natural Resources Defense Council, with DOE funding, began a project to provide technical assistance to the Chongqing Municipal Government to develop regulations for its then newly enacted residential building design standard and to develop an energy code for public and commercial buildings. During the following year, representatives from Chongqing and Beijing participated in a one-week study tour to California on building energy standards. There is also collaborative work with Chongqing Architectural University and other experts on developing a Model Energy Code for the Transitional Climate Zone, as well as discussions with national-level officials in Beijing on a residential building energy code for the transitional climate zone. Lawrence-Berkeley laboratories are providing training in computer energy simulation methods and analysis techniques, as well as assistance in developing detailed hourly weather data.[16]

Additional building activities include the construction of an energy-efficient demonstration building and center in Beijing. A technical feasibility study identifying cost effective energy measures that could reduce a building's energy costs by as much as 40 percent was completed, with design workshops held in Pittsburgh in December 1999 and in Beijing a few months later to enable the technology to be incorporated into the overall building design. The budget for this has also been cooperative, with about $7.57 million provided by the PRC and a total of $4 million by the U.S. private sector and other project participants in cash and or in-kind contributions of professional services, equipment, and materials.

In May 2006, the U.S. Trade and Development Agency (USTDA) provided technical assistance for a contract between America's Caterpillar Corporation and the PRC's Shanxi Jincheng Anthracite Coal Mining Group for the enhancement of clean energy sources; during the following month, the USTDA announced the establishment of grants to encourage clean energy production that will improve air quality in China.[17] In December 2006, China signed on to the FutureGen partnership on clean technology: The billion-dollar government industry project will finance a coal-fired power plant to produce electricity and hydrogen without emitting pollutants such as carbon dioxide and other greenhouse gases. The plant is scheduled to start operations in 2012.[18]

Internationally, the U.S.A. and China are cooperating on an international thermonuclear reaction project (ITER). The acronym, whose Latin meaning is "way," is intended to symbolize an international effort to harness nuclear fusion as a peaceful power source. The U.S.A. has also encouraged China to seek some form of association with the International Energy Agency. The PRC has also joined the international Methane to Market Partnership, whose voluntary, nonbinding framework aims to advance the use of methane as a clean energy source.

Results

Signing protocols, making speeches declaring commitment to worthy goals, drawing up feasibility plans, exchanging personnel, and expending large sums of money do not in themselves constitute progress. There have been some successes. One of these concerns China's strategic petroleum reserve. The Chinese government has accelerated construction of the first phase of the SPR, and expects it to be completed by the end of 2007, or six months ahead of schedule. This will include all four of the project's tank farms, with a total storage capacity of 88 million barrels. As of January 20 2007, the Zhenhai base, near Ningbo, the largest of the four tank farms that make up the first development phase, had been filled.[19] Some energy-efficient buildings have been constructed, and some coal mines are safer.

There have also been numerous frustrations. One is that the fragmented nature of China's energy bureaucracies complicates progress with foreign partners. Policy-setting authority is parceled out among a welter of disparate groups. Since the Energy Ministry was dismantled in 2003, the National Development Reform Commission's Energy Bureau is the nearest the PRC has had to a centralized energy policy-making agency. But there are a wide variety of competing interests in other bureaucracies. China's three major state oil firms have also acquired considerable influence over energy policy. These groups compete to influence the top leadership, many among whom have direct ties to particular energy interests. The result has been a policy-making process that has been described as driven primarily by relationship-building and influence peddling.[20] In 2005, the government created the Energy Leading Group and the State Energy Office to improve the PRC's ability to formulate and implement national energy policy. These may just have added additional players to the already existing plethora. Bureaucratic inertia and vested interests remain entrenched.

Another problem relates to the fragmentation of authority among central, local, and provincial entities. Regulations are being drawn up to clarify the relationship of each to the other, but this does not guarantee compliance. There is a long history of central government directives being circumvented or significantly modified, as is implicit in the age-old saying that "heaven is high and the emperor is far away."

Fears that imposing pollution controls will slow the rate of economic growth to a degree that social stability will be jeopardized have made it difficult to reach a consensus on how stringent regulations should be. So far, the PRC has refused to set limits on carbon dioxide emissions. The Chinese government has also had problems with goals it has set for itself. In early 2007, environmental officials acknowledged that the country failed to meet Premier Wen Jiabao's goal for reducing energy consumption by 4 percent and emissions of pollutants by two percent.[21] Although the stated reason for postponing the imposition of a fuel tax was the high price of oil, the tax was not implemented even after the price of oil dropped.[22] The rush to construct so many buildings and other projects as quickly as possible has often meant that "smart building" technologies are ignored. Where codes exist, code inspectors can be bribed. The prospect that the technologies will pay for themselves in the long run seems less important to most developers than short-run profits. Cost factors are also an issue in implementing other technologies. The head of the China Meteorological Administration, in a discussion that pointed out that the PRC had become one of the worst victims of climate change, stated that the country lacked the money and technology to significantly alter its reliance on highly polluting coal. Observers wondered how this could be, given that the PRC has the world's highest foreign exchange reserves as well as a steadily rising defense budget.[23] A joint U.S.–China study on biomass found that farmers reacted positively to the idea of constructing a conversion facility, but that construction costs were far beyond their ability to finance.[24] Central-regional-local disagreements over cost allocation meant that in most cases very little has been done to implement the study.

An additional problem is that the materials used for biomass conversion are also used as foodstuffs. Making ethanol from corn, for example, reduces the amount of corn that can be eaten. At the end of 2006, after grain prices rose 5 percent in a single month, the government announced controls to limit companies' ability to quickly enter the market for turning crops into transport fuel.[25] Some progress has been made in the use of jatropha, a drought-resistant plant first identified in Africa, whose seeds are inedible. The oil in jatropha seeds burns with one-fifth the emissions of conventional fossil fuels. At the end of 2006, PetroChina signed a memorandum with the Sichuan provincial government to build a jatropha bio-diesel conversion plant capable of producing a hundred thousand tons of fuel annually.[26] Nonetheless, the initial reaction to the apparent promise of jatropha as a fuel was to set off a competition among companies of several nations to gain control over the areas where it was produced. There are fears that poor African nations whose economies could be advantaged by the discovery will be deprived of many of the benefits. Some also fear that, like emu farming a few years before, jatropha could prove just another expensive farming fad that will fail to live up to potential.[27]

For the future

Senator Lieberman's choice of collision versus cooperation notwithstanding, there is not an either/or choice for the U.S.A. and PRC on energy matters. The case for cooperation as opposed to collision is cogent. But speaking realistically rather than rhetorically, the issue is likely to be cooperation versus contention rather than collision, and to involve some degree of both. Cooperative ventures are likely to co-exist with efforts to ensure energy security not only on the part of the U.S.A. and the PRC but other nations as well: The real issue is managing the balance between the two. For example, in spring 2006, Australia not only signed an agreement to supply China with uranium for its nuclear power plants but conferred with the U.S.A., Japan, and Great Britain on China's aggressive purchases of energy assets in Africa and Latin America.[28]

There have been frictions with Japan as well, most recently when Chinese maritime authorities banned shipping traffic in the East China Sea near the median line with Japan while it expands the Pinghu gas field. Tokyo claims that the area straddles the disputed median line between the two countries and extends into waters that Japan considers part of its exclusive economic zone.[29] Japanese sources have expressed disappointment that several efforts at negotiation have achieved so little, with some opining that the Chinese side is simply stalling in order to present Japan with a fait accompli. At the same time, an influential member of the ruling Liberal Democratic Party and cabinet minister-presumptive called for a strategic partnership between China and Japan.[30]

Energy relationships between China and Russia also have aspects of both cooperation and contention. A series of delays from the Russian side due to the need for feasibility studies on building pipelines points up the observation of one analyst: "the paradox that the better the relationship becomes, the more Russians worry about China."[31]

China and the U.S.A. have made substantial strides toward cooperation in energy relationships and have established the basis for a continued constructive partnership that they intend to expand upon, but frictions exist between the two countries, and are likely to continue to do so. Actions speak louder than words. Sovereignty issues remain important. As a case in point, one of the first responses to the discovery of a major oilfield in the Gulf of Mexico in September 2006 was to ask whether it could ensure energy independence for the U.S.A. A carefully worded statement issued at the conclusion of December 2006 discussions between DOE officials and their Chinese counterparts said that the two sides had "made some key energy-related advances ... but differences remain on how to address future energy needs." A DOE official later explained that the crucial point was whether a country had to own resources to actually have access to them.[32] There are complaints that, for all the positive factors in the government's endeavors, the sustainability issue appears to be shaped more by political expediency than a true civil-political engagement. If this continues, China's alternative energy agenda, and its sustainability agenda in general, will suffer as a result.[33]

Just as many Chinese are concerned that Washington uses a desire to establish democracy to disguise its desire for hegemony and many Americans believe that Beijing talks about a China that is peacefully rising while providing its military with unjustifiably large annual budget increases, each side worries that gestures of cooperation may disguise an intent to block fuel supplies to the other. It behooves both China and the U.S.A. to match words with actions, on energy as well as other aspects of behavior.

Notes

1 David Sanger, "China's Big Need for Oil Is High on U.S. Agenda," *New York Times*, April 19, 2006, pp. A1; A8.
2 Wu Lei and Shen Qinyu, "Will China Go To War Over Oil?" *Far Eastern Economic Review*, April 2006, pp. 38–40. The authors' answer is yes, if the U.S.A. were to try to cut off China's overseas oil lifeline "in order to destabilize the country."
3 *Strategic Energy Policy: Challenges for the 21st Century*: Report of an Independent Task Force Sponsored by the James A. Baker III Institute for Public Policy of Rice University and the Council on Foreign Relations, 2001, p. 3.
4 International Energy Agency (IEA), Statistics on the Web, www.iea.org/statist/index.htm
5 Glenn Kessler, "U.S. Says China Must Address Its Intentions: How Its Power is Used is of Concern," *Washington Post*, September 22, 2005, p. A16.
6 Brigadier General Charles J. Dunlap, Jr., U.S.AF, quoted by Michael P. Noonan, "The Future of American Military Strategy: A Conference Report," Foreign Policy Research Institute, February 3, 2006. General Dunlap was speaking in his private capacity. FPRI E-Notes, February 3, 2006. www.fpri.org

7 Senator Richard Lugar quoted in [no author], "U.S. Urged To Work With China On Energy," *Financial Times*, March 14, 2006. http://news.ft.com/cms/s/a0470f9a-b2c6–11da-ab3e-0000779e2340.html

8 [No author], "China 'Not in Arms, Energy Race,'" *Agence France Presse*, January 3, 2007.

9 Joseph I. Lieberman, "China–U.S. Energy Policies: A Choice of Cooperation or Collision," November 30, 2005, http://www.cfr.org/publication/9335/chinaU.S._energy-policies.html

10 Katherine A. Fredriksen, "China's Role in the World: Is China a Responsible Stakeholder?" testimony to U.S.–China Economic and Security Review Commission, August 4, 2006, p. 9. www.U.S.cc.gov

11 Andrzej Zwaniecki, "U.S.–China Cooperation Could Advance Mutual, Global Energy Goals," April 4, 2005, http://unsinfo.state.gov.eap/Archive/2005/April/04–622583.html

12 U.S. Department of Energy, *Fact Sheet: Cooperation with the People's Republic of China*, April 2006. www.pi.energy.gov/pdf/library/ChinaFactSheet042006, pp. 2–5.

13 Katherine A. Fredriksen, "China's Role in the World: Is China a Responsible Stakeholder?" statement before the U.S.–China Economic and Security Review Commission, August 4, 2006, p. 9. www.U.S.cc.gov

14 Jim Robbins, "In the West, a Water Fight Over Quality, Not Quantity," *New York Times*, September 10, 2006, p. A16.

15 Clarissa Oon, "Saving Energy: Call to Take Small Steps," *Straits Times*, March 28, 2006.

16 DOE 2006 Fact Sheet, p. 3.

17 Susan Krause, "Development Grants Promote U.S.–China Environmental Cooperation," June 6, 2006, http://lists.state.gov/scripts/wa-U.S.iainfo.exe

18 Melody Merin, "China, U.S.A. Partner To Advance Clean Energy Technology," U.S. State Department Policy Materials, December 18, 2006. http://U.S.info.state.gov/xarchives/display.html?p-washfile

19 [No author], "China's First Strategic Petroleum Reserve Operational," *China Economic Net*, January 30, 2007, http://en.ce.cn/indU.S.tries/energy&mining200701/30/120070130_10252950.shmtl

20 The Eurasia Group, "China's Overseas Investments in Oil and Gas Production," proprietary study commissioned by the U.S. Economic and Security Review Commission, October 16 2006, www.U.S.cc.gov

21 Shi Jiangtao and Jamil Anderlini, "Nation's Image at Stake in Fight to Cut Emissions," *South China Morning Post*, February 21, 2007.

22 Shi Jiangtao, "Mainland Petrol Price Cut by Four Percent," *South China Morning Post*, January 15, 2007.

23 Shi Jiangtao, "Converting to Clean Energy 'Too Costly,'" *South China Morning Post*, February 7, 2007.

24 Dai Lin, Li Jingming, and Ralph Overend, *Biomass Energy Conversion Technologies in China: Development and Assessment*, Beijing: China Environmental Sciences Press, 1998, p. 213.

25 Michael Richardson, "Putting Food in the Petrol Tank," *South China Morning Post*, December 29, 2006.

26 [No author], "PetroChina Signs MOU To Build Two Energy Plants," *South China Morning Post*, November 14, 2006.

27 Karen Palmer, "Weed's Biofuel Potential Sparks African Land Grab," *Washington Times*, February 21, 2007.

28 *Agence France Presse*, "Secure Energy Supplies to China, India 'Vital,'" *South China Morning Post*, March 27, 2006.

29 [No author], "China Bans Vessels Near Gas Field: Report," *Japan Times* (Tokyo), April 17, 2000, http://search.japantimes.co.jp/egi-bin/nn20060417al.htm

30 [No author], "Japan Talks of 'Strategic Partnership' With China," *Financial Times*,

March 7, 2003m http://new.ft.com/cms/s/862776c4-ad6a-11da-9643-0000779e2340. html

31 [No author], "Moscow Still Wary Despite Closer Ties," *South China Morning Post,* March 24, 2006, quoting Chatham House expert on Russia Lo Bobo.

32 [No author], "Advances Made in U.S. Energy Talks," *Reuters,* December 21, 2006.

33 James Rose, "Confusion Over Energy," *South China Morning Post,* January 8, 2007.

12 China's economic rise

Implications for the U.S.A.

Pieter Bottelier

China's meteoric economic rise caught most China specialists in the U.S.A. by surprise. Since the early 1990s, the economy easily outperformed even the most optimistic expectations such as, for example, those included in the Study Papers submitted to the Joint Economic Committee of Congress in April 1991. Most analysts expected much slower growth in China after the Asian financial crisis of 1997–98 or after the SARS crisis of 2003. The enormous impact of China's rise on the global economy that we are now experiencing was also largely unanticipated. As recently as 1999, Gerald Segal, then director of the International Institute for Strategic Studies in London and a respected China expert, wrote in *Foreign Affairs* that "China is a small market that matters relatively little to the world, especially outside Asia."

We know better today. China's growth – GDP and trade – has in fact accelerated since 2003. China is expected to become the world's second largest trader and third largest economy (after Japan but ahead of Germany) in a few years. In 2006 China was the second largest foreign supplier to the U.S.A. (after Canada) and the largest to the European Union. On *current trends* – a big proviso – China is expected to surpass the U.S.A. as the largest economy well before the middle of this century. No other large economy has grown so fast for so long – over 9 percent per year on average for almost three decades. The purpose of this chapter is to review China's economic growth and social transformation since the start of market reforms, explore implications for the U.S.A., and examine claims that China is "stealing" manufacturing jobs from the U.S.A. and manipulating its exchange rate for unfair trade advantage.

China's growth and transformation

China's rapid economic development and social transformation was accompanied by massive poverty reduction and rapid urbanization but also by serious environmental degradation, growing social inequality and macroeconomic imbalances, raising questions about the sustainability of the country's turbo growth. Following the national accounts revisions of December 2005 based on the results of the nonagricultural national economic census of 2004, average per capita income for 2005 stood at about $1,700. Although this is roughly 2.5 times the corresponding estimate for India, China is still a relatively poor and under-developed country. Because of its huge population, its national income, however, is already larger than that of India, Russia, Pakistan, and ASEAN combined. If and when China's total national income reaches the level of the U.S.A. some time before the middle of this century, its average per capita income will still be only a fraction of that of the U.S.A.

More surprising than China's rapid economic growth and transformation is the fact that it was based on gradual, often unorthodox, home-grown economic reforms and financed from domestic savings. Mao Zedong's state-owned, centrally planned, closed economy has been substantially replaced by a market economy based on competition and diversified ownership. The Chinese call it a "socialist market economy." What "socialist" means in this context has never been precisely explained; it appears to be an evolving concept. Since the early 1990s, China's economy has become increasingly integrated into the global economy. This process accelerated after China joined the World Trade Organization (WTO) in 2001. China's economy is now one of the most "globalized" and open large economies in the world; its trade/GDP ratio in 2006 was over 60 percent. A large proportion of China's trade is accounted for by foreign companies operating in China, including numerous U.S. firms

The reform process was set in motion by Deng Xiaoping in 1978. The state's share in industrial output gradually fell from about 80 percent (the remainder was accounted for by collective enterprises) in 1985 to a little over 30 percent in 2005. Collective farming was gradually discontinued after Mao's death (1976), first on an experimental basis in some remote provinces and then in the entire country. This process was essentially completed by 1982. There are still some state farms, but since the early 1980s more than 90 percent of agricultural output has been produced by individual farmers on private plots leased from local village authorities that own and control agricultural land in China. Rural lease rights are tradable in some parts of the country. Urban land is owned and controlled by municipal governments. Commercial urban land leases (usually for 70 years) were started in 1987 and are now common throughout China. Most urban housing was privatized between 1997 and 2003. Private home-ownership is now more common in China than even in the U.S.A. Price controls on most consumer and producer goods and services were eliminated years ago. The relative importance of private enterprise for output and employment growth, already quite significant, is rapidly growing. The financial sector, however, remains largely state-owned and in need of major further reform.

Through the financial system, state ownership of all land, pro-active control of the exchange rate and most capital account transactions, China's government exercises more control over the economy than its modest (and declining) share in output might suggest. Relatively strong state control is the main reason why the U.S.A., the European Union, and Japan have thus far declined to recognize China as a "market economy," even though many smaller countries have.[1] The pace of development and the degree of state control over economic life is unequal across provinces. Since the start of market reforms, coastal provinces have generally grown faster than inland areas; regional income differentials have grown. Some provinces (Zhejiang, Fujian, and Guangdong, with a combined population of about 166 million) are already largely private sector economies.

China has benefited from a large inflow of foreign direct investment (FDI) – especially from overseas Chinese – and all the technical know-how, management experience, and international market access that came with it. It also benefited from technical assistance and capital from multilateral development agencies such as the World Bank, the IMF, and the Asian Development Bank. In spite of substantial capital inflows, China is one of the few developing countries which, in the aggregate, is a net exporter of capital. In macroeconomic terms this means that China saves more than it invests, which is surprising since China's investment rate is one of the highest in the world (over 40 percent of GDP in recent years). China's external debt is relatively low. Its debt service ratio is under 10 percent and declining. China's sovereign bonds traded in international capital markets are highly rated.

As a result of both current account and capital account surpluses and a relatively fixed exchange rate policy (about which more below), China has accumulated huge foreign exchange reserves ($1.07 trillion at the end of February 2007), the largest in the world. Most of these assets are invested in very secure and highly liquid but low yielding U.S. dollar-denominated financial instruments and hence vulnerable to U.S. dollar depreciation. China now wishes to reduce its *official* foreign exchange reserves by: (1) investing part of them in higher yielding, perhaps less liquid assets that do not count as *official* reserves under the IMF definition, (2) reducing its trade surplus, and (3) promoting direct investment and equity participation outside China. Among nonoil-exporting developing countries, China is already the largest source of outward foreign direct investment (FDI). Since inward FDI is expected to slow or even decline, China may become a source of net FDI outflows to the rest of the world. This could happen in 10–15 years. One of the main factors underlying this expectation is the harmonization of corporate taxation approved by the National People's Congress in early March 2007. Since the beginning of market reforms, most foreign funded enterprises in China had enjoyed significant fiscal incentives in the form of long tax holidays and a lower tax rate than local Chinese enterprises (15 percent instead of 33 percent).

China's external trade has become very unbalanced in recent years. In 2006, it had a trade surplus of about $180 billion. Relative to the size of its economy, China's trade surplus was about as large as America's deficit (about 7 percent of GDP in both countries). China has succeeded in smoothing somewhat the "stop–go" economic growth pattern of the 1980s and early 1990s, but it continues to show a tendency to "over-invest" and to rely too much on external demand instead of domestic consumption growth.

Challenges for the U.S.A. and for China

Challenges for the U.S.A. presented by China's rise are in many ways unique and without precedent. Perceptions of China in the U.S.A. vary from threat to opportunity. Some see both threats *and* opportunities at the same time. As a challenge for the U.S.A., China is clearly very different from the former USSR during the cold war, because: (1) it has voluntarily adopted the principles of a market economy, e.g. through WTO membership, (2) it is wide open to foreign investment and trade – more so than any large developing economy, (3) it does not directly challenge the U.S. militarily, and (4) its one-party political system, though repressive in some respects, is much more open that that of the USSR ever was and communist in name only. The challenges presented by China are also very different from those of Japan when it was perceived as an economic threat to the U.S.A. in the 1980s, because: (1) China's economy is more open than Japan's ever was, (2) China's population is more than ten times that of Japan, and (3) China's economy is thought to have significant growth potential for decades to come, while Japan is still struggling to return to "normal" growth after a decade of stagnation.

If China's rise continues to be peaceful – which depends not only on China – the two main challenges for the U.S.A. are: (1) to accommodate China on the world scene as a major economic and political power, and (2) to make the domestic economic adjustments that are needed to keep the U.S. economy growing, while protecting full employment and international competitiveness. History is full of examples to demonstrate how difficult it is for existing powers to accommodate new ones, but it can be done. The closest example of successful accommodation is the policy of Britain in the late nineteenth century to avoid efforts aimed at frustrating the rise of the U.S.A. With responsible government on both sides, there is nothing inevitable about war between the U.S.A. and China, even though their political systems may continue to differ greatly.[2]

The two main challenges facing the U.S.A. as a result of China's rise are difficult, but they pale in comparison to the challenges facing China which, in spite of all the progress that has been made since the start of market reforms in the late 1970s, is on average still a poor developing country with a population that is more than four times that of the U.S.A. The country's economic system still shows many imperfections and contradictions; its transition from plan to market remains incomplete. Significant further institutional change and legal system development is needed, much of it controversial and enormously complex. China still has to reform, close, or privatize thousands of state-owned enterprises, modernize and privatize its financial system, comply with difficult WTO conditions, draft and implement many new laws and regulations, and – most importantly – absorb hundreds of millions of rural surplus workers into the modern economy over the next few decades. It also has to build much new infrastructure, halt and reverse the process of environmental degradation, reform the social security system, and create strong social safety nets to catch those who are unable to fend for themselves in the massive economic and social restructuring that is ongoing. All of it has to be accomplished while preserving stability and growth momentum. Many of these challenges are unique and without precedent. There are almost no parallels in U.S. history. While China is definitely becoming more active in the international political arena, it is safe to say that domestic concerns will preoccupy the leadership for decades to come.

Political reform in China and the role of the U.S.A.

Though not the main focus of this chapter, the question whether the liberalization and growth of China's economy will be followed by political liberalization
is of great interest to Americans and worthy of some comments here. Some in
the U.S.A. believe that the promotion of democracy in China should be
America's main objective in conducting the bilateral relationship.[3] Others feel
that mutual economic benefits are sufficient to justify a policy of "engagement."
It is generally believed in the West that economic development and democratization go hand-in-hand, but the nature of the links and direction of causality are
not always clear. Moreover, there are many gradations of democracy and different forms of democratic government, which makes it hard to narrowly define
what the political objectives of an "engagement" should be.

International experience suggests that democracy can only thrive, preserve
stability, and promote development, if it is supported by well-established institutions and values, such as respect for human rights, rule-of-law, equality under
the law, and a culture that allows conflicts to be settled through compromise.
Some institutions and values may develop as a result of democracy; others are a
prerequisite. The right to vote is a necessary but certainly not a sufficient condition for democracy. China's only experience with a multi-party democratic
system – immediately following the revolution of 1911 – was brief and traumatic. The system fell apart almost as soon as it was created, because the institutions and values needed to sustain it were not there.

China's current political system is easier to define by what it is not than by
what it is. China is neither democratic nor totalitarian. Contrary to popular
believe in the U.S.A., there have been many changes in the way the country's
political system and government function since the start of market reforms.
Organized political opposition is not allowed, but there is open debate and rule-
based competition within the system. Important government decisions usually
follow serious consultations and efforts at consensus building. There are many
public and a few private think-tanks that feed into policy-making processes.
Public hearings on important new laws and regulations are required by the
system. Numerous domestic and some foreign nongovernment organizations are
now operating in China. Public opinion has become important and cannot be
ignored with impunity, as in the past. The state may try to influence public
opinion through propaganda and media control, but it is no longer the only or
main source of news and information available to the public. A one-party state is
almost inevitably authoritarian and repressive in some ways, as it is in China.
There are insufficient checks on the power of the state, but the promotion of
accountability and transparency in government and in enterprise are priorities of
the leadership. China does not have an independent judiciary, but the system is
becoming more professional and accessible to the public. Chinese citizens can
and do sue their government or individual civil servants for wrongful decisions
or misbehavior and sometimes win their case.

Free markets, as have been created for most goods and most services, are a source of power outside the political system. One of the most important examples is the privatization of most urban housing between 1997 and 2003, and the creation of markets for urban real estate – rental and ownership. China's large and rapidly growing mortgage industry did not exist in 1995. Government "work units" no longer assign their workers to live in state-owned apartments. People now make their own decisions where to work and live, a social change of enormous importance in China. Labor market mobility and upward social mobility have sharply increased. Booming real estate and stock markets have made private wealth accumulation possible on scale never before seen in China. Millions of Chinese citizens now have their own personal passport and travel abroad without government interference. Chinese tourists are reported to be more numerous in Asia now than Japanese tourists. After seven years of debate, the approval by China's legislature in March 2007 of the PRC's first ever "Property Rights Law," which fully recognizes and protects private property, is another milestone in China's social and institutional development.

The pluralization of China's society is progressing fast, but formal democratization is not. The Chinese government and many ordinary citizens argue that China is not yet "ready" for full democracy, because the country's level of development, especially institutional development, is still too low. China's current leadership apparently thinks that democracy is at best a distant goal, but the debate on democracy is alive and well. The preamble of the government's 2005 *White Paper on Political Democracy* states "Democracy is the outcome of the development of political civilization of mankind. It is also the common desire of people all over the world. Democracy of a country is generated internally, not imposed by external forces."[4] Evidently, China's leaders see democracy more as an *outcome* of development than as a precondition. Unless there is a political revolution or utter collapse of the present system, formal democratization in China is likely to remain a very slow process. The ruling Communist Party (CCP) may try to hang on to its power monopoly for a very long time, perhaps indefinitely, but that does not mean that the CCP is anti-reform. One of the paradoxes of China's political system is that the entire economic and social reform process since the late 1970s was guided, or at least sanctioned, by the CCP. If continued rapid growth has become a key source of legitimacy of the party and if sustaining high growth requires further economic liberalization and reductions of state involvement in the economy, the party will have no choice but to further change itself in fairly fundamental ways.

The U.S.A. cannot force democracy on China, but it can promote movement in the right direction by continuing a policy of engagement and, above all, by setting a good example. The likely effect of good example is much greater in the current relationship with China than deliberate pressure though sanctions. Efforts to punish or contain China are bound to fail and may boomerang on the U.S.A. China's reform efforts may get bogged down because of bad Chinese policies, corruption, or adverse circumstances beyond the government's control. It is unlikely to fail because of U.S. actions or policies. A weak or failing China, however, is not something to wish for. China's economy is already so large and so deeply integrated in global markets and supply chains that a crisis in China would have significant international spill-over effects that would adversely affect the U.S. economy. A strong and confident China on the other hand is more likely to also promote development in the U.S.A. China's growth and development is not a zero-sum game for the U.S.A.

China's competiveness and global economic impact

China has quickly become competitive in a wide range of industries and is rapidly moving up the value chain, but its relative competitiveness is falling. In the World Economic Forum's Global Competitiveness Index for 2006 China ranked 54th (down from 48th in 2005). India now ranks ahead of China, but because of its much larger economic size China's competitiveness makes a greater impression on world markets. Reasons for China's *current* competitiveness go well beyond low wages and an undervalued exchange rate. Since the late 1990s, average real wages in urban China, though still very low, have been rising about eight times faster than in the U.S.A. and are already much higher than in India or neighboring Vietnam. Other factors underpinning China's competitiveness are: (1) the large size and growth potential of domestic markets; (2) a surprisingly open trade regime (e.g. most IT components enter duty-free); (3) relatively high quality physical and IT infrastructure; (4) relatively low overheads and capital costs; (5) generous tax incentives for foreign investors (which are about to be removed for new investments as a result of the recently approved corporate tax harmonization act; (6) political and macroeconomic stability; (7) consistency in economic reform policy over an extended period; (8) availability of skilled/highly trainable, disciplined labor; (9) growing availability of managerial and scientific personnel for R&D work; (10) extensive local networks of inter-firm supply chains.

Even if China revalued its currency by 15–25 percent, permitted free labor unions, and complied fully with all international trade rules, it would still be a formidable competitor on the world scene and a threat to many established industries in developed countries. China's entry into the world economy in this age of free trade, capital mobility, low transport costs, and IT for everyone, means nothing less than a relatively sudden enlargement of the global labor force, linked through integrated markets, by an astonishing 25–30 percent. The challenge of absorbing such a huge increase in the globally linked labor force in a relatively short period of time is without precedent.

It is unavoidable that China's economic growth and influence on global markets affects the U.S.A. and other countries linked through trade. The impact is not equally distributed. For example, Mexico is proportionately more deeply affected than the U.S.A.; and so are Taiwan, South Korea and even Japan. In light of the termination of the Multi-Fiber Arrangements (MFA) on January 1, 2005, the *most* affected economies, at least in the short term, are countries that depend heavily on the production and export of garments and textiles – products in which China has a strong comparative advantage – such as Bangladesh and

Morocco. On the other hand, resource-based economies such as Canada, Brazil, Argentina, Chile, Peru, and Australia experience fewer adjustment problems and enjoy more immediate benefits from China's rise. For many African countries China is either a major customer for raw material exports, competitor on consumer markets, an important source of foreign aid and investment, or all of the above.

Neighboring countries in Asia that saw China's rise primarily as a threat only six years ago are now experiencing positive effects as well, especially in trade and investment. To exploit the opportunities more fully, several regional free trade agreements have been negotiated or are under negotiation. Industrialists in Japan and South Korea now fear a possible slowdown in China more than its continued rapid expansion. For both countries, China has become the largest foreign customer. Over the past decade China has not only become one of the most open large developing economies (as measured by the trade/GDP ratio, FDI inflows and outflows), but also an engine of regional and even global growth, along with the U.S.A. China's ferocious appetite for imports accounted for over 30 percent of global export growth in the period 2004–2006. U.S. imports from China and exports to China have both been growing about 23 percent p.a. since 2001, much faster than the bilateral trade with other important trading partners. U.S. imports from and exports to China accounted for 15.5 percent and 5.5 percent respectively of total U.S. commodity imports and exports. Although imports from and exports to China have been growing at comparable rates since 2001, the bilateral trade imbalance has widened significantly, because exports to and imports from China were very unequal in the base year.

Long-term international economic effects of China's rise are harder to predict. Much depends on the outcome of the Doha Round, the containment of rising protectionist sentiments in the U.S.A. and in Europe, and other factors. Having benefited so much from "globalization' thus far, it is likely that China will continue on this route as long as possible, strengthening its global supply and client networks through the promotion of outward FDI and free trade agreements, supported by diplomatic initiatives. Indeed, the now rapidly growing outward flow of FDI from China, especially to other countries in Asia and resource-rich countries in Africa and Latin America, may well become the hall mark of a new phase in the ongoing globalization of China's economy. To secure market share it is likely that Chinese equity investment in its major export markets, including mergers and acquisitions, will also increase in the years ahead.

China's compliance with WTO conditions

China applied for GATT (WTO's predecessor) membership in 1986 and joined the WTO on December 11, 2001. The entry terms were by far the toughest for any new member. The U.S.A., with strong support from the European Union, played a leading role in difficult negotiations which stalled for several years following the Tiananmen Square crackdown of June 1989. The entry bar was raised several times in the course of negotiations. China complained about this but remained committed to complete negotiations. It sought WTO membership mainly for the following reasons: (1) to open up markets for its exports, (2) to attract more FDI, (3) to strengthen the hand of reformers – e.g. former PM Zhu Rongji and former President Jiang Zemin – who pushed for the adoption of international norms for regulating the economy, sometimes over the objection of others in the government or business interest groups; (4) to obtain automatic most favored nation (MFN) status to which WTO members are entitled (MFN was renamed PNTR in the U.S.A. to reflect the fact that MFN is "normal" in a large majority of cases); and (5) to gain international respectability. Membership marks an important milestone in China's reform and modernization process. It has been highly beneficial to China, but it has also benefited the U.S. economy, according to serious economic analysts.[5]

By helping China become a WTO member, the U.S.A. has given itself an additional framework within which to consider bilateral trade issues. We have more than five years of experience with China as a member. The results are mixed, as most had expected, but on balance more positive than negative. China has done well with regard to lowering import and investment barriers, reasonably well with regard to reforming its domestic legal and regulatory systems to ensure consistency with WTO norms, but not well with regard to the removal of some internal subsidies and the enforcement of IPR laws under the TRIPS (Trade-Related International Property Rights) agreement. Successive USTR reports to Congress confirm that key Chinese central government authorities responsible for ensuring compliance with WTO conditions remain committed to but are not always succeeding in their task. Those tasks are formidable by any standard. They involve not only reducing or dismantling external *and* internal trade and investment barriers but also revising or drafting thousands of laws and regulations and retraining tens of thousands of officials at all levels in government. Many implementation problems have arisen at the local level in China, either because local officials are not yet sufficiently familiar with the new requirements or because local financial interests conflict with WTO requirements. To the extent the latter cause of noncompliance prevails, we are dealing with *political economy* problems that will be hard to solve.

In its 2006 Report to Congress on China's WTO Compliance, USTR summarizes the record of China's compliance as follows:

> China has taken significant and often impressive steps to reform its economy since joining the WTO ... China has also taken steps to implement numerous specific commitments pursuant to schedules set forth in its WTO accession agreement ... the U.S.A. – including U.S. workers, businesses, farmers, service providers and consumers – has benefited significantly from these steps ... Nevertheless, despite significant progress in many areas, China's record of implementing WTO commitments is decidedly mixed. China continues to pursue problematic industrial policies that rely

on trade-distorting measures ... China's shortcomings in enforcing laws in areas where detailed WTO disciplines apply, such as intellectual property rights (IPR), have also created serious problems for the United States and its other trading partners.

Similar views were expressed by representatives of the U.S. business community in a survey conducted by the U.S.–China Business Council in July–August 2004. The survey revealed that a majority of USCBC members felt that, on balance, China is making reasonable progress toward WTO compliance, but that more needs to be done. Table 12.1 below shows the percentages of respondents in four categories for 11 compliance areas.

As noted in the table, 65 percent of respondents in the USCBC survey observed at least some progress in IPR enforcement. Is China doing everything it can to address IPR protection problems? Many feel that the government could do a lot more. To meet this criticism and underline its commitment to improving IPR protection, China put Vice Prime Minister Mme Wu Yi, known locally as the "iron lady," in charge of the program. External pressures for better IPR protection are reinforced by complaints from local manufacturers, inventors, artists, etc. whose IPR are also being violated. Early 2005 China introduced new IPR protection measures; it lowered the threshold for criminal prosecution in case of IPR violations, including on-line copyright piracy and export/import of counterfeit goods.

China is, of course, not the only WTO member with IPR protection problems, nor are the perpetrators always Chinese. The first to be jailed in China under the new measures that were introduced in 2005 were two Americans who were caught by Shanghai police trying to sell fake DVDs on the Internet. Enforcement of IPR protection laws is especially difficult in poor countries with weak administrations and a local population that does not appreciate the critical importance of IPR for development. Another factor is that mark-ups for IPR

Table 12.1 Responses by USCBC members to questions about problems of doing business with China

	Now resolved	*Progress*	*No progress*	*New problems*
Distribution rights	5	68	25	4
IPR enforcement	0	65	35	0
IPR legal framework	0	70	26	4
Trading rights	11	62	29	0
Nontariff measures	0	53	16	31
Transparency	0	78	13	9
Market access services	7	43	36	14
Technical standards	0	71	12	17
Taxation	7	57	29	7
Customs and trade admin.	0	50	20	30
National treatment	0	42	29	29

included in the price of Western products (e.g. pharmaceuticals, DVDs) are related to Western income levels and seem unreasonably high to local people. Financial incentives and opportunities for piracy and counterfeiting in China are abundant. With the connivance of local authorities, production and distribution of counterfeit products can be concealed relatively easily. Taiwan had a massive IPR protection problem only 15 years ago and still struggles with residual elements. It is not likely that the massive IPR protection problem in China will be resolved soon.

Two kinds of IPR

In considering the consequences for the U.S.A. of China's poor record in IPR protection, it is useful to distinguish between (1) the copying and counterfeiting of final consumer goods such as DVDs, Gucci bags, Hermes ties or Rolex watches; and (2) the "stealing" of patented production technologies or (bio) chemical formulas. The first form of piracy is annoying and harmful to the financial interests of particular industries, designers, and artists, but it is not a serious threat to "innovation" or to the U.S. economy as a whole. Even the U.S. government or local administrations within the U.S.A. do not punish the vendors of pirated goods on U.S. streets. Similarly, one of the world's largest purveyors of pirated goods – eBay, a U.S. company – is allowed to operate unchecked.[6] The negative consequences for the U.S.A. (and other advanced industrial nations) of the second form of piracy, however, are potentially more serious, because: (1) the market value of many large U.S. technology corporations depends significantly on the IP component of their assets, and (2) it may threaten the quality and pace of technological "innovation" and thus long-term economic development in the U.S.A. In bilateral discussions with the Chinese on IPR enforcement, greater emphasis should be placed on the protection of patented production technologies, (bio) chemical formulas, seeds, etc.

Financial system reform and trade distortions

USTR reports to the Congress on China's WTO Compliance typically focus on *access* by U.S. financial companies to China's financial services market, not on financial system regulation and banking supervision in China. The latter is not an area of WTO compliance, but it is important for the protection of American producers against possible unfair competition from Chinese companies. Due to the lack of hard budget constraints on some Chinese companies, it is in some situations still possible for some exporters to cut prices to gain market share by off-loading losses on their banks. In addition, China may provide indirect subsidies to certain exporters or import substitution industries through discriminatory tax arrangements or favorable terms for loans from state banks.

These forms of unfair competition are often hard to detect. But when confirmed they should be challenged, if necessary through the WTO dispute settlement mechanism. There are no explicit WTO conditions on the health of

China's banking system, only implicit ones resulting from China's commitment to open its market fully to international competition by December 2006 and to give "*national treatment*" to foreign banks. Trade distortions resulting from soft budget constraints will not disappear until China's banking system has been fully reformed and subjected to strict supervision. China is making progress in this direction, but additional action on the part of the government and its regulatory agencies is needed.

The relatively low cost of bank loans in China and inadequate banking supervision contribute to periodic over-investment in many industries. China's extraordinarily high domestic savings rate and high bank liquidity are the main factors underlying China's relatively low interest rates, not government policy. China's tendency to over-invest and its growing export surplus in recent years appear to be related problems. With China's increasing participation in international trade, excess capacity in many industries may generate trade frictions in the international arena. A restoration of macroeconomic balance in China requires greater reliance on domestic consumption to support high growth and reduced reliance on external demand. Successful pursuit of such policies, which requires a faster appreciation of China's currency (as will be discussed below), will automatically reduce China's excess savings over investment.

Twin economic engines: the U.S.A. and China – a sustainable model?

China and the U.S.A. together accounted for over 50 percent of global import growth in 2004 and 2005 and for the lion's share of commodity price increases. In that sense they were the twin engines for global economic growth in recent years. China's growth is primarily investment-driven, whereas the U.S.A. relies more on consumption-driven growth, some of it debt-financed. The U.S.A. has been spending more than it earns for many years. This is reflected in the current account deficit – about 7 percent of GDP in 2006. China typically has a current account surplus. It was never very large – between 1–3 percent of GDP during the decade 1994–2004, but it suddenly swelled in recent years to an astonishing 9.5 percent of GDP in 2006. This is a clear indication of China's excessive dependence on external demand to support high domestic growth, a dependence that is almost certainly related to China's over-investment problem.

Current American and Chinese macroeconomic imbalances are each other's mirror images. China finances part of the U.S. current account deficit by buying U.S. Treasury bonds and other U.S. securities, or by investing in U.S. companies or through M&A. The flow of financial resources from China to the U.S.A. is much greater than the reverse. After the Asian financial crisis of 1997–98, many other countries in Asia also developed current account surpluses; together with China they financed close to 50 percent of the U.S. current account deficit in recent years. The global economic model that has developed since the crisis of 1997–98, depends on a huge net flow of financial resources from Asia (and to a lesser extent from Europe and oil exporting countries) to the U.S.A.

The global economic model described above is stable as long as foreigners (in particular Asian central banks) are willing to increase their holdings of US$-denominated financial instruments. Since this willingness cannot be taken for granted, the current global growth model depending on growing trade imbalances, particularly in the U.S.A. and China is not sustainable. The U.S.A. has to reduce its external deficit and China has to reduce its external surplus. For the U.S.A. this means that for some years at least, consumption growth has to be lower than GDP growth, and for China it means the opposite.

The U.S.–China bilateral trade gap – various interpretations

Widening of the U.S.–China bilateral trade imbalance is mainly due to changes in intra-Asia trade and investment flows, not to factors that are exclusively related to China. Instead of exporting directly to the U.S.A., many Pacific Rim countries now export indirectly, after processing in China. For example, Kodak moved production of its digital cameras from Japan to China in 2004 and now exports from there. This has reduced the U.S. trade deficit with Japan, while simultaneously increasing the deficit with China. China has become the processing hub and a vital link in the supply chain for numerous Japanese, Taiwanese, Hong Kong, South Korean, Philippine, Thai, and other Pacific Rim-based manufacturing firms, including many American ones. The shift in trade patterns is reflected in the rise of China's share in U.S. imports from 5.8 percent in 1995 to 15.5 percent in 2006, while the share of other Pacific Rim countries, including Japan, fell from 34 percent to about 20 percent during the same period.

The U.S. economy benefits from this new *triangular* trading pattern based on China's low production costs. It permits generous distribution margins for U.S. importers and wholesalers while still permitting lower retail prices. Moreover, and in spite of the recent recalls of toys and some other consumer goods imported from China, the quality of products made in China has generally improved over the years. U.S. firms involved in the China import trade usually control a much larger share of the value chain than their Chinese counterparts. Andie Xie, a prominent analyst in Hong Kong, estimated that corporate America earned some $60–80 billion in profits from the trade with China in 2004, accounting for 10–15 percent of S&P 500 profits that year.[7] He also estimated that some 4–8 million jobs in the U.S.A. were related to adding value to imports from China and that this value added accounted for some 3–5 percent of U.S. GDP in 2004.

According to Xie and other analysts, domestic value added in China on exports to the U.S.A. is a fraction of the value added in the U.S.A. on imports from China. The reverse is not true: U.S. exports to China represent an estimated 80–90 percent value added in the U.S. while China adds relatively little value to typical imports from the U.S. Though the bilateral U.S.–China *trade balance* is heavily in China's favor (it grew from $100 billion in 2001 to $233 billion in 2006),[8] a result of the factors mentioned above, the bilateral *value added balance* generated by that trade is almost certainly in favor of the U.S.A. This contrast between the bilateral *trade balance* and the bilateral *value added* balance is probably unique to the U.S.–China trade. It has received no serious attention in U.S. political circles, but is the subject of much discussion in China.

Until 2004, China's large and growing trade surpluses with the U.S.A. and the E.U. were more or less balanced by trade deficits with countries in Asia. Its overall trade surplus was generally less than 3 percent of GDP until recently. As mentioned, China's overall trade surplus grew to about $125 billion in 2005 and $180 billion (about 7 percent of China's GDP) in 2006 and its current account surplus was even larger. It grew to about 9.5 percent of GDP in 2006, which for a large economy is probably a record and an indication of unsustainable macro imbalances in the Chinese economy. Whereas the U.S.A. remains the epicenter of global trade imbalances in absolute terms, it is clear that China has become an important part of the problem in recent years.

While China is a growing factor in global trade imbalances, it is important to note that wholly Chinese-owned enterprises account for only about 35 percent of China's exports and that a large part of China's foreign trade is "processing trade" which, beyond employment, generates relatively little value added in China. Most of China's "processing trade" is conducted by foreign-invested enterprises located in China. The "processing trade," based on imported materials and components that are assembled in China, generates almost automatically its own trade surplus; otherwise such trade would not be profitable.[9] As long as the "processing trade" accounts for a large part of China's exports, there is likely to be an overall trade surplus. The surplus is therefore structural in nature; it reflects the high degree to which China's manufacturing sector (which accounts for the bulk of all exports) has become integrated with global supply chains.

According to China's Ministry of Commerce, the share of foreign-invested enterprises located in China rose from almost nothing 20 years ago to over 60 percent in 2005. Their share in exports to the U.S.A. is even higher (65.8 percent in 2004)[10]. International and U.S. involvement in China's manufacturing and manufactured exports is far greater than it is in Japan or any other large economy. The globalization of China's economy is the result of massive FDI inflows since the early 1990s, the opening up of China's economy which accelerated when China joined the WTO, China's extraordinary domestic savings performance, and policies aimed at export promotion or import substitution.

The U.S. bilateral trade deficit with China has grown in parallel with the growth of "affiliated" sales (domestic sales and exports) by U.S.-owned companies located in China. In 2005 the dollar value of sales from U.S. enterprises located in China was estimated at about three times the value of direct U.S. exports to China. Since part of the "affiliated" sales from U.S.-owned enterprises located in China represents U.S. imports from China, one could argue that part of the U.S. bilateral trade deficit with China is a deficit with itself. This ironic situation illustrates the usual nature and the complexity of U.S.–China trade relations and underlines the degree to which the two economies have become intertwined. As mentioned, the U.S.A. will have to reduce its trade deficit with the rest of the world and China has to reduce its surplus, but that does not imply that the U.S. bilateral trade deficit is a central issue in this matter.

U.S. manufacturing job losses

The question of U.S. manufacturing job losses to China is also a very complex matter. Adjustment to the emergence of China (and other large, low-cost countries) on the international economic scene in a globalizing world must be expected to lead to shifts in the composition of production and employment in the U.S.A. It is obvious that the U.S.A. has lost manufacturing jobs to China, but that does not mean that this is necessarily a bad thing for the U.S. economy as a whole, that U.S. manufacturing is in decline, or that China's manufacturing employment expanded by the number of manufacturing jobs lost in the U.S.A. The answer to all three questions is negative. The U.S. economy has continued to grow faster than most other advanced economies and the unemployment rate has remained relatively low. Furthermore, as Table 12.2 below shows, U.S. manufacturing valued added has continued to grow year after year, in spite of industrial outsourcing and plant relocation to China and other low-cost producers. In fact, the share of manufacturing value added in U.S. GDP in 2005 was slightly higher than in 1990.

With regard to China, it is worth noting that total manufacturing employment in that country fell by an estimated 18 million jobs between 1998 and 2003 in spite of very high output growth rates.[11] It was a period of intensive economic restructuring in China, including massive lay-offs by overstaffed state-owned industries and many plant closures. It was only after 2003 that China began to see very modest increases in manufacturing employment again.

It does not make a lot of sense to hold China responsible for job losses in U.S. manufacturing. More important factors are: (1) the *overall* U.S. current account deficit and (2) the fact the overall U.S. trade deficit is matched – almost dollar for dollar – by the trade deficit in manufactured goods. The manufacturing sector is generally more vulnerable to international competition than service sectors. However, even services are increasingly becoming "tradable," especially through broadband connections.

In spite of outsourcing and the relocation of some manufacturing plants to China, the U.S.A. remains the world's largest manufacturer and, as mentioned, domestic output has continued to grow at a reasonable rate. As shown in Table 12.3 below, the U.S. share of global manufacturing in 2005 was just over 22 percent – the same as it was in 1995. Japan's share dropped, while China's share almost doubled to 8 percent in 2005.

Table 12.2 U.S. GDP and manufacturing value added (trillions of constant 2000 dollars) and the share of manufacturing in GDP

	1990	*1995*	*2000*	*2005*
US GDP	7.1	8.0	9.8	11.0
Manufacturing value added	0.9	1.1	1.4	1.5
Manufacturing/GDP	12.9%	13.6%	14.5%	13.8%

Source: Bureau of Economic Analysis, *Real Value Added by Industry*, www.bea.gov/bea/industry/gpotables/gpo_action.cfm

Table 12.3 Share of global manufacturing output

	1995	2005 (provisional)
U.S.A.	22.3%	22.4%
Japan	21.1%	17.8%
China	4.2%	8.0%

Source: UNIDO

Those who argue that U.S. manufacturing is in decline are usually referring to the long-term decline in manufacturing employment. Some blame trade with China for the decline in U.S. manufacturing employment. However, the statistics show that U.S. employment in manufacturing was already falling long before China became a factor. Productivity growth was and remains by far the most important explanation. The ongoing structural economic shift from labor-intensive manufacturing to capital-intensive manufacturing and from manufacturing to service industries in the U.S.A., as in all advanced economies, will continue to reduce the share of manufacturing in total employment. As shown in the chart below, it accounted for just under 10 percent of U.S. employment in 2005, compared to 16.5 percent in 1987. The China factor was unimportant in explaining this long-term relative decline, even after China joined the WTO in 2001.

Most economists agree that the expansion of U.S.–China trade and investment is yielding significant net economic benefits for both nations. However, the benefits are not equally distributed across sectors; adjustment pains in individual

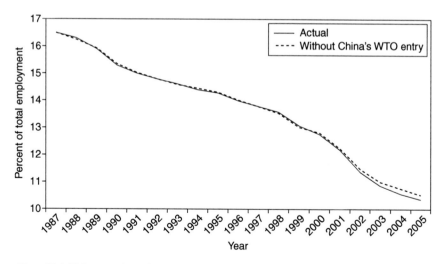

Chart 12.1 U.S. manufacturing employment share (source: Oxford Economics and The Signal Group, *Assessing the Impact on the U.S. Economy of Trade and Investment with China*, The China Business Forum, educational and research arm of the U.S. China Business Council, January 2006).

industries can be serious. In their recent study for the U.S.-China Business Council, Oxford Economics and The Signal Group estimate that 500,000 manufacturing jobs will be lost in the U.S.A. between 2001 and 2010 as a result of the China trade. By comparison, the normal "job turnover" rate in the U.S.A. – old jobs being replaced by new ones, mostly in skill-intensive service industries – is estimated at millions per year.

Major challenges undoubtedly exist for some U.S. manufacturing sectors, especially those that compete directly with imports from China or other low-cost sources. Foreign competition, as well as high energy and healthcare costs, mean that these manufacturers must find ways to improve competitiveness or shift to new fields. Industries that made the shift have tended to phase out low-skill manufacturing jobs while creating high-skill ones. Although the U.S.A. is not a planned economy and never will be, policy-makers should be examining ways to assist this transition for businesses and workers. Increased protection is not the answer.

Bilateral trade imbalances, such as the U.S. deficit with China, may be politically uncomfortable, but they are not negative economic factors per se. The real issue is a country's overall external balance. Economic considerations suggest that the U.S.A., like any importer, should procure its import needs from the most economic and most reliable sources. If that source is China, so be it. Artificial trade diversion aimed at cutting the bilateral deficit with a particular supplier is, on balance, harmful to the U.S. economy. The U.S.A. should, of course, not relax in its efforts to enforce fair trade rules with China using legitimate tools to fight against *unfair* competition from China.

Is the RMB undervalued? Does China "manipulate" its exchange rate?

By most indicators the RMB is undervalued relative to a long-term equilibrium level, but that does not necessarily mean that China's exchange rate is a major factor in explaining the country's external surplus or the U.S. bilateral trade deficit with China. Nor does it mean that the U.S.A. would gain if China adjusted its exchange rate immediately or quickly to its long-term equilibrium level. The opposite is in fact more likely. Moreover, it is not uncommon for exchange rates to be undervalued or overvalued relative to their long-term equilibrium level for extended periods.[12]

Economists do not agree on how to measure the precise degree of undervaluation of China's currency. There are several different methodologies that produce very different results.[13] Many in the U.S.A. have argued that China should "float" its currency, but it is possible that the RMB would then *depreciate* in spite of its current undervaluation relative to a long-term equilibrium level. If a floating currency system were suddenly introduced, many Chinese might try to move their savings abroad.[14] The exchange rate is only one of many factors that influences international trade flows and it may not even be the most important one. The U.S. trade deficit with China was growing long before the RMB was thought to be undervalued.

Some currency appreciation would probably help to reduce China's external surplus, which has become uncomfortably large in recent years, as even Chinese officials now agree.[15] The IMF has been urging China for years to make its exchange rate regime more *flexible* as a first priority. When China changed its exchange rate regime on July 21 2005 by adopting a link to a basket of currencies (instead of just the U.S. dollar) while revaluing by 2.1 percent (relative to the U.S. dollar) on the same day, there was an expectation that the RMB would appreciate more rapidly than it did. If a basket reference rate was used to adjust the RMB/US$ rate, the weight of the U.S. dollar in that basket was much higher than the share of the U.S.A. in China's external trade. By the end of February 2007, the nominal RMB/US$ exchange rate had appreciated by only about 7 percent, while China's trade-weighted real effective exchange rate had in fact slightly depreciated.

From the perspective of the U.S. economy, an appreciation of China's currency would be much more helpful if it were accompanied by similar action in the East Asian region, but in fact, the Japanese yen, Asia's most important currency, moved in the opposite direction in 2006. Since China's exports are on average very import-intensive and because most component imports originate from other East Asian countries, unilateral RMB appreciation against the U.S. dollar will do little to reduce China's export competitiveness in the "processing trade."

When and how did China's relatively fixed exchange rate system come about? It was not China's intention to have a fixed exchange rate when it rationalized its messy, multiple exchange rate system on January 1, 1994 and unified the various rates at the then prevailing free market RMB/US$ rate of 8.7. On the same date China abolished the Foreign Exchange Certificate (FEC)[16] and introduced a "managed, market-driven float system." Soon thereafter it created the Shanghai interbank foreign exchange market to serve as a guide for exchange rate management by the central bank. For some period after exchange rate unification, the rate was allowed to appreciate slowly against the U.S. dollar (about 5 percent) in line with market signals. The rate was frozen at 8.28 to the U.S. dollar (with a very narrow trading band) in December 1997, following the financial collapse of South Korea during the Asian financial crisis. This measure was taken to protect the Chinese economy against instability and to signal that China would not devalue, as was widely expected at the time. The measure was seen by the international community as constructive, because a fixed RMB/US$ rate served as an anchor in the region, making it easier for the regional crisis economies to recover. There was zero international pressure on China to change its new de-facto fixed exchange rate system until 2002. That was the time when China's foreign exchange reserves began to mount very quickly, mainly as a result of a sudden reversal of speculative international capital flows – from capital flight out of China to large "hot" money inflows into China. This reversal in capital flows was probably related to increased international confidence in China's economy following the country's entry into the WTO (2001) and the booming housing market in Shanghai and other cities following the privatization of most urban housing in China that had started in the late 1990s. In wasn't until 2006 that China's trade surplus became a more important factor than speculative capital flows in explaining the rising level of official reserves.

So, when did China's exchange rate policy become unconstructive or "*manipulative*," as some analysts allege? Even though the RMB is thought to be undervalued by most, the prevailing international perspective on this question is that the widening U.S. trade deficit since 2001, including the gap with China, is more related to domestic monetary and fiscal policies in the U.S.A. than to China's exchange rate policy. Relaxed monetary policy combined with large fiscal deficits helped sustain domestic demand in the U.S.A. and prevent a deep recession after the collapse of the NASDAQ in 2000, while at the same time causing the gap between imports and exports to widen. In macroeconomic terms, a country's current account deficit (or surplus) necessarily reflects the gap between its domestic saving and investment rate. For many years the U.S.A. has in fact been spending more than it earned, financing the deficit with net capital inflows from abroad, including China. In other words, China's excess savings (or underconsumption) helped compensate for the domestic savings shortfall in the U.S.A. which ensured lower interest rates than otherwise would have prevailed. Lower interest rates in the U.S.A. helped economic recovery from 2001 and sustained an unprecedented housing boom until recently. So who was subsidizing whom? If it is fair to accuse China of currency manipulation, it is not unfair to accuse the U.S.A. of profligate fiscal and monetary policies.

It was sensible for China to unify its multiple exchange rate system in 1994, to fix its exchange rate against the U.S. dollar in December 1997, and not to devalue at that time. It was also sensible for China not to immediately revalue when capital flows suddenly reversed in 2002, contributing to sharp foreign exchange accumulation from then on. Since that time China's macroeconomic imbalances have grown worse and now threaten the sustainability of its growth model. China has become too dependent on external trade surpluses and excessively high investment levels to maintain high growth. These two factors – excess investment and overdependence on export growth – may well be related as the two sides of a coin. To restore balance, China has to increase the share of consumption in GDP while reducing its saving rate and its external surplus. This will require more than exchange rate adjustment, but RMB appreciation will help to push the economy in the right direction. The rate at which China can afford to appreciate the RMB while maintaining domestic stability is to some extent a matter of political judgment. A big, one-step adjustment, as demanded by some U.S. politicians, could trigger large-scale unemployment in agriculture (producing import competing products), and in low-margin export-oriented manufacturing using primarily domestic inputs (e.g. textiles and garments). It could trigger a recession in China that would also adversely affect the U.S. economy.

The currency decision of July 21, 2005 was a step in the right direction, but it was only a very small step. While serious macro imbalances persist, it is in

China's interest to allow for somewhat faster RMB appreciation. Meanwhile, the U.S.A. should concentrate on restoring macroeconomic balances in its own economy. China's exchange rate has little to do with that.

Prospects and conclusions

If the experience of the past 25 years is any guide, it seems reasonable to expect that China's modernization, urbanization, and the internationalization of its economy will continue. Its relative economic importance in the world will grow before it stabilizes. The U.S.–China economic relationship will continue to grow in both absolute and relative importance. China's GDP growth rate will undoubtedly come down over time as diminishing returns to capital begin to take effect. The household savings rate, which is at present very high, will decline (even without exchange rate action) due to the aging of China's population, growing urbanization, and increasing availability of consumer credit. Crises may occur, but it seems unlikely that China's economy will collapse as a result of economic factors, or turn into the *Economic Monster of Frankenstein* that some critics make it out to be. The direct role of the state in China's economy will further decline and reliance on modern macroeconomic management tools to influence aggregate demand will grow. China will undoubtedly press the U.S.A., the European Union, and Japan to be recognized as a "market economy" for application of their anti-dumping laws.

Many of the cost advantages that producers in China currently enjoy (labor, land, capital, utilities, taxes, overheads) will only be temporary. The enormous spurt in productivity growth that accompanied the massive industrial restructuring since the mid-1990s, which explains a significant part of China's recent export success, is also temporary. In 15 years the situation will be very different. Unit production costs will probably rise as it seems implausible that productivity growth will continue to outpace labor and other cost increases as it did since the mid-1990s. The prices of many other so called non-tradable inputs will undoubtedly move toward international levels as a result of the internationalization of China's economy. Corporate tax advantages for foreign firms will gradually disappear as a result of the recent decision to harmonize tax rates for firms regardless of ownership. The pressure on China to adjust to shifting comparative advantage will become as great as it is on the U.S.A. today. As China's competitive edge in many lines of production declines, it is likely that countries like Vietnam, India, and Bangladesh will take over. This process is already observable. China's international competitive ranking by the World Economic Forum has been falling for several years.

The track record of economists in predicting China's growth is not good. What we can say about the future with some confidence is that some of the factors which played a key role in China's meteoric economic rise during the past 15 years are still present today. We should not forget, however, that China's market reforms remain incomplete and that the country is facing daunting challenges such as the need to find employment in cities and towns for hundreds of millions of farmers over the next few decades. China is also facing severe water shortages in the Northern Plain, other environmental problems, and the need for further social security reform to help redress at least some of the very serious social inequality that has arisen. The recently approved 11th Five-Year Plan gives priority to "harmonious" and "balanced" development, but market forces may continue to push in the opposite direction.

The two most important factors that will make the difference between a successful and a failing China are related: the quality of leadership and domestic political reform. Since the emergence of Deng Xiaoping as top leader in the late 1970s, China had, with few exceptions, high quality leadership at the center. Will that continue to be the case...? One thing is sure: American and Chinese economic interests are already deeply intertwined. The U.S.A. has a big stake in a successful economic transition in China. A prosperous and stable China is not only good for the U.S.A., but also for Asia and the rest of the world. The global structural economic changes which are unfolding as a result of China's rise do indeed pose significant challenges for the U.S.A., but these challenges have to be recognized for what they are. To maintain long-term growth momentum, the U.S.A. will have to protect the sources of its innovative culture and the dynamism of competitiveness. This will require changes in many areas, including fiscal policy, national energy, education, and health policies, tort litigation, small business, and export promotion, job retraining, and the organization of social security systems. The quality of the U.S.–China relationship will be very important for both countries for the remainder of this century and beyond. The U.S.A. and China may never become friends or allies, but the notion that they are destined to become enemies, held by some in the U.S.A. and in China, is not only plain wrong, it is a dangerous and baseless fantasy.

Notes

1 Such recognition is primarily important for the application of national anti-dumping laws. In early 2007 China had been recognized as a market economy by Australia, New Zealand, South Korea, Brazil, Argentina, Venezuela, Chile, Nigeria, and many other African countries.
2 The analysis by John J. Mearsheimer in *The Tragedy of Great Power Politics*, 2001, is of great historical interest, but application of his theory to the evolution of U.S.–China relations is spurious, mainly because the globalization of the Chinese and the American economies has created many critical interdependencies that previously did not exist.
3 This includes James Mann who argued in his recent book, *The China Fantasy. How Our Leaders Explain Away Chinese Repression*, New York: Viking 2007, that many political and business leaders in the U.S.A. naively (perhaps even cynically) justify a policy of engagement with China on the basis of a "soothing scenario" in which economic liberalization is linked to democratization. Because he thinks that this assumed link is a fallacy in the case of China, he recommends a fundamental rethink of U.S.–China relations
4 State Council Information Office, October 19, 2005.
5 A report by Oxford Economics and The Signal Group for the U.S.–China Business Council in January 2006, *The China Effect: Assessing the Impact on the U.S.*

Economy of Trade and Investment with China, calculates that by 2010 U.S. GDP will be 0.7 percent higher, U.S. consumer prices 0.8 percent lower, and per capita disposable income $1,000 higher as a result of increased trade and investment with China since 2001. Similar conclusions are reached in C. Fred Bergsten et al., *China: The Balance Sheet*, New York: Public Affairs, 2006.

6 C. Fred Bergsten et al., *China: The Balance Sheet*. New York: Public Affairs, 2006, p. 97.

7 Andy Xie, "Don't Fear U.S. Backlash," JP Morgan Chase (Equity Research), January 12, 2005. Wal-Mart is reported to have imported some $18 billion worth of goods from China in 2004, $3 billion more than the U.K. and almost twice as much as France.

8 Chinese trade statistics show a much smaller surplus with the U.S.A. than the deficit shown in U.S. trade statistics for reasons that have been explained in various reports by Nicholas Lardy and by the USCBC.

9 The U.S. International Trade Commission distinguishes between two kinds of "processing exports": processing with imported materials and assembly of imported components. According to ITC Working Paper no. 2006–07-A, July 2006, the two categories together accounted for 67.1 percent of China's exports to the U.S.A. in 2004, which corresponds closely to the share of foreign-invested enterprises in China's exports to the U.S.A. in 2004, estimated by ITC at 65.8 percent. The ITC report does not estimate how much of the 65.8 percent is accounted for by U.S.-owned companies located in China, but it is probably not less than one-third, which would mean that at least 22 percent of China's exports to the U.S.A. is accounted for by U.S.-owned companies.

10 Alexander B. Hammer, *The Dynamic Structure of U.S.–China Trade, 1995–2004*. U.S. International Trade Commission, working paper N0. 2006–07-A, July 2006.

11 This estimate is based on the work of Judith Banister and will be reflected in a forthcoming publication of the Conference Board.

12 Jeffrey Frankel, "On the Yuan: the choice between adjustment under a fixed exchange rate and adjustment under a flexible rate," CESifo Economic Studies, 2006, http://ksghome.harvard.edu/~jfrankel/currentpubsspeeches.htm

13 Government Accountability Office, *Treasury Assessments Have Not Found Currency Manipulation, but Concerns about Exchange Rates Continue*, April 2005, (GAO-05–351).

14 Neither the IMF nor the U.S. Treasury recommend that China should make its currency fully convertible immediately or open the capital account fully at once. To avoid dangerous shocks to the financial system, they recommend a phased dismantling of remaining capital account restrictions combined with intensified banking reform and interest rate liberalization, prior to the adoption of full convertibility. This is also China's policy.

15 Announcing China's trade results for 2006, Bo Xilai, China's minister of commerce, mentioned to the press that reducing the country's trade surplus had become a high priority.

16 The FEC was a special currency for foreign residents and tourists in China. Its exchange rate was fixed at the same rate as the official RMB/US$ exchange rate.

13 China, the U.S.A., and Japan
Reconfiguring relations in Southeast Asia

Elizabeth Economy

During the past few decades, China's foreign policy has undergone a remarkable transformation from one predicated on China as a developing country consumed with issues of domestic concern to one that acknowledges and even celebrates China's potential as a regional and global power. Particularly since the turn of the century, China's economic success has enabled it to pursue a greater role on the international stage, backing up its claims to regional and global leadership with growing economic and military might. Nowhere is China's presence more keenly felt than within Southeast Asia, where increasing Chinese activism is met with a combination of both enthusiasm and significant trepidation.

There are clear signs of China's more active diplomacy, including growing trade relations, the signing of numerous cooperative agreements, and an increasing number of high level visits to the region by senior Chinese officials. Chinese trade officials have trumped their Japanese counterparts, marching through Asia to structure a regional free trade agreement. Chinese development assistance is flowing freely to Laos, Myanmar, and Cambodia, and China is becoming the destination of choice for foreign direct investment (FDI) and trade from its wealthier East Asia neighbors. In the security realm, China has put forth several proposals to develop new security arrangements based on principles of mutual cooperation and security and is pursuing bilateral security arrangements throughout the region. Even in the arena of transnational issues, such as public health, drug trafficking and the environment, a source of significant contention between China and many of its neighbors, Chinese officials have been promising and delivering on new initiatives. Moreover, in ways not seen previously, the Chinese leadership is tapping into the overseas Chinese community throughout Asia to play an important role diplomatically and economically in furthering the mainland's interests.

China's diplomatic offensive in Southeast Asia has raised questions in the U.S.A. and throughout Asia concerning the nature of China's rise and its implications. Advocates of a China threat scenario have long argued that China desires regional hegemony and that U.S.–China relations in this regard are a zero-sum game. Analogies are made between the rise of China and that of Nazi Germany or Imperial Japan: China's rise will necessarily be highly disruptive to U.S. preeminence in the global system, stability in Asia, and the international system writ large. Others paint a picture of China returning to the glory days of the Middle Kingdom, using its economic might to establish an empire with tentacles reaching out throughout most of Asia and transforming its neighbors into little more than vassal states. Still other analysts argue forcefully that China's rise can be managed through integrating the country into international norms and regimes, thereby ensuring that China has a stake in preserving the status quo.[1] In this scenario, as the Chinese themselves have insisted, China's rise will be peaceful, serving an ameliorative function in international affairs: enhancing global security, promoting peaceful trade, and addressing transnational challenges.

Such debate arises against the backdrop of a perception among some scholars that China's aggressive engagement with Asia contrasts starkly with a policy of relative neglect by the U.S.A., the region's traditional hegemon. The Asia strategy President Bush enunciated at the outset of his term focused overwhelmingly on East Asia: militating against the rise of China, ensuring peaceful relations between Taiwan and the mainland, and enhancing ties with America's traditional allies and trading partners, South Korea, Taiwan, and Japan. Relations between Southeast Asia and the U.S.A. were perhaps well described as "a policy without a strategy."[2] While U.S. relations with Southeast Asia, as with most of the world, seemed to develop common purpose in the wake of the terrorist attacks in New York and Washington, D.C. on September 11, 2001; over time, much of this shared sense of purpose has dissipated. The White House's doctrine of preemption, unilateralism, and invasion of Iraq led to a precipitous decline in America's reputation among many publics throughout the world, including those in Southeast Asia. Moreover, President Bush's singular focus on security issues during the past five APEC forums has done little to persuade many regional leaders that the White House understands the region's priorities of domestic economic development and political stability.

The contrast between the perceived "rise of China" and "decline of the U.S.A." makes it easy to reach the conclusion that China is staking its claim as the region's hegemon, that the region welcomes China's advances, and that the U.S.A. is ill-positioned to meet this challenge. Still, we need to question whether such an assessment is accurate. And, if it is, does it matter? And if we answer both in the affirmative, what are the long-term implications for the U.S.A.?

Does it matter?

To take perhaps the most important question first: Does it matter who holds top billing in Asia? At some point it might not, but right now it clearly does.

The economic and security significance of Southeast Asia to the U.S.A. is well established. Southeast Asia is home to almost 600 million people, commands a GDP of greater than $880 billion, and is the U.S.A.'s fourth-largest trading partner. From a strategic perspective, the region hosts some of the world's most critical sea-lanes, most notably the Strait of Malacca, through which nearly a quarter of the world's trade passes, including 80 persent of East Asia's oil shipments. Perhaps most important in the current political context,

U.S. leaders view Southeast Asia as a fertile breeding ground for terrorist activities.

The preeminent role of the U.S.A. in Asia, moreover, has permitted the U.S.A. to help shape regional politics in ways that directly serve U.S interests. For example, in 2001, in the immediate wake of the terrorist attacks against the U.S.A., President Bush successfully reoriented the agenda of the APEC leaders' summit in Shanghai away from trade and investment to terrorism. It is a focus that has remained in each APEC summit since, despite the grumblings of many members. And, at the APEC 2003 summit, APEC members enshrined the war on terror in the final declaration, stating that transnational terrorism and the proliferation of weapons of mass destruction pose "direct and profound challenges to APEC's vision of free, open and prosperous economies." They further agreed to commit APEC "not only to advancing the prosperity of our economies but also the complementary mission of ensuring the security of our people."[3]

Within Asia more broadly, the U.S.A. has played a critical role in trying to ensure the security of the region. The initial impulse of the Bush administration, for example, to engage all five other relevant nations – particularly China – to support the six-party talks on the North Korea nuclear threat has been essential to reengaging North Korea in a manner that increases the likelihood of a verifiable and enforceable agreement.

Moreover, while the U.S.A. has lost some credibility globally as a leader over the past several years, it nonetheless will remain an essential force in shaping issues such as public health, environmental protection, human rights, and drug trafficking in the region. Asia needs the U.S.A. for its commitment to transparency, openness, and human rights protection; a commitment that China does not evidence consistently, at least at the present time. And finally, as already noted, Asia's role in shaping the future of the U.S. economy also argues for the U.S.A. to retain a dominant role in the region.

Is it true?

What is the reality of China's new diplomacy and what does it portend for U.S. influence in the region? China's rise to date appears to be much less about the "inevitable conflict of rising power" theory popular in some circles than about creeping power transition. Chinese thinkers themselves have recognized that the international community is concerned over the potential implications of China's rise and have taken pains to ensure that China's rise is perceived as nonthreatening.[4]

In spring 2003, China's leaders signaled a dramatic shift in the country's foreign-policy approach. Senior Party adviser Zheng Bijian publicly articulated the leaders' new vision as *heping jueqi* or the peaceful rise of China. According to Zheng, this rise has been occurring since 1978 and will continue until the mid twenty-first century. The pronouncement acknowledged a transition from a foreign policy that had been predicated on China as a developing country consumed with issues of domestic concern to one that declared China's potential as a regional and global power. At the same time, within China, it was viewed as an important counterweight to the prevalent "China threat" or "China collapse" theories in the West. One of the central tenets is that China will never seek hegemony. Li Junru, vice-president of the Central Party School, explicitly outlined the benefits to China's neighbors, stating, "China's rise will not damage the interests of other Asian countries. That is because as China rises, it provides a huge market for its neighbors. At the same time, the achievements of China's development will allow it to support the progress of others in the region."[5] Asserting such a strategy was a diplomatically skilful move calculated not only to declare China's intentions but also to reassure others concerned about China's growing economic and military strength.

To realize this peaceful rise, China is using a sophisticated blend of trade, confidence building measures, and even development assistance to establish itself as an important regional leader. Even though it is far from supplanting either Japan or the U.S.A. as the most important regional player in economic or security affairs, it is steadily building bridges with other countries in the region and demonstrating a willingness to step into the breach when American or Japanese leaders hesitate to take action. Over the past few years, China has received much acclaim in the region for its multilateral approach, its ability to understand the needs of regional actors, and its desire to address the region's concerns.

China's interest in multilateralism is manifested in its role in the growing number of institutions in the region. These institutions provide new opportunities to engage in diplomatic activism in addition to China's growing economic and military influence. China has become a driving force in the Shanghai Cooperation Organization, the East Asia Summit, and other regional groupings. The country's economic presence also wields significant influence on Southeast Asia, particularly as it pushes ahead with a China–ASEAN FTA in defiance of regional calls for a more inclusive trade pact. These developments suggest China is embarking on a strategy to form alliances and create broader regional groupings that will be beneficial to its core strategic interests.

At the same time, many in the region remain wary of China's growing activism, fearing the PRC will swamp the region economically and over time use its military might to establish a much more active role in policing the region. China's relations with the countries of the region vary significantly from close economic and military ties with Myanmar to growing economic linkages and lingering suspicions with Vietnam.

Moreover, discussions with officials throughout the region suggest that China has yet to assume a real leadership role outside the realm of trade. With regard to transnational issues – health, crime, and environment, among others – China is often a major contributor, if not the primary source of the challenge.

Driving regional economic growth

China's greatest advances in the region have come in the economic realm. In 2000, former Philippine President Estrada said, "Frankly, I think China wants to take over Asia."[6] But China has worked hard to assuage such fears. Yang Jiechi, China's ambassador to the U.S.A., stated that the "rising tide lifts all boats," intimating that as China succeeds so too will the rest of Southeast Asia.[7] While some regional officials and analysts were initially skeptical, China's actions to a large extent appear to support such rhetoric. In 2006, Malaysian Prime Minister Abduallah Ahmad Badawi stated, "Perceiving China as a threat has been wrong. We have always regarded China as an opportunity."[8]

Yang and Badawi's claims are supported by China's growing role as an engine of economic growth for the region. From 1990 to 2005, China-ASEAN trade volume grew an average of 22 percent annually;[9] trade reached $130.4 billion in 2005, up from $105 billion in 2004.[10] At least one estimate indicates China-ASEAN trade could surpass $200 billion by 2008.[11] From the perspective of Southeast Asia, China's trading patterns are particularly beneficial; in 2005, ASEAN maintained a trade surplus with China of US$20 billion, largely from its enormous exports of raw materials and precision machinery.[12]

At the same time, China has been actively pushing for a regional free trade agreement that will encompass Brunei, Indonesia, Malaysia, the Philippines, Singapore, and Thailand in 2010 and incorporate Vietnam, Laos, Myanmar and Cambodia by 2015. Experts have suggested that once the China–ASEAN FTA is established in 2010, China's exports to ASEAN will grow by $10.6 billion or 55.1 percent, and ASEAN's exports to China will surge by $13 billion or 48 percent. The total trade volume will reach $1.2 trillion.[13] China also agreed to an "Early Harvest Package" that is perceived by the region as "largely a concession by China" to provide early benefits through tariff reductions on 573 products including agricultural and manufactured goods.[14] Individual Chinese entrepreneurs are also expanding China's economic reach throughout Laos and Myanmar. In some areas, locals use only the yuan and speak Chinese.

Still, skeptics could point to the fact that both Japan's current trade with ASEAN (more than $155 billion in 2005) and that of the U.S.A. (more than $149 billion in 2005) exceed that of China. And the response to China's growing economic presence in the region has not been uniformly positive. In some sectors, China's expansion is not welcome: electronics, furniture, motorcycles, and fruits and vegetables are just some of the areas in which Chinese goods have begun to supplant those traditionally produced in Southeast Asia;[15] and in both Indonesia and Malaysia, people complain that jobs are being lost to China. A growing Chinese economic presence could also fuel latent resentment against the sizable population of Chinese economic elites in the region.

Overall, however, trends suggest that both China and Japan are offering growing markets for Southeast Asian goods and producing more goods desired by Southeast Asian countries. Japan–ASEAN trade jumped from $136 billion in 2004 to $155 billion in 2005, while U.S.–ASEAN trade has remained relatively stagnant, increasing from roughly $137 billion in 2004 to $149 billion in 2005.[16] Such trends are likely to continue as China outpaces both the U.S.A. and Japan in developing free trade agreements with regional actors. Thus far, the U.S.A. has only established a bilateral free trade agreement with Singapore, although it is currently negotiating another FTA with Malaysia. In August 2006, the U.S.A. announced it would begin talks establishing a less-comprehensive trade and investment framework agreement with ASEAN members. U.S. agricultural subsidies, however, and concerns of most of the poorer countries in Asia over rules concerning foreign investment, antitrust regulation, and transparency in government procurement are likely to slow any additional bilateral trade negotiations with the U.S.A.

Recently, Japan has been more aggressive in pursuing its own bilateral FTAs, with an eye toward the formation of a regional FTA in the future. It has signed bilateral free trade agreements with Singapore, the Philippines, Malaysia, and Mexico, and has finalized another agreement with Thailand. As competition with China increases, Japan has embarked on a spate of new FTA negotiations with countries including Indonesia, Chile, Australia, South Korea, Brunei, and Vietnam. In contrast to China, however, Japan talks less about what a regional free trade agreement will bring to the region, and – perhaps for domestic consumption – more about the overwhelming benefits that it will bring to the Japanese economy, which already runs a trade surplus with the region. The Japanese government believes that a free trade agreement with ASEAN would bring as much as $18 billion to Japan's GDP and create as many as 260,000 jobs.[17]

While China has made rapid strides in expanding its trade relations with Southeast Asia, not surprisingly its role as a source of investment for the region has been far slower. Still, it has taken steps to assert itself in this arena as well. It has committed US$100 million in aid and investment to Myanmar, and is developing Indonesian natural gas reserves, investing in infrastructure development in the Philippines, establishing rail and highway links with Cambodia, Thailand, and Singapore, and promising to dredge part of the Mekong River in Laos and Myanmar to make it suitable for commercial navigation.

In terms of development assistance, China still lags far behind the regional leader, Japan. Japan is the top aid donor to ASEAN members; in 2001, Japan pledged $2.1 billion to ASEAN countries, comprising almost 30 percent of Japan's aid worldwide and 60 percent of the development assistance to the region.[18] China is increasing aid to ASEAN countries: Major aid initiatives include $2 billion in loans to the Philippines, undercutting Japan's offer of $1 billion and dwarfing $200 million offers from the World Bank and Asian Development Bank.[19]

Finally, in the wake of the Asian financial crisis, many actors, particularly Japan, have been paying increasing attention to issues revolving around the stability of Asian currencies. As is well known, during the financial crisis, China not only refrained from devaluing the yuan but also provided a US$1 billion loan bailout of Thailand. In contrast, many in Southeast Asia complained that the U.S.A. was interested only in imposing an IMF straitjacket. American efforts at the 2003 APEC summit to persuade Asian allies to criticize China's exchange rate policy were received poorly by the region. Since that time, China has tried to appear accommodating, repeatedly promising more flexibility with its currency practices, and at the 2004 APEC leaders' summit announcing the establishment of an Asia-Pacific Finance and Development Center to facilitate exchanges and capacity building within the region.[20]

With Japanese leadership, the region has moved forward to develop a range of regionally-based currency arrangements that exclude the U.S.A. Brunei, Indonesia, Japan, the Philippines, Thailand, and Vietnam are exchanging data on short-term capital flows. The regional economies are attempting to establish an early warning system that would involve monitoring balance of payments, exchange rate regimes, and levels of foreign borrowing. At the same time, the Chiang Mai Initiative, launched in 1999, has contributed to a flurry of bilateral swaps, worth $17 billion dollars, involving Japan–Korea, Japan–Thailand, Japan–Philippines, Japan–Malaysia, China–Thailand, and Japan–China. Other agreements are in the works, including two involving China: China–Malaysia and China–Philippines. Despite objections by the IMF and the U.S.A., in June 2003 "China and ten other Asia-Pacific countries, including five ASEAN members, agreed ... to establish an Asian Bond Fund worth more than $1 billion" to help "bail out economies in crisis."[21] This was followed by a second bond fund initiative implemented in April 2005 for an additional $2 billion fund to invest in Asian currency-denominated government bonds.[22]

Such developments strengthen the sense of an Asia for Asians, and an Asia that does not necessarily involve the U.S.A. While Japan has played a leadership role in developing these new currency arrangements, China will likely become an increasingly important force. As China takes steps to make its currency convertible, it may well emerge as the dominant regional currency. According to one analysis, Japan's banking and debt crisis makes the yen "less suitable as a vehicle for wider Asian monetary integration," and the U.S. dollar may not retain its dominance in a trade regime "dominated ... by links with China."[23]

The reality then is that China is assuming a leadership role in the regional economy and aggressively pursuing an ASEAN + China free trade agreement. Yet Japan's investments in ASEAN are ten times that of China, it retains a larger trade relationship, and drives the currency negotiations within the region. Japan and the U.S.A. continue to be the region's most important trading partners, but the stagnant level of trade between the U.S.A. and ASEAN suggests that the U.S.A. may be finding other markets, such as China, more attractive. Unless greater attention is paid to contributing to Southeast Asia's continued economic growth, the U.S.A. will rapidly lose its stature as a key trading partner to the region.

Securing the region

While China has moved aggressively to promote closer economic relations with Southeast Asia, its initiatives in the security arena have been more tentative, although Chinese political analysts are increasingly acknowledging the potential for China to play a more far-reaching role in the region's security. As Vice Director of the China Institute of International Studies Ruan Zongze has noted:

The development of China is conducive to security and stability in the region. China lies at the joint of the "curve of turbulence" through the Eurasia continent to northeast Asia and this region is where the interests of major powers converge and therefore has a lot of "hotspots." A stronger China would have more leverage in mediating regional conflicts, and thus contributing to cooperation.[24]

The basic thrust of China's approach has been to identify its regional security outlook more closely with that of other regional actors. For example, China signed on to ASEAN's 1976 Treaty of Amity and Cooperation, the essence of which is a set of commitments to respect the ideals of sovereignty and noninterference in others' internal affairs, and to settle disputes peacefully. President Hu has also proposed a new Security Policy Conference that would be comprised of senior military as well as civilian officials from the 23 ASEAN Regional Forum (ARF) countries. The objective would be to draft a new security pact to promote peace and stability in the region on the basis of "mutual trust, mutual benefit, quality and coordination."[25] In concrete terms, China has established a listening post in Myanmar; and in 2002 China signed its first ever border agreement with Vietnam. The two countries also conducted a joint campaign to clear all the landmines along their border, resulting in an increase in border trade of 4 billion yuan.

Yet challenges remain. Taiwan in particular has the potential to undermine the PRC's image as an accommodating and benign rising power. In July 2004, Singapore Deputy Prime-Minister Lee Hsien Loong, son of Singapore's former leader Lee Kuan Yew, visited Taiwan, prompting a sharp response from the PRC, which cancelled a visit by China's Central Bank Governor Zhou Xiaochuan and suspended a number of other government talks.

In addition, China pledged to accede to the Southeast Asia Nuclear Weapon Free Zone (a regime that the U.S.A. rejects). In a surprising move, however, in fall 2004, ASEAN rejected China's bid to join the accord on the grounds that it would prefer that all nuclear powers join at the same time. This might signal some desire on the part of ASEAN that China does not assume a high profile role on the security front without the simultaneous engagement of the other regional powers.

At the same time, negotiating China's claims to the islands and resources (particularly oil and natural gas) of the South China Sea remains the greatest area of concern for most Southeast Asian states. Approximately 25 percent of the world's shipping moves through the Sea, and the South China Sea is an area that engages most of the regional actors: It is bordered by China and Taiwan on the north, Vietnam on the West, Malaysia, Indonesia and Brunei on the South, and the Philippines on the east. To date, Vietnam controls the largest number of islands in the largest island grouping, the Spratlys, but in 1987 China set up an observation station there and five years later the National People's Congress passed a law declaring sovereignty over the entire South China Sea. There have been sporadic conflicts between the Philippines, China, Taiwan, Malaysia, and

Vietnam over control of the islands. China has also long rejected any multilateral code of conduct that would restrict its access to the resources of the Sea.

Yet in August 2002, to the great surprise of many in the region, China signed a declaration of conduct that essentially promised to discuss joint development in the South China Sea. China did not, however, agree to sign a code of conduct. In September 2004, Vietnam accused China and the Philippines of planning surveying operations in its territorial jurisdiction; one month later, China retaliated, accusing Vietnam of violating its territorial sovereignty by inviting bids for oil exploration in the Spratlys.[26] Premier Wen Jiabao appeared to try to defuse the situation by proposing greater regional consultation: At the China-ASEAN summit in November 2004, he suggested the establishment of a senior-level working group to work through the issues of joint development.[27] In 2005, in a step in a positive direction, the national oil companies of China, the Philippines, and Vietnam signed a joint accord to conduct marine seismic activities in the Spratlys. Some analysts argue that a combination of a previous agreement by both countries to settle disputes through negotiation and rapidly rising trade relations will mitigate any potential negative fallout from the Spratlys dispute.[28]

The U.S.A., while perhaps making less headway rhetorically in furthering regional security, has moved aggressively to shore up its bilateral military-to-military relations with a number of countries in the region. Since the late 1990s, the U.S.A. has taken steps to enhance some security relationships and re-establish others, such as those with the Philippines. Such efforts received new impetus after the terrorist attacks against the U.S.A. on September 11, 2001. The Bush administration labeled Southeast Asia the "second front" in the war on terror. Evidence indicates that Malaysia, Singapore, Indonesia, and Thailand all have served as meeting grounds for terrorists with links to al-Qaeda. In early January 2002, Singapore arrested 13 such terrorists, eight with direct links to al-Qaeda. Thus, the war on terror has reinforced a sense of urgency in deepening U.S. military ties throughout the region. The U.S.A. has forged strong security relationships with Thailand, the Philippines, and Australia, all of which it considers major non-NATO allies. It has also taken steps to begin negotiating a framework agreement with Singapore to establish a strategic partnership in defense and security. The U.S.A. is working with Thailand to improve port security and expending significant resources to train and arm the Philippine military in its anti-terrorism work, among other things. The U.S.A. has particularly targeted the Philippines for military assistance. Total military assistance jumped from $31 million in 2001 to $91 million in 2005.[29] While there is a ban on military-to-military relations with Indonesia, the U.S.A. is providing assistance to the Indonesian police to improve their counter-terrorism capacity. While Malaysia rejected the presence of U.S. troops redeployed from Japan and South Korea for the sake of "national dignity and sovereignty," since 2002 Malaysia has nonetheless been engaged in a series of training exercises with U.S. naval forces, as have Brunei, Thailand, Indonesia, Singapore, and the Philippines. China has participated as an observer in some of these exercises.

Overall, the states in Southeast Asia play a critical role in "providing intelligence, undertaking surveillance of suspicious groups, and, in some cases, watching over US freight craft and warships laden with military and other supplies for the war and post-war effort in Afghanistan."[30]

Still, the recent heightened U.S. interest and military presence in the region has been received by distrust in some quarters in Southeast Asia. Scholars, policy-makers, and track-two participants in security dialogues have voiced several concerns. First, that the U.S.A. interest is ephemeral: as soon as interest in terrorism wanes, the U.S.A. will again forget about Southeast Asia. Second, that the war against terrorism may be used by authoritarian governments such as that in Malaysia to strengthen its own hand by eliminating legitimate opposition groups, such as the Pan Malaysian Islamic Party or Islam Se-Malaysia. And finally, that the U.S.A. did not consult other countries in its pursuit of the war against terrorism, but acted largely unilaterally, demanding that countries fall in behind the U.S.A. or risk being labeled "not with us."[31]

Certainly, the U.S. focus on preemption and regime change, especially as revealed in the 2002 National Security Strategy, has become a source of significant concern among Asian publics. Asian countries have traditionally been strong supporters of the norms of sovereignty, territorial integrity and nonintervention. Already in Indonesia, 74 percent of Indonesians have been worried that the U.S.A. might become a military threat to their country. The Indonesian vice-president, Hamzah Haz, stated in 2003, "Who is the real terrorist? Well, it's America ... In fact, the US is the king of terrorists because of its war crimes in Iraq. The U.S. condemns terrorists but itself carries out terror acts on Iraq." In the Philippines, Vice-President Teofisto Guingona reportedly resigned as foreign minister as a result of the growing military ties between the Philippines and the U.S.A. He argued, "America should stop bullying countries like the Philippines. We became independent, but ... we are still under their rules and supervision."[32] The Pew Foundation's 2006 Global Attitudes Project reported that in Indonesia, the percentage of Indonesians who held a positive image of the U.S.A. fell from 75 percent in 2000 to 30 percent by the summer of 2006.[33]

Moreover, regional analysts are concerned that the focus of the Bush administration on a military response to the terrorist challenge is misguided, and that the U.S.A. must embrace more nuanced political strategies. Singapore defense analyst Kumar Ramakrishna has argued, "It is a strategic inefficiency to physically eliminate scattered terrorist groups without addressing the roots of the anti-Americanism that animates them." Chinese strategic analyst Guo Xinning also points out in his assessment that the U.S. military presence in the region is not likely to diminish the increasing anti-American sentiments among Muslims in the region.[34] Such concerns were reinforced at a June 2006 security conference for Asian defense ministers, in which then U.S. Secretary of Defense Rumsfeld reiterated White House demands that Asian countries improve their effort to counter terrorism, particularly criticizing Iran's participation in the Shanghai Cooperation Organization. And Singapore analyst Simon Tay has written eloquently about the disturbing evolution of U.S. relations with Southeast Asia from one of partnership to one of primacy. In his assessment, if the U.S.A. lives up to its own values – "championing aspirations of human dignity," "igniting a new era of global economic growth," and "expanding the circle of development by opening societies and building the infrastructure of democracy," U.S. leadership will be much more acceptable to the people of the region.[35]

The White House may have recognized the damage done to its reputation by its overwhelming focus on the war on terror and Iraq. During January 2005, the U.S.A. assumed a leadership role in responding to the humanitarian crisis in Southeast and South Asia brought on by the devastating tsunami. This represented perhaps one step toward recapturing some of what Tay and others have called for in U.S. leadership.

The picture that emerges in the security realm is thus a mixed one. While China has not asserted itself as an alternative to U.S. leadership, the potential exists. Despite strengthened military ties between the U.S.A. and some regional actors, a strong reservoir of distrust and enmity exists toward the U.S.A. in many of the region's publics. It is plausible that over time, China's message of non-interference, cooperative security, and the diminution of the role of the U.S.A. that is implied by China's approach will gain in popularity, although the U.S.A. may yet again broaden its approach to security and regain territory it has lost.

Environment, drugs, health, and governance: China confronts itself

While China's economic and security diplomacy has advanced China's reputation within the region, its relative lack of transparency in addressing transnational issues has been a continued source of angst among regional actors. Across the board on such issues as environmental protection, public health, drug trafficking, and governance, China generally has been less of a positive force than a challenge for other regional actors to negotiate. Still, there are signs of change in the willingness of the Chinese leadership to work more openly and cooperatively with its neighbors on these issues.

In May 2002, the Chinese government issued a position paper at the ARF outlining the necessity of improving cooperation on nontraditional security issues, such as terrorism, drug trafficking, HIV/AIDS, illegal migration and the environment. While the paper was short on specifics, it highlighted the complex transnational nature of these challenges and committed China to play an integral role in working with other countries to resolve them.[36]

In some respects, this commitment has been manifested on the ground. After years of refusing to cooperate in international efforts to combat drugs, for example, China is now playing a far more constructive role, particularly in addressing the drug trafficking in heroin and amphetamines, among other illicit drugs, that are crossing the border from Myanmar through China to Hong Kong, Taiwan, and beyond. China signed onto three major U.N. drug conventions and hosted a meeting in Beijing in May 2002, with the United Nations Drug Control Program, as well as Laos, Thailand, Myanmar, and Cambodia to discuss strategies. Over the past decade, Beijing has become increasingly concerned about the drug problem within its own borders and links between drug traffickers and broader organized crime efforts, as well as the relationship between drug use and China's growing problem of HIV/AIDS. In October 2005, China hosted a conference for over 200 prosecutors from throughout ASEAN as well as U.N. officials on combating drug trafficking.[37] Still, Beijing is likely to have a difficult time clamping down effectively: A recent report by an analyst within China's State Council indicated that local governments in China are increasingly dependent on the revenues from organized crime, such as drug trafficking and prostitution, making local officials reluctant to prosecute criminals.

China's interest in cooperation on transboundary health issues also received new impetus with the advent of Severe Acute Respiratory Syndrome (SARS), which the government acknowledged as an epidemic during spring 2003. While the Chinese government initially refused to admit to the severity of the problem, once it did, it moved quickly to rein in the negative publicity. In April, 2003, at a Special China-ASEAN Leaders' Meeting on SARS, Chinese Premier Wen Jiabao called for much deeper cooperation on health issues: a reporting mechanism for future epidemics with a rapid response program; cooperation on SARS research with an investment of Y10 million (US$1.2 million) by China; and a future meeting on SARS to be hosted by Beijing.[38] The response from the region to Wen's remarks was quite positive. And China's apparent openness concerning the outbreak of Avian flu during summer 2004 was also well received. Still, China's record on communicating the nature of its HIV/AID's problem – both to its own citizens and to the international community – suggests that reforms in the public health sector and openness about the nature of these problems will continue to remain a challenge.

In the environmental arena, China has long been perceived as the source of several regional problems. South Korea and Japan, for example, have worked for many years to assist China in improving its efforts at controlling the SO_2 emissions that cause acid rain. Despite significant funding assistance, close cooperation on monitoring emissions, and commitment on the part of China's environmental officials, China's rapid economic growth and weak environmental enforcement have yielded little improvement.

In addition, on more sensitive issues, China has proved a more recalcitrant actor. This is perhaps nowhere more evident than in China's development of the Mekong River. According to one report, 20 percent of the waters of the Mekong originate in China; during the dry season this figure jumps to 70 percent.[39] China already has one dam operating on the upper reaches of the river and a second, Dachaoshan, under construction. A third is planned for 2012. For countries downstream, including Thailand, Laos, Cambodia, and Vietnam, China's dam development is already having negative consequences. During summer 2004, the Mekong was at its lowest level ever, with serious consequences for fisheries and rice production, both significant income sources for communities within all of the downstream countries. Cambodia's fish catch dropped by almost 50 percent from the prior year.[40] At the same time, the water level fluctuates wildly depending on dam operations. While the Mekong River Commission has attempted to engage China, the Chinese have demonstrated interest neither in participating in the work of the commission nor in listening to the concerns of its neighbors.[41] China is also a major source of biodiversity loss throughout South-east Asia. Rare turtles, tigers, and seahorses, among other wildlife, are being consumed voraciously by China; one analyst reports that the problem has only become worse with China's growing wealth. Business people are now willing to pay $1,000 rather than $100 for illegal wildlife parts, providing even more incentive for illegal wildlife trade. Moreover, China has become one of the world's largest importers of tropical timber from the region, and Chinese logging firms have developed a reputation for their illegal practices, contributing to the decimation of forests in Myanmar and Indonesia.[42]

Finally, in the broader political realm of governance – transparency, rule of law, and human rights – China's record has been mixed. China's strong relations with some of the more brutal of the region's regimes, such as Myanmar, make it a potentially important partner for other nations interested in taking action to improve the region's overall practices. In June 2003, for example, ASEAN rejected its traditional reluctance to interfere in the domestic affairs of other countries and condemned Myanmar's human rights practices, in particular its detention of the pro-democracy leader Aung San Suu Kyi and attacks on her supporters. At the 2003 APEC leaders' summit, APEC's host, Thai leader Thaksin Shinawatra, stated that China should be party to any discussions of progress toward democracy in Myanmar. Soon thereafter in April 2004, China took the surprising step of supporting a resolution in the United Nations Human Rights Commission urging the government of Myanmar to restore democracy. Yet three years later, in January 2007, China vetoed a draft U.N. Security Council resolution condemning Myanmar's treatment of political opponents.

Thus, although it is unlikely that China will be able to assume a leadership role in promoting good governance in the very near future, and even though the region undoubtedly recognizes the limitations of China as a leader on such issues, China's role as a contributor to transnational problems dictates its presence at the table. To the extent that China is reforming its own practices and increasingly behaving in a responsible manner both domestically and internationally, the opportunity for China to assume a leadership role will increase exponentially.

Conclusion

China's efforts to assuage the fears of its neighbors by adopting a foreign-policy approach that is active, nonthreatening, and generally aligned with the economic and security interests of the region is clearly making headway. The substance underlying the positive diplomacy is most notable in the trade realm, where China is rapidly emerging as an engine of regional economic growth and integration that may well challenge Japanese and American dominance in the next three to five years. China's role as an important source of FDI for the region and player in regional currency schemes is also likely to grow rapidly.

In the security realm, China's diplomacy, while likely rhetorically appealing to regional actors, has yet to make significant inroads in a regional security structure dominated by the U.S.A. and its bilateral security relationships. More-over, while China has signed a declaration of conduct governing the South China Sea, how the region moves forward to develop the resources of the Sea will depend significantly on the actual measures that China takes to ensure that ventures are cooperative and equally developed. Still, if nascent anti-American sentiment within the region continues to grow, China may find more room to maneuver as it attempts to develop a regional security architecture that mini-mizes American influence.

If China is to emerge as a real leader within Southeast Asia, it will also need to assume more of the social and political burden that leadership entails. Throughout Southeast Asia, the U.S.A., for all its misadventures, has generally been perceived as a champion of democracy and human rights. Public opinion polls and statements by various Southeast Asian analysts and officials suggest that this reputation has been tarnished during the Bush administration. Yet, there is no other country willing or able to claim the mantle of such leadership. While Premier Wen's post-SARS call to arms for regional action to combat this deadly disease was heartening to the region and the world, it also was prompted by significant international condemnation of China's initial decision not to acknow-ledge the severity of the problem. As China continues to advance itself as a regional leader, its policies on issues such as health, drugs, the environment, and human rights will face additional scrutiny not only for their impact on the region but also for the more profound question they raise concerning the potential of China's moral leadership.

China's rise within the region also suggests a larger, longer-term struggle to define the nature of Asian relations. Many of China's initiatives promote a far more integrated Asia than currently exists. Such a future may seem unlikely. It is a region marked by disparate geography, languages, political systems, stand-ards of living, and degrees of integration with the outside world. In addition, if China and Japan were to assert a collective leadership role, it would necessitate a far more cooperative relationship between the two countries than is the case today. Moreover, unlike in the case of the European Union, there is no single, agreed-upon threat in Asia. Southeast Asian leaders appear torn between their long-term concerns over a bullying U.S.A., a hegemonic China, or a resurgent Japan. As Muthaih Alagappa has argued, "The primary purpose of the state-centered regional security order in Asia is to consolidate the nation-state, enhance its international power and influence, and create a safe and predictable environment."[43]

Asian integration also presumes a much deeper set of integrated policies and norms than currently exist. Moving from a forum that encourages free trade to a regional free trade agreement requires one significant expansion in cooperation; progressing from an Asian monetary fund to a common currency requires yet another. In the security arena, advancing from a largely stagnant set of talks to a regional code of conduct in the South China Sea represents one advance in coordination, while moving to a formal treaty governing sovereignty over the resources of the South China Sea demands a far more intrusive set of obligations, potentially requiring a far more demanding leadership role on the part of China.

Moreover, in many respects, Southeast Asian leaders appear eager to maintain an identity independent of China, Japan, and the U.S.A. While Western analysts sometimes dismiss ASEAN as primarily a forum for discussion, officials from member states repeatedly indicate that ASEAN offers them an opportunity to negotiate on a more equal footing with the potential regional hegemons. Moreover, for a country such as Vietnam, regional organizations such as ASEAN and APEC offer an important opportunity for more outward looking ministries such as the Ministry of Foreign Affairs to push for greater integration with the global community under the cover of ASEAN or APEC. Still, 50 years ago, no political analyst would likely have predicted the establishment of the European Union.

For the U.S.A., in the best case scenario, a more activist China will share leadership with the U.S.A. and Japan, helping to forge consensus within a more active and integrated region to address its political, security, and economic challenges. Such an Asia would likely have a better chance of either pressuring or inducing change in some of the more recalcitrant actors in the region such as Myanmar and North Korea. There might also be an opportunity for regional actors to relieve the U.S.A. of some of the burden of leadership in the region by assuming a more proactive role in responding to regional crises such as the humanitarian crisis brought on by the tsunami in South Asia in 2004, political unrest in Indonesia, or in coordinating a response on transnational or global threats such as terrorism. In addition, as Asia increasingly contemplates its own security arrangements, "keeping America in" may prove a continued necessity for Japan or other Asian states still concerned about a rising China, much as France believed its interest to be better served by reliance on NATO to balance closer integration with Germany during European unification.[44]

A second scenario, less attractive from the perspective of the U.S.A., suggests a traditional balancing act, in which the nations of Asia use China to ignore the U.S.A. on selective issues, developing alternative approaches to security and political and economic affairs in ways that perhaps more directly serve their domestic interests.

In a worst case scenario, as China assumes a more dominant economic, political, and even security role in the region, the U.S.A. will confront an Asia less likely to respond favorably to U.S. security initiatives, less dependent on U.S. economic leadership and U.S.-run financial institutions, and potentially less open to the full range of U.S. diplomatic initiatives on issues such as human rights and terrorism. With an intra-Asian monetary fund, for example, may come less potential for the U.S.A. to press its agenda for continued domestic economic reform in countries such as China and Vietnam. A regional free trade agreement could prove discriminatory to U.S. products and trade initiatives. If China and Japan become the France, Germany and Britain of Asia, U.S. security priorities such as ensuring Taiwan's security will likely find less support than if the U.S.A. remains the dominant military actor in the region. Certainly, too, while some of the luster has come off America's reputation as the dominant supporter for human rights and democracy in Asia, it is a mantle that no other country in Asia appears ready or capable of assuming. Given the precarious state of democracy in a number of Southeast Asian countries and the struggle to emerge in a number of others, the predominance of the U.S.A. in this capacity is particularly critical.

At least in the initial phase of what appears to be a long-term trajectory of growing Chinese influence in Southeast Asia, the U.S.A. remains a critical partner; a force for regional security; and proponent of greater political transparency and human rights protection for the region. Japan, in turn, is the dominant trading partner, source of development assistance, and architect of new regional currency practices and institutions. While China is in no position to displace either the U.S.A. or Japan – nor is the region as a whole necessarily interested in seeing this come to pass – China's greater presence and activism suggest at the very least that the U.S.A. and Japan cannot remain complacent about the status quo that has governed political, economic, and security relations for the past few decades. Shared leadership within Southeast Asia will likely include China in the near future, with all the potential benefits and challenges that such leadership will entail.

Notes

1 Aaron L. Friedberg, "Ripe for Rivalry: Prospects for Peace in a Multipolar Asia," *International Security*, vol. 18, no. 3, Winter 1993–94, pp. 5–33; Juan T. Gatbonton, "China Moves in as East Asia's Core-State," *Manila Times*, January 8, 2004; Eric Teo Chu Cheow, "An Ancient Model for China's New Power; paying Tribute to Beijing," *International Herald Tribune*, January 21, 2004, p. 6; Elizabeth Economy and Michel Oksenberg, eds, *China Joins the World: Progress and Prospects*, New York, NY: Council on Foreign Relations Press, 1999.
2 Rommel C. Banlaoi, "Southeast Asian Perspectives on the Rise of China: Regional Security after 9/11," *Parameters*, Summer 2003.
3 Geoffrey Barker Bangkok, "APEC Heads Unite in War on Terror," *Australian Financial Review*, October 22, 2003, p. 1.
4 Ruan Zongze, "What are the Implications of China's Peaceful Rise to the World?" http://www.crf.org.cn/peaceful rise/ruanzongze2.htm
5 Jifang Zan, "Peaceful Rise," *Beijing Review* http://www.bjreview.com.cn/200416/BoaoSpecial-200416(B).htm
6 David Lamb, "China Works to Improve Relations with Southeast Asian Neighbors," *Los Angeles Times*, November 15, 2000.
7 Personal note of Jiechi Yang speech at the Asia Society, New York, NY, December 3, 2002.
8 Donald Greenlees, "ASEAN Hails Benefit of Friendship with China," *International Herald Tribune*, November 2, 2006.
9 "China-ASEAN Trade Expected to Reach 200 Billion USD by 2008," *People's Daily*, October 30, 2006. http://english.peopledaily.com.cn/200610/30/eng 20061030_316319.html
10 "China–ASEAN Trade for 2005 Forecast to Reach $120 Billion," *Asian Economic News*, October 24, 2005.

11 "China-ASEAN Trade Expected to Reach 200 Billion USD by 2008," *People's Daily*, October 30, 2006. http://english.peopledaily.com.cn/200610/30/eng20061030_316319.html

12 "Southeast Asia Not Ready to Concede Jobs to China," *Taipei Times*, March 1, 2006. http://www.taipeitimes.com/News/biz/archives/2006/03/01/2003295230

13 Hongmei Shen, "Knocking Down Asian Trade Barriers," *Beijing Review*, April 17, 2003, p. 42.

14 Zaidi Isham Ismail, "ASEAN, China to complete Talks by June," *Business Times*, March 30, 2004, p. 2.

15 Denis D. Gray, "Anxiety and Opportunities Mount as Chinese Colossus Exerts Influence on Southeast Asia," Associated Press, March 30, 2004.

16 "Japan Asked to Extend Economic Pact to All ASEAN Members," *People's Daily*, December 14, 2005; ASEAN-Japan Trade Up 7.9% in 2005, *People's Daily*, August, 24, 2006, http://english.peopledaily.com.cn/200608/24/eng20060824_296202.html "US, ASEAN Sign Trade and Investment Framework Agreement," U.S. State Department, August 25, 2006. http://usinfo.state.gov/xarchives/display.html?p=washfile-english&y=2006&m=August&x=20060825175510ASesuarK0.8261988

17 Audrey McAvoy, "Fearing Rivalry with China, Free Trade Agreements are Suddenly the Rage in Japan," Associated Press, April 2, 2004.

18 "Japan Talks Trade at ASEAN Summit," December 10, 2003, www.cnn.com/2003/world/asiapcf/east/12/10/japan.asean.summit.ap/

19 Evelyn Goh, "China and Southeast Asia," Foreign Policy in Focus, December 16, 2006. http://www.fpif.org/fpiftxt/3780

20 Huang Xingwei, "Hu Expounds China's Stance on Asia-Pacific Regional Cooperation on APEC's Future Development," Xinua General News Service, November 21, 2004.

21 Lyall Breckon, "SARS and a New Security Initiative from China," *Comparative Connections*, 103, July 2003, p. 76.

22 "Asia-Pacific Central Banks to Launch New Fund for Regional Bonds," Japan Economic Newswire, December 16, 2004.

23 Michael Vatikiotis and Bertil Lintner, "New Asian Dollar: The Growing Reach of China's RMB," http://tawainsecurity.ag/news/2003/feer-052903.htm

24 Zongze Ruan, "What are the Implications of China's Peaceful Rise to the World?" http://www.cfr.org.cn/peacefulrise/ruanzongze2.htm

25 Brad Glosserman, "China's Smile Diplomacy," *South China Morning Post*, April 1, 2004, p. 13.

26 Willy Wo-Lap Lam, "China Aiming for 'Peaceful Rise,'" February 6, 2004; CNN.com/20040WORLD/asiapcf/02/02/willy.column; Gilbert Felongco, "Manila Unfazed by Spratly Isles Tensions," *Financial Times Information*, September 11, 2004. "China Protests Vietnam's Bid in South China Sea," Agence France Presse, October 20, 2004.

27 "Major Points of Premier Wen's Speech at the 8th China-ASEAN Summit," Xinhua News Agency, November 30, 2004.

28 Ray Cheung, "Verbal Sparring Eases Tensions over Spratlys," *South China Morning Post*, November 15, 2004, p. 6.

29 Philippines, *Center for Defense Information*, 2007. http://www.cdi.org/PDFs/philippines.pdf

30 M.J. Hassan, "Terrorism: Southeast Asia's Response," January 3, 2002, Pacific Forum CSIS, PacNet 1, via e-mail from pacforum@hawaii.rr.com in Rosemary Foot, "Human Rights and Counter-terrorism in America's Asia Policy," *Adelphi Paper* 363, International Institute for Strategic Studies, 2004, p. 46.

31 Author interviews with officials and scholars in Singapore, Vietnam, and Thailand, November 2002.

32 Mark Baker, "Southeast Asia Turns on Bush," *The Age*, March 20, 2004, p. 4.

33 "America's Image Slips, But Allies Share Concern over Iran, Hamas," *The Global*

Attitudes Project, The Pew Research Center for People and the Press, June 2006. http://pewglobal.org/reports/display.php?ReportID=252

34 Xinning Guo, "Strategic Premium," *Beijing Review*, March 18, 2004, p. 17.

35 Simon S. C. Tay, "Asia and the U.S.A. after 9/11: Primacy and Partnership in the Pacific," *The Fletcher Forum of World Affairs*, vol. 28: Winter 2004, p. 1.

36 "China's Position paper on Enhanced Cooperation in the Field of Non-Traditional Security Issues," May 2002. http://www.fmprc.gov.cn/eng/wjb/zzjg/gjs/gjzzyhy/2612/2614/tl5318.htm#

37 "China-ASEAN Prosecutors-General Conference Opens," Xinhua News Agency, July 8, 2004.

38 "Speech by Premier Wen Jiabao of China at the Special China Leaders' Meeting on SARS," April 29, 2003. www.fmprc.gov.cn/eng/topics/zgcydyhz/zgdmfdtbhy/t26292.htm

39 Alex Liebman, "Washed Down the Mekong," *South China Morning Post*, July 21, 2004.

40 "Damming of the Mekong Sparks Fear for Farmers," *South China Morning Post*, June 30, 2004.

41 John Vidal, "China Mekong Dams Worry Downstream Nations," The *Guardian*, March 25, 2004.

42 Dennis D. Gray, "Illegal Trade Derailing Southeast Asia Wildlife," Associated Press, March 28, 2004; Elizabeth Economy, *The River Runs Black: The Environmental Challenges to China's Future*, Ithaca, NY: Cornell University Press, 2004, p. 122.

43 Muthaih Alagappa, "Constructing Security Order in Asia," in Alagappa, ed., *Asian Security Order*, Stanford, CA; Stanford University Press, 2003, p. 79.

44 Alyson Bailes, "Europe's Defense Challenge," *Foreign Affairs*, January/February 1997, p. 16.

Index

CPSIA information can be obtained at www.ICGtesting.com
Printed in the USA
BVOW03s0936110913

330883BV00004B/39/P